Conflict and Change

What happens to the traditional work practices of Japanese firms when they are taken over by European and American firms? How do the employees react? What lessons can be learned from examples of successful and unsuccessful acquisitions?

Ten years ago, such questions would never have been asked, simply because the incidence of takeovers of Japanese firms by foreign companies was virtually non-existent. However, in the past decade, a number of major Japanese companies have come under the control of foreign firms. *Conflict and Change* focuses on five Japanese companies acquired by foreign firms in the last ten years (including Nissan, Chugai Pharmaceutical and Shinsei Bank) to show how takeovers by foreign companies have changed HR and organisational practices traditionally associated with Japanese firms. This provides invaluable information for researchers and managers about the choices and challenges associated with the cross-border acquisitions of firms that are embedded in "institutionally distant" frameworks.

GEORGE OLCOTT is Senior Fellow at the Judge Business School, University of Cambridge. Before this he held a number of senior management roles in Japan with SG Warburg. During this time, he became involved in the takeover of a wholly Japanese firm, experiencing at first hand the impact of introducing significant organisational change.

Conflict and Change: Foreign Ownership and the Japanese Firm

GEORGE OLCOTT

CAMBRIDGE
UNIVERSITY PRESS

CAMBRIDGE UNIVERSITY PRESS
Cambridge, New York, Melbourne, Madrid, Cape Town, Singapore,
São Paulo, Delhi, Dubai, Tokyo

Cambridge University Press
The Edinburgh Building, Cambridge CB2 8RU, UK

Published in the United States of America by Cambridge University Press, New York

www.cambridge.org
Information on this title: www.cambridge.org/9780521878708

First published 2009

Printed in the United Kingdom at the University Press, Cambridge

A catalogue record for this publication is available from the British Library

Library of Congress Cataloguing in Publication data
Olcott, George, 1955–
    Conflict and change : foreign ownership and the Japanese firm / George Olcott.
        p.   cm.
    ISBN 978-0-521-87870-8 (hbk.)
    1. Corporations, foreign–Japan.   2. International business
enterprises–Japan–Cross-cultural studies.   3. Corporate
culture–Japan.   4. Industrial management–Japan–Cross-cultural
studies.   5. Organizational change–Japan.   I. Title.
HD2907.O48 2009
338.8′30952–dc22   2009033921

ISBN 978-0-521-87870-8 Hardback

For Caroline

Contents

Figures

Tables

Acknowledgements

This study involved a large number of interviews at nine Japanese companies, five that had been taken over by foreign firms and, for comparative purposes, four that had not. This meant that I was very reliant on the assistance of a large number of people, those who helped to coordinate and set up the interviewees, as well as the interviewees themselves. Without the help of these people, this book would never have been completed. In particular, at Nissan, Thierry Moulonguet (who is now back at Renault), at Chugai Pharmaceutical, Osamu Nagayama and, at Shinsei Bank, Masamoto Yashiro, Koiichiro Nakaya and Tom Pedersen were all instrumental in assisting me to set up interviews. At two case companies whose identities are not revealed and at four Japanese firms, there were people who I would like to acknowledge but am unable to. In all cases, they extended to me every possible courtesy and helped me enormously with my fieldwork. I hope that in some small way I will one day be able to repay the debt I owe them. I would like to thank the Ministry of Finance's Policy Research Institute for hosting me as a Visiting Scholar in the spring of 2004. In addition to those who provided me with direct help, there were a number of people whose support "behind the scenes" was particularly valuable. In particular I would like to single out Messrs Yoshiyuki Kasai and Aki Katagiri, who were, and remain, a never-ending source of inspiration and moral support. I would like to thank them for their interest in my project, their constant encouragement and their friendship. The original inspiration for this book was provided by my spell at what used to be LTCB Investment Management (a subsidiary of the Long Term Credit Bank of Japan), which was taken over by UBS in 1998. The alliance between LTCB and UBS ultimately failed due to the collapse of LTCB but was in my view a genuine attempt by a Japanese bank to find a new way of globalising its operations. There were many people from whom I learned a great deal during that period, such as Katsunobu Onogi, Koji Hirao, the late Takashi Uehara and the employees of LTCB Investment Management, including Yuji Kage.

At the Judge Business School, I would like to express my sincere thanks to my mentor, Professor Nick Oliver, now head of the University of Edinburgh Business School. Without his consistent support and guidance throughout the research process, I would never have been able to complete this work. His perceptive guidance and his enthusiasm have been an inspiration. I should also thank John Roberts who read an early draft and provided helpful comments. A number of other academics have kindly read the manuscript and provided helpful and candid advice. In particular, Ron Dore, whose past work has provided so much of the intellectual framework of the book, has been extremely generous with his time in offering constructive criticism as well as a huge amount of enthusiastic encouragement. I am also indebted to Chris Ahmadjian and Gillian Tett for kindly agreeing to review the book. The Foundation for Management Education generously provided a fellowship during the period of writing this book and I would like to thank in particular Director Mike Jones for his support and encouragement, as well as John Wybrew and Bob Lintott.

Finally, I would like to thank my family for their love and support. My mother kindly put me up on my many visits to Tokyo. My wife Caroline and my children Flora, George and Ellie put up with long periods when I was away on fieldwork and were constant in their enthusiastic support and encouragement.

Introduction

"There are those that are concerned that
if we abandon the concept of equality that
is emphasised in HR policy at Japanese
companies, 'salaryman' society will
become stratified and income differentials
will grow. In the end, we will become a
criminal society such as the US."
(Yashiro, N., "Get rid of the HR
Department!" 1998, p. 218)

THIS BOOK is about employment systems, their relationship with national corporate governance regimes and how pressure for change to the latter causes shifts in work practices and organisational structures. Specifically, it is about the Japanese employment system, the way in which large Japanese corporations align their organisational structures and HR practices and how these might change following a takeover by a company whose own practices are embedded in an "institutionally distant" employment system and corporate governance framework. Prior to the late 1990s there were very few examples of large-scale takeovers of Japanese companies by foreign firms. Although foreign firms had operated in Japan for decades, their employment practices were seen to be quite distinct from those at traditional Japanese firms.[1] Since the late 1990s, however, foreign takeovers have been a growing phenomenon and have attracted considerable attention. There has been a great deal of speculation as to what impact these takeovers will have on economic life in Japan, in particular its employment system. As is illustrated

---

[1] There are some notable exceptions, such as IBM or Showa Shell, companies with a long history in Japan whose practices were seen as deeply embedded in the Japanese system.

in the quotation from Yashiro above, there are many that consider
the maintenance of the traditions and the underlying philosophy of
the Japanese employment system to be fundamental to the continuity of civilised life itself. On the other hand, there are many others,
including Yashiro himself, who see Japanese employment practices
as a significant barrier to economic progress and who seek reform.
By and large, these authors emphasise greater individual accountability, a more performance-based organisational culture where rewards
are based more on individual, rather than group, effort, or age and
seniority. For this reason, the study of the organisational impact of
foreign takeovers on Japanese companies is of considerable interest
and importance, both to academics interested in employment systems,
as well as practitioners who are involved in the management of multinational firms and for whom acquisition has become an increasingly
feasible alternative to establishing a presence in hitherto "institutionally distant" corporate societies such as Japan.

   Some time during the summer of 1991, when I was working in the
Corporate Finance Department of SG Warburg & Co in Tokyo, I was
telephoned by the CFO of one of my Japanese clients, a large and successful manufacturing company. He said to me:

"Look here, Olcott-san, I've been hearing from a lot of my friends at our
competitors about this 'investor relations' thing. It sounds like something
that we've got to take seriously, so I've asked my team to design a brochure
in English so that we can inform overseas investors more effectively about
our activities. Could you come over and have a look at it?"

The next day, I visited him at the company's headquarters and examined the document, which was already at proof stage. It was glossy,
with photographs of the company's various products and factories,
and a good deal of text explaining the company's history and strategy.
At the top of the first page was a photograph of the President, with
"A Message to Our Stakeholders" underneath. As the concept of the
"stakeholder" had hardly caught on in the UK, let alone Japan, this
was a promising beginning. For "employees", they promised a stable
and rewarding workplace; for "clients", the best products at reasonable prices; for suppliers, a long-term relationship based on trust; and
for "society", a sense of corporate responsibility towards the population at large and the environment in particular.

"There appears to be one important stakeholder missing here," I told the CFO.

"And who would that be?" he asked.

"Shareholders?" I suggested tentatively.

"*Naruhodo* ... yes, of course!" he exclaimed. "I thought there was something missing!" His subordinate shifted uncomfortably in his seat and undertook to add a message to shareholders right away. A few days later, he duly sent me a revised version, complete with a new section promising shareholders a stable dividend policy and high standards of disclosure.

I relate this episode not to cause amusement, but to illustrate a number of points. First, it demonstrated the historical tendency for shareholders not to demand managerial attention at large Japanese companies; second, that there were forces at work as early as the early 1990s causing management to rebalance stakeholder priorities (hence the new brochure) and that, third, this re-evaluation was still in its very early stages, and changes were limited largely to symbolic gestures that were not accompanied by changes in attitude. It was interesting, for example, that the company originally intended to produce the brochure only in English, and to distribute it to institutional investors based outside Japan. There appeared to be a clear understanding that foreign institutional shareholders were an entirely different species to domestic ones and needed to be approached accordingly. Indeed this episode was only one among a host of examples which seemed to support the proposition, forcefully put by a number of commentators since the 1950s (e.g. Abegglen, 1958; Ouchi, 1981; Vogel, 1979), that there was a distinct version of Japanese capitalism, underpinned by fundamental attitudinal differences about the very purpose of the firm.

At the time, the consequences of non-engagement with foreign institutions did not seem to be serious. Although the stock market bubble had burst at the beginning of 1990, property prices were still on the rise and the economy was still growing. Most felt that Japan would soon be back on track. Foreigners had never owned more than around 5 per cent of the Japanese stock market. There were of course a large number of foreign firms operating in Japan. There were examples of large and successful firms, such as IBM, Coca-Cola and Showa Shell (the result of a merger between Shell and Showa Oil), that had long been established in Japan and had become part of the domestic scene, with employment practices to match. There were even examples of acquisitions by foreigners of listed Japanese firms. SG Warburg & Co had acted on two large acquisitions of Japanese firms by foreigners during the early 1980s: the acquisition of Banyu Pharmaceutical by Merck and that of Osaka Sanso by BOC. Large stakes had been taken by foreign firms, such as Ford's holding in Mazda. However, these were invariably "friendly" transactions involving the full cooperation of the Japanese company's main banks and, more often than not, the bureaucracy, usually in the form of MITI. They were also very rare. On the whole foreign firms such as the one for which I worked operated at the margins, occupying niches and sweeping up and living off the crumbs left to us by our Japanese competitors. Japanese and foreign firms had parallel, but separate, lives. The strength of the Japanese economy, the global success of many Japanese companies and the esteem which "Japanese management" was held in internationally suggested that there was no reason for a drastic change of direction.

By the late 1990s, however, the landscape had undergone a dramatic transformation and, for the first time since the post-war period, serious questions were being asked about the suitability and sustainability of the Japanese version of capitalism. By this time Japan's economy had endured a period of stagnation of unprecedented duration in the post-war era. The "bubble economy" that had inflated asset prices to extraordinary levels by the late 1980s had burst and equity prices had fallen almost continuously since the beginning of 1990. Land prices started falling somewhat later, in 1992–1993, but had fallen even more sharply. The weakness of the entire financial sector was exposed and in late 1997 there were a number of major bankruptcies, including Hokkaido Takushoku Bank, one of the smaller city banks, and Yamaichi Securities, one of the "Big Four" securities firms.

It was argued by many that the Japanese model of capitalism, which gave a broad range of stakeholders a claim on the fruits of the country's economic success, was outmoded and needed to be replaced with a more orthodox, Anglo-Saxon style of capitalism that rewarded winners and had no place for losers (e.g. Porter *et al.*, 2000). Capital was the lifeblood of companies, and shareholders, who had put up the equity capital and who held all the residual risk, had to be properly rewarded. Arguments that Japan was somehow exceptional, which were mostly culturalist in nature and which held that Japanese society was organised in a way that supported a different mode of capitalism (e.g. Fujiwara, 2005; Funabiki, 2002), were, it was claimed, no longer valid.

While it is possible to interpret declining Japanese asset prices and extreme weakness in the financial sector as harbingers of permanent decline for Japan, many foreign companies saw these events as presenting major opportunities for investment. Japan was, and still is, a large and sophisticated market, with many industrial sectors at the forefront of technological innovation. Moreover, it seemed possible, even likely, that the long period of economic decline might bring about the kind of environment that would make the Japanese authorities, corporations and society at large more sympathetic to a more orthodox capitalistic and shareholder-friendly mode of operation.

However, there still remained the question of how to enter and expand in the Japanese market. As we have noted above, despite Japan's position as a major global exporter and decades of gradual integration with the global economy, there had hitherto been very little inbound mergers and acquisitions (M&A) (i.e. cases of foreign companies buying Japanese companies) and most foreign companies had entered Japan either through green field investments or joint ventures. While the reasons for this will be explored in later chapters, by the mid-1990s, with banks in straightened circumstances and beginning to unwind their substantial portfolios of cross-held shares (Okabe, 2001) and with the valuations of Japanese companies at historic lows (especially relative to their international peers), it was clear that buying a Japanese company was going to be easier for a foreign firm than it had ever been. It can be seen from Figure 0.1 that, from a very low base, the volume of inbound[2] M&A took off sharply from around 1996.

The firm for which I worked was among those who saw the considerable potential of the Japanese market. I had returned to London in 1993 and, two years later, SG Warburg was bought by Swiss Bank Corporation (SBC). In the summer of 1997, SBC announced a wide-ranging alliance with a Japanese bank, the Long Term Credit Bank of Japan (LTCB), to pool their respective investment banking and institutional asset management businesses, and start jointly a new private

---

[2] In Figure 0.1 "out-in" refers to inbound M&A, or foreign companies taking over Japanese companies. "In-out" is the opposite – Japanese companies taking over foreign companies.

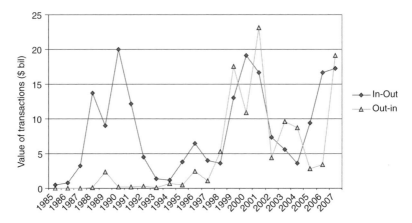

Figure 0.1 Trend of M&A transactions: Japan 1985–2007
Source: Thompson One Banker (2005)

banking business in Japan. Thus, although SBC did not take control
of LTCB, it saw its alliance as a means of establishing a presence in
Japan which would give the company direct access to a large pool
of corporate and institutional clients, as well as private savings – an
effort that would have taken years, perhaps decades, to build up
organically. I was told that I would shortly move over to the asset
management side of SBC to become the SBC representative in the
asset management joint venture with LTCB.

I started work at the asset management joint venture in Tokyo in
September. The joint venture was in fact an existing LTCB subsidiary,
LTCB Investment Management, which had been set up fifteen years
earlier, which managed ¥1 trillion ($10 billion) of Japanese pension
fund assets and which had 80 employees. SBC bought 50% of the
company. It was a classic joint venture of the old style: the local company providing human resources and the client base, the foreigner
providing technological know-how.

I had lived and worked in Japan for many years and, even though I
had never worked for a Japanese company, I felt that I knew my way
around. Yes, Japanese firms looked and felt different from the foreign
firms I had worked for, but I felt the gap would not be so great and
that I could act as an effective "bridge". It would be easy.

The fact that it was not was brought home soon enough. In a particularly bizarre episode, I found myself writing a series of memos …

to myself. There was one particularly contentious issue which arose from various commitments that LTCB had made to distribute mutual fund products of our competitors through their branch network, something that deregulation of the financial markets was going to permit from 1 December 1997. These arrangements had been made prior to the announcement of the LTCB–SBC alliance and, in any event, SBC would not have any products ready for distribution by 1 December. My superiors (who were located in Chicago) were not at all happy about this arrangement and saw it as a betrayal. I was asked by my boss in Chicago to draft a letter to LTCB emphasising our displeasure and telling them to desist. "You know the Japanese", he said; "couch it in the right way". I duly drafted a letter which was faxed from Chicago to LTCB's Tokyo headquarters. The next day, I received a call from my counterpart at LTCB, who told me he had received the fax. He explained the situation and stressed that it was not their intention to "betray" us. He was not going to change his mind. I told him that while I had understood and perhaps even sympathised with his point of view, our position was as my boss had explained it. I suggested he write back outlining their position, putting some apologetic language at the end of the letter and hopefully that would be the end of the matter. To my surprise, he asked me to draft the letter. "You know the Americans", he said. "You will know how to put it." I duly drafted a letter for him. I ended up drafting two more letters, one from each side, before the issue faded away.

There were many such incidents and, while some were just differences of opinion based on simple considerations of economic interest, many others were due to different interpretations, based on cultural factors, as to what and how things should be done. Whilst the role of the "bridge" – interpreting and explaining cultural differences and how they impact on business decisions to culturally distant partners – was important, it would only get me so far. We needed to establish a cultural frame of reference which would serve as a basis for organisational design and routines. Would our organisational structure and practices be based on Japanese principles? Or should we transform the company into a "foreign" firm? If we did the latter, what would be the impact on the employees and on the business?

Even at the outset, SBC were given considerable leeway to reorganise the company. The company was now 50% foreign owned, but when I started work it looked and felt just like my perception of a Japanese company. There were eight directors for a company of 80 employees. They had all been sent by the parent company and were therefore commercial bankers by background. Some, such as the President, Yuji Kage, had remained with the subsidiary for a considerable period and had in the process become highly professionalised, but others had little experience of asset management and I was under the distinct impression that they had been "parked" there to await retirement. There was also a group of very bright young employees who had also been sent by the parent company to acquire skills in a strategically important area for the firm (i.e. asset management). There was also a group of female clerical staff who had been recruited directly by the subsidiary. The layout of the office clearly reflected the office hierarchy: directors' and general managers' desks lined up by the window facing inwards. In front of them the managers' desks, also facing inwards, and in front of the managers, ranks of desks facing each other, with employees getting more junior the further they got from the window, with the (uniformed) office ladies at the very end.

The behaviour of the employees was quite different from the Japanese with whom I had worked at foreign firms in Japan, who had always been regarded as "mavericks" and "outsiders" (see Kang, 1991). There was, at least on the surface, a respect for authority that was almost military. As SBC's representative, I was the Deputy CEO of the firm. Employees bowed before entering my office, and bowed again before leaving.

The HR practices were also in line with what I had imagined to be typical for white-collar workers at a large Japanese company (see Beck and Beck, 1994). Recruitment of the executives had taken place exclusively at the elite universities. Training had been of a general kind, aimed at creating solidarity among cohort members. Careers had followed a generalist path, with employees moving from head office to a branch, back to head office to a lending department or a currency or bond dealing desk, then into the planning or personnel department, back to a branch, and so on. A few had been sent overseas, either to work in a branch or to do an MBA at a US or UK university. These employees spoke good English but seemed reluctant to use it, for fear of embarrassing their non-English-speaking colleagues, who represented the great majority, or so I was told. This was very different behaviour from the Japanese who worked at foreign firms. Two employees who might have joined the company at exactly the same time fifteen or twenty years ago would often be paid, to the nearest yen, exactly the same salary, despite manifest differences in ability. Bonuses were a fixed proportion of salary and hardly changed from one year to the next. Company or individual performance had almost no bearing on the bonus the employees received – a practice totally alien to someone who had worked at a foreign financial institution.

Authority appeared to be delegated to the lower reaches of the organisation and the traditional consensus-building mechanisms were in place, with the *ringi* process being vigorously followed. The *ringi* process dispersed responsibility through the organisation, and it was not clear who was accountable for any one decision.

Although these observations, particularly from an Anglo-Saxon perspective, might leave an unfavourable impression, this would be misleading. There was, for one thing, a remarkable sense of cohesiveness in the organisation that was entirely missing in the foreign firms operating in Japan, especially in the financial sector. Yes, it was hierarchical and bureaucratic, but it also had a sense of order and discipline. Employees identified strongly with the firm and with its parent, LTCB, despite its manifest financial problems, and this sense of identity seemed to function as a source of pride and long-term commitment to the organisation. This was not only true of the front office elite, but also the clerical staff, who were highly dedicated and professional and who, in most cases, were generally earning half of what they might have been paid at a foreign firm. It was also true to say that the nature of the relationships that existed between the firm and its clients was different. The company had over 100 clients, many of whom had never dealt with a foreign firm and with whom it would have taken SBC years, perhaps decades, to develop a relationship on their own. However, many of the clients were very small, and would have been considered too marginal for coverage by a foreign asset manager. Relationships were highly structured and ran much deeper than would have been the case at a foreign firm.

Notwithstanding these positive attributes, our instinct was to bring practices into line with what might be considered best practice at a western firm. We therefore set about making drastic organisational changes and radically altered the HR system to bring it into line with that of other foreign financial institutions. There would be no more rotation, employees would have to specialise, rewards would be strictly on merit and bonuses would vary considerably according to individual and company performance. Clear job descriptions would be issued outlining the scope of individual responsibilities. The hierarchical arrangements were simplified and the organisation flattened. The size of the board was cut drastically.

Within six months of the inauguration of the joint venture, LTCB collapsed and SBC took full control of the company.[3] Within this short period, the employees of the old LTCB Investment Management had seen their employer change from a 100% Japanese company to a 100% foreign firm, via the intermediate step of a 50/50 joint venture. As if this was not enough drama for the employees, SBC was at this time merging with UBS, the largest of Switzerland's "Big Three" banks. UBS had an established asset management business in Japan. Their employees were typical of those Japanese working in foreign firms and they provided a remarkable contrast with the employees of the former LTCB Investment Management.

LTCB Investment Management was now called UBS Asset Management Japan (its third name in six months) and, despite the fact that the employees were the same, it was beginning to feel like a very different operation. I wondered what the links were between employee behaviour and HR practices and what the impact the changes in HR practices we had begun to implement would be on the behaviour of the old LTCB employees. There were media reports of radical organisational change occurring at other Japanese firms taken over by foreign companies and I reflected on the impact that changes in underlying corporate governance attitudes would have on deeply embedded Japanese organisational practices, especially when the changes were brought about by the "shock" of a takeover by a foreign firm. For, despite the debate alluded to above about the fundamental nature of Japanese capitalism and calls for a far greater emphasis on "shareholder value", there was little sign of change in Japanese companies (e.g. Morgan and Takahashi, 2002), many of whom argued that the Japanese system was still a source of competitive advantage. Many of the institutions regarded as typical features in Japanese companies, such as the reward and decision-making systems, and which I had found in abundance at

---

[3] For an excellent account of the story of LTCB and especially its demise, see Tett (2004).

LTCB Investment Management, appeared to be remarkably enduring aspects of the wider Japanese corporate landscape.

Perhaps the cultural explanation of organisations (e.g. Hampden-Turner and Trompenaars, 1993; Hofstede, 1994), that they reflect deeply rooted social norms and beliefs that were the bedrock of national identity, was correct: the cultural foundations upon which Japanese organisations, and the institutional context into which they were embedded, were constructed in such a way that change was extremely difficult, if not impossible. I was therefore intrigued to comprehend what might happen to a Japanese organisation when it received what might be considered the ultimate "jolt" – a change of ownership to a single, foreign, shareholder.

Ahmadjian and Robbins (2005) have already shown that the higher the proportion of foreign institutional shareholders a Japanese company has, the more likely it is to introduce "shareholder-friendly" policies, such as taking more drastic downsizing measures in a downturn. These shareholders, however, only exert indirect pressure on companies, through the exercise of voting rights at shareholders' annual general meetings. They do not *control*. In Japan, ownership of 33.4% of a company's outstanding share capital gives effective control, which I define as "the power to determine the broad policies guiding the corporation, including decisions regarding capital structure (such as equity, debt, profits, and cash flow), geographic expansion, product diversification, corporate structure, and mergers" (Fligstein, 2001, p. 125),[4] as well as decisions which affect the broad distribution of surplus value.

Therefore, the questions I am asking are:

- How do Japanese companies change when they are taken over by foreigners?
- What factors might account for any differences that are observed between one takeover and another?
- How do we know that the change is attributable to the influence of foreigners, or, to put it another way, how do we know the same changes are not occurring at Japanese companies?

---

[4] Thus, the controlling foreign firms own at least 33.4% of the shares of the Japanese case study firms I examine. Some, though not all, have acquired more than 50%.

- By investigating what is happening at Japanese firms, what can we learn about the process of organisational change in Japan?

I had already gained some valuable insights at LTCB Investment Management, which had turned into UBS Asset Management. However, I would clearly need to look not only at other foreign, or "western,"[5] firms, but also at "pure" Japanese firms, to ensure the same changes were not also occurring there.

Why was such a study of interest? It was interesting not only because the takeover of major Japanese companies by foreign firms was a relatively new and unstudied phenomenon, but also because such a study might shed some light on what it was about Japanese organisations, and indeed organisations in general, that caused traditional practices and organisational forms to survive for so long.

Scope of research

This is a wide-ranging study and cuts across a large number of disciplines within the scope of organisational behaviour. There are potentially many theoretical doors to open. For example, while it is a study of organisational change, it is a study that encompasses corporate governance, national culture, models of capitalism, Japanese organisations, mergers and acquisitions, HR practices including recruitment, training, reward systems, gender issues and many more. I was not able to look through all of these different lenses. Rather, I propose to examine all of these perspectives through the literature on Japanese organisations, with particular reference to Dore's notion (1973) of the Japanese firm as a "welfare corporatist" organisation, and attempt to tie it together using institutional theory as my conceptual framework.

---

[5] I do not intend here to differentiate between various models of capitalism except that of Japan and those of other western countries, fully recognising that each country will have developed its own particular brand that can differ considerably from that of even a neighbouring country. Thus, the status of the shareholder in the governance hierarchy is quite different in say the US, compared with say Germany, and the employment systems of those two countries are quite different. My assertion is that, in post-war Japan, shareholders have had particularly low status and that a distinction between Japanese and "western" forms of capitalism is valid, even if there are a number of "western" varieties.

What is attractive about the institutional framework? First, because much of the institutional literature, particularly the cultural-cognitive elements that flow from Berger and Luckmann (1966) which emphasise the process whereby humans construct for themselves a stable environment through the creation of a "widening sphere of taken-for-granted routines", seems an appropriate way to view the embeddedness of organisational structure and practices. Culture is a notoriously difficult concept, criticised for being impossible to measure and useless as a predictive or diagnostic tool. Geertz (1993, p. 5) wrote: "man is an animal suspended in webs of significance he himself has spun, I take culture to be those webs, and the analysis of it to be therefore not an experimental science in search of law but an interpretive one in search of meaning". By linking the concept of culture to the creation of institutions through the cultural-cognitive framework (Scott, 2001), institutional theory shows us why those self-spun webs are so strong and resistant to encroachment and under what conditions they may break down.

Second, with the idea of organisational fields, institutional theory provides a versatile way of conceptualising organisations and enabling varying levels of analysis. Cultural values underpin both world-systems or societal sectors (Scott and Meyer, 1991) at the macro level and organisations and organisational sub-systems at the micro level (e.g. Selznick, 1949). "Organisational fields", which DiMaggio and Powell (1983, p. 148) define as "those organisations that, in the aggregate, constitute a recognized area of institutional life", fit in between the macro societal level and the individual organisation (Scott, 2001). Japanese organisations, broadly speaking, are the field we are examining, and the Japanese employment system, the "institutional project" (Fligstein, 2001), into which they are embedded.

Third, if there is a "hole" in institutional theory, it is that empirical studies of "deinstitutionalisation", the process whereby an existing set of arrangements or practices are replaced with new ones, are "relatively rare" (Scott, 2001, p. 183). This work intends to help fill this gap. In particular, during the last ten years there has been some interesting literature on the impact of "institutional distance" on the relationship of subsidiaries of multinational firms with their headquarters as well as the way the institutional distance of a target acquisition may affect the way the multinational firm integrates it into its global operations. By examining the extent to which traditional practices at Japanese firms become deinstitutionalised after being acquired by foreign firms, I hope to add to the debate on the effects of institutional distance.

I should emphasise at this stage that this is not an all-encompassing study of the Japanese organisation and employment system. I am looking at a particularly narrow, although important, segment of Japanese organisational life: elite white-collar workers at large Japanese companies.[6] It is often said that Japan has two employment systems, one for those employed either in the public sector or at large corporations, where employees enjoy all the advantages of the protection afforded by "welfare corporatism", and those who work at small and medium-sized enterprises, who have to put up with a much higher degree of uncertainty and instability, as well as generally lower wages (Cole, 1971; Whittaker, 1994). While there are those who also argue (e.g. Yashiro, 1998) that it is not appropriate to draw a distinction between the HR practices of large and small companies and that small companies endeavour to offer stable, long-term careers just as much as large companies but often do not have the resources to do so,[7] I will not attempt to enter this debate in this book.

I will also not be looking at blue-collar workers. Again, while theoretically the distinction between white-collar (*shain*, or "employees") and blue-collar workers (*kōin*, or "worker") was abolished in the 1950s (Gordon, 1998) and while blue-collar workers at large Japanese companies enjoy stability of employment just as much as their white-collar counterparts, they are still a distinct set of employees, with different recruitment, training, career patterns and reward criteria (Beck and Beck, 1994; Cole, 1971; Dore, 1973). Thus, while elite white-collar employees all enter the company union, they all leave it eventually, mostly on reaching the rank of manager. I will therefore not be looking closely at union-related issues.[8]

---

[6] The Japan Institute of Labor (JIL) defines "large" as a company with over 1,000 employees and I will stick to this definition.

[7] Abegglen (1958, p. 17) argues "it is no less difficult for the small firm to lay off or fire than for the large firm; indeed, in many ways it is more difficult".

[8] I had been curious about the role of the unions in relation to companies taken over by foreign firms and one of my questions to employees was about union activity. There was almost without exception no knowledge (or even interest in most cases) about union activity and how it might be faring under foreign ownership. A study that incorporated an analysis

Although I try in the conclusion to speculate on the impact of the acquirer's nationality on the post-merger integration process, I have in general consciously avoided using the nationality of the acquirer as a factor in explaining the process of change. I accept that an argument could be made that nationality has some bearing on the outcome. Thus, a French company taking over a Japanese company may, because it is French, have taken a different approach to organisational modifications compared to, say, an American company. However, there are not enough examples of foreign companies taking over Japanese firms and the number of case studies in this book are too few to draw definitive conclusions. Moreover, my supposition is that whatever the nationality of the acquiring firm, their main objective in making the acquisition is to enhance shareholder returns and the organisational changes that result from the acquisition are made with this in mind.

This study is about organisational change resulting from "institutionally distant" mergers and how employees react to their new circumstances. Some of the case companies have been successful, while some have not. In the final chapter, I have tried to highlight some common features of the successful firms, but they do not amount to a recipe for successful integration strategies in cross-border M&A. I should also emphasise that I am not attempting in this book to pass any judgement on whether the Japanese employment system and organisational form is either "good" or "bad": this is simply not possible from such a limited number of cases. I hope I do show, however, that the fear that is evident in many corporate and government quarters as to the pernicious effects of a foreign takeover are not justified.

Structure of the book

In Chapters 1 and 2 I will examine the literature on the Japanese organisation and its historical context, as well as set out my conceptual framework based on institutional theory, including the ways in which institutional theory might relate to the development of Japanese organisations. In Chapter 2, I explain my research methodology and offer a brief introduction of the case study and comparator companies. Chapters 3 to 7 are my empirical chapters in which I attempt to

---

of the blue-collar workforce would obviously produce a different result. Two of the five case study companies were not unionised.

verify, first, that Japanese companies still show a strong resemblance
to Dore's welfare corporatist organisation and, second, that, once
taken over by foreign firms, Japanese organisations abandon many of
the traditional practices typical of the welfare corporatist organisation. In Chapter 8, I lay out a summary and my conclusions.

References

Abegglen, J.C. (1958) *The Japanese Factory: Aspects of Its Social
    Organisation.* Boston, MA: Massachusetts Institute of Technology
    Press
Ahmadjian, C.L. and Robbins, G.E. (2005) "A Clash of Capitalisms: Foreign
    Shareholders and Corporate Restructuring in 1990s Japan", *American
    Sociological Review,* 70: 451–471
Beck, J.C. and Beck, M.N. (1994) *The Change of a Lifetime: Employment
    Patterns among Japan's Managerial Elite.* Honolulu, HI: University of
    Hawaii Press
Berger, P.L. and Luckmann, T. (1966) *The Social Construction of Reality.*
    New York, NY: Doubleday
Cole, R.E. (1971) *Japanese Blue Collar: The Changing Tradition.* Berkeley,
    CA: University of California Press
DiMaggio, P.J. and Powell, W.W. (1983) "The Iron Cage Revisited:
    Institutional Isomorphism and Collective Rationality in Organizational
    Fields", *American Sociological Review,* 48: 147–160
Dore, R. (1973) *British Factory–Japanese Factory: The Origins of
    National Diversity in Industrial Relations.* Berkeley, CA: University
    of California Press
Fligstein, N. (2001) *The Architecture of Markets: An Economic Sociology
    of Twenty-First Century Capitalist Societies.* Princeton, NJ: Princeton
    University Press
Fujiwara, M. (2005) *Kokka No Hinkaku (The Dignity of the State).*
    Tokyo: Shinchosha
Funabiki, T. (2002) *"Nihonjinron" Saikou (Reconsidering "Nihonjinron").*
    Tokyo: NHK Shuppansha
Geertz, C. (1993) *The Interpretations of Cultures: Selected Essays.*
    London: Fontana Press
Gordon, A. (1998) *The Wages of Affluence: Labor and Management in
    Postwar Japan.* Cambridge, MA: Harvard University Press
Hampden-Turner, C. and Trompenaars, F. (1993) *The Seven Cultures of
    Capitalism: Value Systems for Creating Wealth in the United States,
    Britain, Japan, Germany, France, Sweden and the Netherlands.*
    London: Piatkus

Hofstede, G. (1994) *Culture and Organizations: Software of the Mind.* London: HarperCollins

Kang, T. W. (1991) *Gaishi: The Foreign Company in Japan.* Tokyo: Tuttle

Morgan, G. and Takahashi, Y. (2002) "Shareholder Value in the Japanese Context", *Competition and Change*, 6: 169–191

Ouchi, W. (1981) *Theory Z: How American Business Can Meet the Japanese Challenge.* Reading, MA: Addison-Wesley

Porter, M. E., Takeuchi, H. and Sakakibara, M. (2000) *Can Japan Compete?* London: Macmillan

Scott, W. R. (2001) *Institutions and Organizations.* Thousand Oaks, CA: Sage

 and Meyer, J. W. (1991) "The Organization of Societal Sectors". In W. W. Powell and P. J. DiMaggio (eds.) *The New Institutionalism in Organizational Analysis.* Chicago, IL: University of Chicago Press

Selznick, P. (1949) *TVA and the Grass Roots: A Study in the Sociology of Formal Organization.* Berkeley, CA: University of California Press

Tett, G. (2004) *Saving the Sun: Shinsei and the Battle for Japan's Future.* London: Random House

Vogel, E. F. (1979) *Japan as Number One.* Cambridge, MA: Harvard University Press

Whittaker, D. H. (1994) "SMEs, Entry Barriers and 'Strategic Alliances'". In M. Aoki and R. Dore (eds.) *The Japanese Firm: Sources of Competitive Strength.* Oxford: Oxford University Press

Yashiro, N. (1998) *Jinjibu Wa Mou Iranai (Who Needs an HR Department Any More?).* Tokyo: Kodansha

1 | *Japanese institutions: are they different?*

A S MENTIONED in the Introduction the purpose of this book is to examine organisational change at Japanese firms taken over by foreign firms. The aim of this chapter is to establish an understanding of the Japanese employment system, to examine its institutional underpinnings and to determine in what way the practices that constitute the system are distinctive. From this we can build a model of a Japanese firm from which we might speculate how practices might diverge if the firm were to be taken over by an organisation embedded in a different institutional framework. We will also examine the pressures that the Japanese system has been under in recent years and the extent to which the institutions that make up the Japanese form of capitalism may have been undermined.

This chapter is divided into two sections. In the first section I give a broad overview of Japanese organisations, presenting it in an institutional framework, focusing on the development of the communitarian firm in the decades following the end of World War II. In the second section, I describe recent developments which have affected the Japanese organisational model, again offering an institutional lens to view the process of change that appears to have taken place during the last decade and a half.

Japan, varieties of capitalism and institutional distinctiveness

Interest in the idea that there are varieties of capitalism grew with the rising economic profile of Japan and Germany in the post-war era. As early as the 1950s, writers such as Abegglen (1958) and Levine (1958) identified organisational processes and structures that differed markedly from those that characterised American companies. In recent years, academics have devoted their efforts to identifying separate "types" of capitalism based on distinctive governance structures which emphasise in differing degrees the role that the various stakeholders play in various "business systems". The distinctive varieties are generally broken down into two types. The first, variously described as "shareholder-" or "market-oriented", "liberal market economies" and the other as "organisation-" or "stakeholder-oriented", "coordinated market economies" (Dore, 2000; Hall and Soskice, 2001). Anglo-Saxon countries are held out as exemplars of the former, Japan and Germany of the latter.

Coordinated market economies are characterised by the existence of dense business networks, with finance and a strong monitoring function provided historically by banks which maintained close links with their borrowers, participative labour relations with an emphasis on high levels of skill formation based on intensive training and internal labour markets, relatively egalitarian pay scales and the constrained ability for unilateral action by senior management, with an emphasis on consensual decision making. Firms operating in liberal market economies, on the other hand, are not likely to be bound by intimate business networks; are more beholden to the equity markets which is the main source of monitoring; are more likely to be attentive to short-term performance indicators to which the share price is sensitive, and operate in highly fluid labour markets where rewards are determined by market forces with much wider gaps between senior management and the rest; and have a tendency for more power to be concentrated in, and exercised by, the top ranks of the firm.

The economic, social and political institutions that constitute individual business systems have produced distinctive mechanisms for coordination, both in terms of the role of the state in coordinating economic activity and in the way the firms coordinate among themselves (Whitley, 1991). Contrasting regimes of competition have developed, as well as sharply differing attitudes towards mergers and acquisitions, particularly those of a hostile nature. Crucially, it is believed that these differences lead to the development of comparative institutional advantage, the idea that distinctive national institutional frameworks give rise to certain advantages in discrete areas of economic activity, such as production, innovation, the provision of services, etc. (Hall and Soskice, 2001).

The Japanese organisation: an institutional perspective

Institutional theory emphasises the role of the institutional environment as a key determinant of organisational form and behaviour and posits that the degree of legitimacy with which the organisation is held in its institutional environment is vital to organisational survival. Organisations will therefore tend to adopt practices and routines that are seen as legitimate in their particular environmental context, as opposed to necessarily the most efficient. Historic continuity of an institutionalised practice leads to its widespread acceptance and in effect it becomes a "social given", part of a "widening sphere of taken-for-granted routines [where] many actions are possible on a low level of attention" (Berger and Luckmann, 1966, p. 57). Formal structure has symbolic, as well as action-generating, meaning, and many elements of formal structure "function as myths". Technologies are institutionalised, becoming myths that bind an organisation. Thus, as Meyer and Rowan (1977, p. 344) write:

Technical procedures of production, accounting, personnel selection, or data processing become taken-for-granted means to accomplish organisational ends. Quite apart from their possible efficiency, such institutionalised techniques establish an organisation as appropriate, rational, and modern. Their use displays responsibility and avoids claims of negligence.

It follows that organisations sharing the same institutional environment will be subject to similar institutional pressures and will have inherent isomorphic tendencies to enhance legitimacy[1] and survival prospects (DiMaggio and Powell, 1983).

[1] It is perhaps worth emphasising at this point that "legitimacy" in the institutional context does not refer only to its most commonly understood form, that is to say *moral* legitimacy, which in an organisation reflects a "positive normative evaluation" of its activities by its audience. Suchman (1995) identifies two further forms: "pragmatic" legitimacy, which "rests on the self-interested calculations of an organisation's most immediate audiences", where members of the audience calculate the benefit to themselves before subscribing to a set of policies or practices; and "cognitive" legitimacy, which involves "mere acceptance of the organisation as necessary or inevitable based on some taken-for-granted cultural account" (p. 582), where members of the audience come to believe that any alternative form is "unthinkable". See also Barron (1998).

Institutionalisation occurs through a process in phases, from externalisation (taking action), objectivation (linked with the property of "exteriority", which determines the extent to which "reciprocal typifications" are "experienced as possessing a reality of their own, a reality that confronts the individual as an external and coercive fact") and internalisation (the construction of subjective consciousness) (Berger and Luckmann, 1966). The endless process of "typifications" gives rise to shared systems of meaning and contributes significantly to the establishment of boundaries for sets of organisations and organisational practices which, according to Selznick, may become "infused with value beyond the technical requirements of the task at hand" (1957, p. 17).

Organisations are inherently isomorphic by nature; that is to say that their practices and structures have a tendency to resemble those of other organisations in order to enhance legitimacy and survival prospects. DiMaggio and Powell (1983) identify three types of isomorphic behaviour – mimetic, normative and coercive – each of which in their different ways cause organisations to conform to certain standards (e.g. "benchmarking") or to mimic certain organisations for reasons other than the efficiency imperative.

Organisational communities, or "fields" (Scott and Meyer, 1991), eager to create order and reduce instability, turn reciprocally shared understandings into formal rules which permit ordered exchanges, from which markets and the systems that regulate them develop. Although, in the earlier institutional literature, fields tended to consist of public or at least not-for-profit organisational groupings such as schools or art galleries, it became clear that institutional pressures worked in similar ways on economic structures where the efficiency motive and the requirement for technical rationality were more explicit. Structured markets are an example of an organisational field, one which is controlled in large part by dominant firms and which interprets market institutions such as governance structures, rules of exchange and property rights as instruments to preserve the existing order, enhancing the survival prospects of existing players rather than explicitly promoting profit maximisation (Fligstein, 2001). Employment systems are an "institutional project", the outcomes of political interactions between sets of actors that make up the structure of employment relations, namely labour, capital and the state, formed at "crucial points in time, [when] power constellations in society and differentiated patterns in education have crystallised and been 'frozen' into institutions that have continued to shape employment systems even after those initial conditions have changed' (Fligstein, 2001, p. 109). The idea of the employment system as an "institutional field" held together by a coalition of groups who have a large amount at stake in maintaining the status quo will be helpful in enabling us to understand the longevity of the Japanese employment system, itself "crystallised" in the critical post-war years.

In what way then is the Japanese employment system institutionally distinctive? If differences with other employment systems do exist, do these differences spring from deep-rooted cultural factors which were aligned in such a way that the only possible result was the Japanese organisational form, or were they deliberately and rationally arrived at by organisational architects striving to come up with a template for industrial supremacy? What, if anything, is the link between the Japanese organisational design and low inward FDI? Let us first view the various historical perspectives before examining the nature of Japanese firms in detail.

Japanese organisations in historical context: culturalist vs rationalist interpretations

Reflecting the broad division in organisational literature between rationalist and culturalist explanations, there are competing interpretations of the origins of the Japanese organisational form. Studies of Japanese organisations have tended to emphasise a highly integrated "system" at work (e.g. Aoki, 1994; Itoh, 1994). At the macro level, for example, government, bureaucracy and business are tightly connected (e.g. Johnson, 1982), members of industrial groups are interdependent, centred around the main bank (Aoki, 1988; Hoshi, 1994; Sheard, 1994), and the Japanese employment system consists of a series of interlocking attributes (Aoki, 1994). At the level of the firm, the integrated system has been characterised by a system of lifetime employment, seniority-based pay and all the recruitment, socialisation and training practices that are designed to elicit long-term commitment from employees (Lincoln and Kalleberg, 1990).

The idea of the uniqueness of the Japanese is embedded in the ideas of *nihonjinron*, a theory of Japanese culture that can be traced back to the Tokugawa period. *Nihonjinron* emphasises the distinctiveness of the Japanese race, its linguistic, psychological and even physiological make-up, which developed in isolation on the island nation over the millennia. Japanese social structures reflect the dominance of the group, emphasised homogeneity and down-played the role of the individual. Whilst not coming close in any way to the particularism of *nihonjinron*, the early post-war anthropological literature offered predominantly culturalist explanations for the existence of Japanese social systems and practices, with pioneering anthropological and sociological works by the likes of Benedict (1967) and Nakane (1970), which highlight cultural values, such as the emphasis on harmony, duty, loyalty and the subordination of the individual to the group. Confucian values are often referred to, even in analyses of business organisations. For example, Imai and Komiya (1994) wrote:

> it is clear that traditional Japanese principles for the formation of organisations and the Confucian concept of *seniores priores* – precedence to the old over the young – have been influential in producing those features of Japanese firms that we have referred to … as the lifetime employment system and the *nenkō* system. (p. 23)

The early works presaged a number of studies by anthropologists, sociologists and business academics that laid heavy emphasis on culture as the key explanatory variable to Japanese organisational form and employment practices (e.g. Abegglen, 1958; Levine, 1958; Ouchi, 1981; Pascale and Athos, 1981; Rohlen, 1974; Vogel, 1979), in particular a system of values instilled through close clan and kinship ties.

The rationalist explanation

As a reaction against the idea of "Japanese firms … regarded as culturally unique and somewhat aberrational compared with the Anglo-Saxon orthodoxy of capitalism" (Aoki, 1994, p. 11) a set of literature has developed in the last twenty years that attempts to apply neoclassical economic tools to gain insights into the Japanese organisational form and set it against the backdrop of economic rationality. Perhaps the most significant argument made against the cultural school is the fact that the Japanese version of capitalism in the inter-war period was very different to that which appeared in the post-war era, with much more power exercised by shareholders and a more fluid external labour market, especially for blue-collar workers, thus undermining the cultural argument (Jacoby, 1979; Okazaki, 1994; Sugayama, 1995).

At the macro level, the rational school analysis of *keiretsu* relationships ranges from the explanations based on transaction cost theory and exercise of monopoly power (Itoh, 1994) to the more recent assertions that, far from being a key element in Japanese economic development in the post-war period, they never existed in the first place and were merely a "figment of the academic imagination" (Miwa and Ramseyer, 2002). At the micro level, Koike (1994), in referring to the "myth concerning teamwork or group-oriented behaviour", draws upon incentive theory to reject the notion of cultural uniqueness. He attributes high work performance to the way Japanese employees are trained, evaluated and rewarded, a system that promotes intense competition among workers. He asserts that "the skill is basically an individual one", rather than being based in some innate ability of Japanese workers to work harmoniously with each other. Okabe, in a study comparing the work attitudes of British and Japanese workers (2002), found that cultural differences between British and Japanese workers were not as large as were generally perceived and that attitudinal difference emerged from rational responses to different employment practices. Marsh and Mannari (1976) went further, arguing that the distinctiveness of the employment systems themselves (in this case, the Japanese and US systems) was greatly exaggerated, reflected in similar attitudes towards work by US and Japanese workers.

Another important argument made by those who oppose the culturalist argument is that Japan has a "dual economy" and that the traditional understanding of the Japanese employment system only applies to large companies, employing over 1,000 workers. For small and medium-sized enterprises ("SMEs") which account for 70% of employees and 50% of Japan's output (Cole, 1971) recruitment from universities (let alone the elite ones) is harder (Whittaker, 1994), worker loyalty is less evident, evidenced by higher employee turnover (Watanabe and Sato, 2000), and trust relationships harder to engender (Chalmers, 1989).

An influential subset of the rational school is the "control school". Advocates (e.g. Gordon, 1998; Kamata, 1982; van Wolferen, 1993) assert that the present Japanese employment system emerged from the bitter post-war labour-management conflicts in which the power of the managerial class was considerably strengthened in return for concessions to labour on long-term job security. This literature tends to interpret Japanese organisational innovations such as quality circles and *kaizen* as instruments of Japanese management surveillance and control over the workforce (Morris *et al.*, 2000) where membership, voluntary on the surface, is effectively compulsory (Gordon, 1998). In a questionnaire-based survey, Sullivan and Peterson (1991) found some support for the control model. Gordon describes the lifetime employment and seniority wage systems as "misnomers" and emphasises that managers have in practice an array of devices to reduce the labour force, particularly targeting overpaid elderly workers. Still others dispute the concept of the inherently loyal Japanese worker; the rigid job market and frequent job rotation are deliberately formulated by a management bent on preventing employee mobility (Hirakubo, 1999). A number of studies of work practices of Japanese companies' overseas operations have also reinforced the "control" hypothesis (Besser, 1995; Morris *et al.*, 2000).

There are, then, problems in applying either a purely rationalist or a purely culturalist analysis and neither offers a completely satisfactory explanation as to why Japanese organisations have developed as they have. Culture is traditionally served up as the remedy for the "undersocialised" and "Panglossian" nature of functionalism (Granovetter, 1985), its over-reliance on economic and technical factors and its overly deterministic orientation. Cultural interpretations, however, are also fraught with problems. Culture only has meaning through interpretation and these meanings are also often applied with inconsistency. As we have seen, absolutist cultural arguments are relatively simple to undermine when examining the "before" and "after" in cases of major social upheaval such as occurred in Japan during and in the immediate aftermath of World War II. Ultimately, it is difficult to accept that the true explanation of the origins of the Japanese organisational form and employment system lies at either extreme of the spectrum of a purely culturalist or rational foundation and that a combination of factors must be responsible. Indeed, this is the position of most commentators. In an exhaustive study of the work organisations and attitudes in the US and Japan, Lincoln and Kalleberg (1990) conclude that:

the role of culture is not trivial, it is primarily: (a) indirect through the role it presently plays and the residues it has historically left in the concrete organisation of firms; and (b) additive in the sense that it contributes to attitude and behavioural differences between Japanese and US workers but does not markedly condition the ways employees respond to their jobs or other facets of their employment. (p. 251)

The advent of "welfare corporatism": 1945–late 1990s

Today, thirty-six years after its first publication, there is still no better description of what we consider to be the classic Japanese firm than Ron Dore's *British Factory – Japanese Factory* (1973). While we will explore in this and later chapters the extent to which Japanese organisations have moved on from the Hitachi archetype depicted in this book, the concept of "welfare corporatism" developed by Dore describes perfectly the employment philosophy of large Japanese firms in the half century or so after the end of World War II. "Welfare corporatism" is, of course, contrasted to "welfare statism" and could refer generally to an employee-centred stakeholder-based corporate governance structure present in other countries, such as those in Scandinavia, but Dore emphasises that the way Japanese welfare corporatism developed has made it take on a very different appearance from that which may be present elsewhere (Dore, 1973, pp. 370–371). Since the 1980s, the welfare role played by large Japanese firms may have diminished, but those who believe that the basic philosophy that underpins Japanese organisational practices remains unchanged refer to them as "organisationally oriented", contrasted to the "market-oriented" practices of Anglo-Saxon firms.

According to Dore, there is also a strong element of rational design in the Japanese organisational form. He asserts that the origins of the welfare corporatism that shaped the post-war Japanese industrial organisational form could be explained by the "late developer" hypothesis. In much the same way that the major institutions in Meiji Japan such as the postal system and the press were adaptations of what were perceived to be the most successful models then in existence in Europe and the US (Westney, 1987), this theory maintains that countries that embark late on the process of industrialisation have at their disposal a number of models of industrial production, technology and indeed industrial society from which to choose. Thus the system took shape and formed the basis of the Japanese employment system, what Dore termed the Japanese "welfare corporatist organisation".

At the root of welfare corporatism is the idea that the company exists to serve a broad stakeholder base, but with the employees playing a much more prominent role in the governance hierarchy than in western corporations (Fliaster and Marr, 2001). This idea has profound implications for the shape of the Japanese employment system and organisational form. The alignment of interests of managers is closer to that of employees than with shareholders:

in Japan, hitherto, there has been little doubt that employees come a clear first ... the stakeholder which is of overwhelming importance to a Japanese manager is the community of *sha-in*,[2] the "members of the enterprise community": the firm's regular employees who, like himself, joined the firm, mostly at a very early age, in the expectation of making a career in it. (Dore, 2000, p. 10)

In contrast to the emphasis on lifetime membership of the Japanese firm "the paradigm of employment in the British firm is the contract, specific in its obligations and limited in time by a specified period of notice" (Dore, 1973).

Both inside the firm and as a societal phenomenon in general, the idea of equality was an important guiding principle in the construction of Japanese institutions in the post-war period. An "'equality of condition' for all adults at the expense of earlier conceptions of society as naturally divided into a ruling class and an underclass" (Dore, 1973, p. 339) took root "backed by the full authority of the occupying army before union-management relations had acquired any institutional rigidity". The embeddedness of this sense of equality, both in government policy and corporate human resource philosophy, was considered an important factor in raising the commitment of the workforce (Abegglen and Stalk, 1985) and is evidenced at the workplace by a number of symbols that downplay status differentials between blue- and white-collar workers, and between management and others, such as dining arrangements, uniforms and so on (Lincoln and Kalleberg, 1990).

There was little evidence of the concept of the employee-favouring company prior to World War II, with little hesitation on the part of shareholders to exert influence and 30–40% of company funds being raised in the capital markets compared with 10% in the post-war period (Hoshi and Kashyap, 2001; Okazaki, 1994). However, the war proved to be a decisive moment in the balance of power between the owners and employees. With the emphasis on increasing production and productivity, the wartime administration not only introduced

[2] I.e., employees.

measures to get the general public to increase savings (which effectively suppressed the role of direct finance) but also explicitly raised the status of the worker at the expense of the shareholder. In the "Outline of the Establishment of a New Labour System" published in 1940, it was made clear that "the firm should not be the property of the stockholders but rather, a communal organisation composed of managers, office clerks, and workers – in short, everybody who worked for the firm" (Okazaki, 1994, p. 369). When the war ended, the emphasis that the occupation administration laid on the democratisation of labour meant that the shift in the balance of power from stockholders to employees went through a smooth transition into the post-war era, with little adjustment. The widespread adoption of the *densangata chingin* system, designed to guarantee a minimum living standard for the workforce, but which formed the cornerstone of the seniority system as older workers' financial needs would be greater as their family circumstances changed and the labour-management consensus reached in the late 1950s that promised stability of employment in return for flexible work practices (Gordon, 1998), were important "crystallising" events (Fligstein, 2001) that solidified the foundations of the Japanese employment system.

The shareholding structure of Japanese firms, as well as the motives of Japanese shareholders, was contrasted by Clark (1979) to owners of US and UK firms. Whereas Anglo-Saxon shareholders were predominantly pension funds, unit trusts and insurance companies who held shares in the expectation of dividend and capital gain, "in Japan, by contrast, the institutional shareholders are usually the banks and trading partners of a company whose shares they own. They have bought their shares not so much for dividends as to ensure the co-operation of the company as a borrower or customer or supplier" (p. 102).

"Employee sovereignty": corporate "insiderism"

Once the system became institutionalised, legitimacy constraints operated both on shareholders and on the managers who were in theory their agents in the running of the company as the "Japanese view the corporation as a societal institution whose mission goes well beyond mere profit-making and share-price appreciation" (Lincoln, 1997, p. 33). Itami (1994) develops the idea of "employee sovereignty" and concludes that "the firm belongs to the people who have committed themselves to it and worked in it for long periods. They are the hold-ers of 'sovereign power'. In other words, they are the people who have the right to make the decisions of basic importance to the firm and they have priority rights in the distribution of the economic products of the firm's activities." Itami appeals to both economic efficiency and social legitimacy arguments to defend his position. Employee sover-eignty is economically efficient because it represents a "coincidence of interests" between the personal goals of the employee and the goals of the organisation itself (employees are the ultimate beneficiaries of the company doing well, therefore it motivates them to work hard for the company). Employee sovereignty is also economically efficient because it promotes "information efficiency in decision making". Important decisions on matters such as investment are made by those who are at the front line, who have "some sense of shop-floor realities", and therefore are likely to be more informed decisions. Employee sover-eignty is more legitimate because, in Itami's view, the risk burden on the employee is far greater than that of the shareholder in the event that the firm's fortunes decline or collapse completely. Ultimately, it is a matter of supply and demand of scarce resources: "if the people, the essential resource, are of high quality, the money will come to them. Good people are scarcer than money, and that is why I would say the shareholders do not make the essential contribution" (p. 81).

In a survey of employees of large listed companies with widely diversified ownership in five countries, Yoshimori (1995) found that that there were considerable attitudinal differences concerning gov-ernance hierarchy between Japanese, French, German, US and UK employees. Figure 1.1 illustrates the gulf in perception concerning the underlying assumptions of the purpose of the company that exists between Japanese and US and UK employees. Just 2.9% of Japanese respondents thought that shareholders should take first priority com-pared with over 75% of US respondents. The positioning of French and German respondents is interesting, with a closer alignment to the Japanese than the Anglo-Saxon mentality.

In line with what one might expect in an employee-dominated governance hierarchy in times of economic difficulty, it is the share-holders who are expected to show flexibility, not the employees: divi-dends are cut, salaries may even be cut, but not the headcount of core long-term employees (Dore, 1997). In a welfare corporatist organisa-tion, the lifetime commitment means that in periods of adjustment

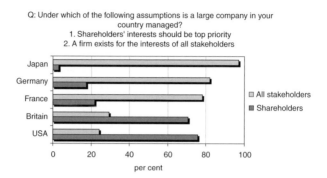

Figure 1.1 Shareholder vs stakeholder orientation
Source: Yoshimori (1995)

"the market processes play a much smaller, and administrative processes a much larger part, in adjustment than in most other societies.
Cyclical adjustment is more a matter of adjusting work hours, less a
matter of hire and fire" (Dore *et al.*, 1989). "Employee adjustment"
in the Japanese sense is based on relative flexibility in nominal and
real wages (Hamada and Kurosaka, 1986), widespread hiring and
dismissal of temporary staff and temporary laying off of full-time
employees (Hashimoto, 1993; Higuchi, 1997). In Yoshimori's 1995
survey, Japanese and Anglo-Saxon employees respond very differently to questions of whether the company should consider dividend
or headcount reduction in financially straitened times.

From the concept of employee sovereignty and the distinctive framework of Japanese corporate governance emerge all the other features
of Japanese organisational form that make up the welfare corporatist
organisation. The result is an employment system whose component
parts are strongly inter-linked (Itoh, 1994) and which has emerged
from "choices made in historical context with constraints imposed by
existing institutional factors" (Morishima, 1995, p. 618). Above all, the
Japanese system of corporate governance and the employment system
which flows from it are based on the principle of "internalism", which
overwhelmingly protects the interests of insiders (Buchanan, 2007).
The communitarian firm (Dore, 1973; Inagami and Whittaker, 2005),
and the system of recruitment, reward and lifetime employment stability that underpins it, fosters a sense of a common purpose and a long-
term commitment to the organisation (Lincoln and Kalleberg, 1990).
There is little incentive to permit infiltration from the outside (Itoh,

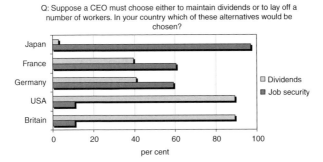

Figure 1.2 Dividends vs layoffs
Source: Yoshimori (1995)

1994): the vast majority of board members are insiders (Ahmadjian, 2001) and the CEO feels that the support of his employees is far more important than that of shareholders (Yoshimori, 1995). As the firm's shareholders are also predominantly insiders, other Japanese firms with whom the company has intimate business or financial links, there has been an absence of pressure from the legal owners of the firm to alter the balance of stakeholder influence. There are external board members on many boards, but they are invariably heavily outnumbered by internal appointees and in any case are usually "friendly" appointments whose views as outsiders may be valued, but are not viewed as representative of shareholders' interests (Clark, 1979). With the lack of effective separation of executive and monitoring functions at board level, in the past it has been left to the company's main bank in its role as principal creditor to provide a certain level of external monitoring of company management (Sheard, 1994). From time to time, banks were responsible for CEO and senior management transition, or forcing the company to merge in cases of serious corporate failure.[3]

The fact that virtually all corporate CEOs and executive directors are home grown has led to an absence of a properly functioning external labour market for senior management. As there is no market, there is no effective "market price" for executive talent. During the

---

[3] Examples include the forced merger in 1992 of the trading company Itoman with Sumitomo Metals arranged by Sumitomo Bank, or the intervention by the Industrial Bank of Japan to bring in the CEO of Nissan Diesel to become CEO of Fuji Heavy Industries to turn the company around in 1990.

period 1976–2001, directors' emoluments including bonus as a multiple of employees' wages hovered in the extraordinarily narrow range of 2.44x and 2.68x. According to a report by Towers Perrin average CEO pay for large Japanese companies in 2003 was $457,000. In US firms it was $2.2 million.[4] Reflecting the long climb up the corporate ladder to the rank of CEO, the average age of newly appointed CEOs at Japanese firms was 58.4 years in 2004, compared with 49.1 years at US firms.[5] The relatively narrow pay differentials, plus the feeling that the directors of the firm represent a "committee of elders" (Dore, 2000), has enhanced the internalist nature of Japanese organisations.

Isomorphic tendencies of Japanese organisations

If ever there was a society that took isomorphism seriously, it must be Japan. The concept is particularly useful in enabling us to understand the institutionalisation process of the Japanese employment system. Indeed, there is a word used in common parlance which describes perfectly the isomorphistic process: *yokonarabi* (横並び). *Yokonarabi* refers to the process, before making a decision, of stopping to look what other participants in the same domain or institutional field are doing and then deciding to do pretty much the same thing. It is variously translated as "copying" or "follow the leader" and at its most basic level it can refer to the simple act of emulation. However, its use as a word to describe a behavioural predisposition as in *yokonarabi shikō* (横並び志向) illustrates a deep-seated mimetic tendency where the legitimacy of an organisation's actions can be enhanced by putting it into the wider context of the institutional field rather than through demonstrable claims to logic or rationality. The communitarian nature of Japanese capitalism gave rise to a form of "cooperatively competitive" behaviour, *yokonarabi kyōsō* (横並び競争), which have spawned similar, or even pooled, research agenda, *yokonarabi kenkyū* (横並び研究).

Orrù *et al.* (1991, p. 375) identify strong isomorphic pressures at work in Japanese industrial organisations: "what is embodied in the isomorphism of Japanese enterprise groups is not simply organisational

[4] See www.allbusiness.com/human-resources/compensation-salary/207587 1.html.
[5] See *Nihon Keizai Shimbun*, 9 July 2004, p. 1.

efficiency and effectiveness in the Western sense, but also a unique concern with group solidarity and cooperation". They refer to this particular brand of isomorphism as "coercive" pertaining to "the cultural expectations in the society within which organisations function" (DiMaggio and Powell, 1983, p. 150). Enactment of a communitarian ideal is part of the fulfilment of these cultural expectations and the decision-making process in business organisations reflects the same emphasis on what is best for the collectivity, rather than individual firms. Whitley (1990, 1991) also identifies major differences in organisational form among east Asian nations and emphasises that the "social constructions" of business systems are neither a cultural relativist phenomenon nor a reflection of market pressures and the efficiency imperative.

Westney (1987) has noted the mimetic process by which the Japanese in the Meiji period built up key institutions such as the newspaper media and the police force virtually from scratch. We have also noted Dore's observation that Japan, as a "late developer", was able to adopt organisational structures and routines which were judged to suit the country's particular cultural and physical attributes.

The idea of the "employee-favouring" company and the importance of the concept of equality in the design of the substructure of the Japanese employment system took root during the post-war period (Hoshi and Kashyap, 2001; Okazaki, 1994). The isomorphic tendencies of large Japanese corporations is illustrated by the speed with which the new system acquired legitimacy, even if initial resistance from the labour movement meant the process was not always a smooth one (Gordon, 1998). By the late 1950s the labour unions had achieved their most important objective, long-term security of employment, and the practices that constituted the community firm became thoroughly institutionalised. The component parts of the communitarian model took on the "taken-for-granted" characteristics that are so important in the institutional landscape (Berger and Luckmann, 1966; Zucker, 1977). There is evidence of strong isomorphic pressures as systems of recruitment, training and career development spread in the decades after the war. The "Japanese employment system" was thus established and, whilst practices varied somewhat from industry to industry, the strength of legitimacy constraints was such that there was little deviance from the norm. The system was reinforced by a legal framework, which in turn was strongly supported by judicial interpretation.

Equally significant was the great emphasis placed on symbols and ceremony in large Japanese companies in which work practices and organisational form were embedded (John W. Meyer and Rowan, 1977). There is evidence of an advanced level of "sedimentation" from the recruitment process, where large Japanese firms looked to the same elite universities when hiring graduates, in the initiation and socialisation process designed to augment cohort solidarity and cohesion, through to the design of career structures and reward structures. This is the ultimate stage of Berger and Luckmann's process of institutionalisation.

As we have seen, many commentators argue that there is a rational basis for Japanese organisational form and practices. An institutional interpretation on the other hand would posit that while this might have been the case at the moment of the system's crystallisation in the aftermath of World War II and might explain its widespread adoption in the immediate post-war era, it has endured despite increasing claims that it does not represent the most efficient form of organising. Once an organisational field and the templates for organising within it become imbued with a "taken-for-granted" quality, strong inertial forces build up that discourage the challenging of the legitimate order (Oliver, 1992; Tolbert and Zucker, 1983). The events of the last fifteen years, however, have provided a very stern test for the Japanese employment system's institutional foundations.

Pressure for change: is "welfare corporatism" dead?

The legitimacy of the concept of the "employee-favouring firm" became increasingly undermined during the 1990s as pressure built up, a point that was not lost on Dore (2000, pp. 9–10): "the transformation on the agenda may be variously described – from employee sovereignty to shareholder sovereignty; from the employee-favouring firm to the shareholder-favouring firm; from pseudo-capitalism to genuine capitalism. They all mean the same thing: the transformation of firms run primarily for the benefit of their employees into firms run primarily, even exclusively, for the benefit of their shareholders."

The last fifteen years have seen a reversion to the theme of the irrationality of the Japanese employment system and a growing consensus that, for Japan to remain competitive, a fundamental shift is required. Questions are being asked about the very philosophical basis upon which the foundations of welfare corporatism lie. In particular, a number of commentators (e.g. Yashiro, 1998) have expressed the view that the nature of the equality emphasised in the post-war social consensus has hindered, rather than promoted, economic development. Taichi Sakaiya, a former MITI official and Director General of the Economic Planning Agency and now an influential writer, has called for changes in the attitudes and expectations of society and the individual:

In post-war Japan the idea of social justice was associated with three principles: efficiency, equality and security ... In particular, during the 1970s the principle of equality became more and more important to the extent that differentials among individuals were negatively considered ... However, in Japan, equality was not interpreted as equality of opportunity or equality in front of the law, but as equality of outcome ... As for security, this was mainly conceived in terms of peace, health and public order. In this framework, freedom was not even considered as a fundamental principle of social justice ... As a result, when freedom conflicted with efficiency, equality and security, the former had to be sacrificed. (Sakaiya, 1999, quoted in Molteni, 2000, p. 6)

It is claimed that "insiderism" inherent in Japanese organisations and the deeply embedded nature of the concept of equality in the employment system reduces income disparity and thereby fosters a strong sense of solidarity, but this is also cited as one of the key causes of resistance to change. The trade-off between freedom and this type of equality, often referred to as *akubyōdō* or "bad equality", is, as we shall see, a theme that emerged frequently during the fieldwork.

In the 1990s, the performance of many Japanese firms declined dramatically, especially financial institutions and those that were over-exposed to the domestic market. This was accompanied by a collapse in the share prices of Japanese companies. The rigidity of the Japanese labour market meant that revenues were falling, but costs were not. The problem was particularly acute in the white-collar sector. Overheads rose rapidly as a percentage of total costs because Japanese managers had paid attention only to production costs, not to selling, general and administrative expenses (Hori, 1993). The weakness of the financial sector, and of the banks in particular, raised questions as to the effectiveness of the main bank system (Scher, 1997) which had hitherto provided the main monitoring function of the management of Japanese companies (Aoki, 1990; Hoshi and Kashyap, 2001; Sheard, 1994) in continuing its key role in the corporate governance process. This left a void which required the more active participation of shareholders (METI, 2003). There have been strong calls on Japanese firms to recognise more explicitly shareholders' status as owners and to put more emphasis on "shareholder value". To many, this means a sharper focus on the cost base which in turn implies curbing levels of investment and a more flexible labour policy (e.g. Smithers, 2006). In a Ministry of Finance survey carried out in 2002, nearly 50% of Japanese pension funds and more than 70% of trustee organisations felt that the Japanese employment system represented an obstacle to corporate revival (Ministry of Finance of Japan, 2002).

As a result, many observers during the late 1990s (e.g. Hirakubo, 1999; Mroczkowski and Hanaoka, 1998; Ornatowski, 1998) went as far as forecasting the imminent demise of the Japanese employment system. At the same time, however, many questioned how deep convictions about shareholder value were among Japanese managers (e.g. Morgan and Takahashi, 2002; Yoshikawa and Phan, 2001), which in turn led others to doubt that such deeply institutionalised practices could be transformed so easily (Dedoussis, 2001; Molteni, 2000).

Particularly during the Koizumi premiership, government policy has been to address what it perceives as Japan's structural shortcomings and there have been a number of initiatives to promote liberalisation and competition in a broad range of sectors such as finance, post and telecommunications, transportation and retail industries. These measures have been supplemented with changes in labour laws, the commercial code and accounting practices to increase flexibility and enhance transparency and managerial accountability. The sense of urgency that led to these reforms was not only brought about by the long period of economic stagnation, but also by demographic shifts which have left Japan particularly exposed to the effects of an ageing population.

An important component of the economic restructuring that has taken place during the last fifteen years has been the transformation in the structure of ownership of Japanese listed companies. The persistent weakness of Japanese banks and life insurance companies, as

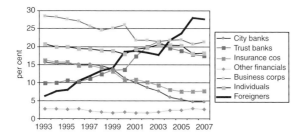

Figure 1.3 Share ownership of TSE by market value
Source: TSE Handbook (2008)

well as changes in accounting regulations, have forced companies to reduce substantially their cross-shareholdings. As Figure 1.3 above shows, the combined shareholding of Japanese city banks and life insurance companies listed on the Tokyo Stock Exchange fell from around 32% in 1993 to approximately 12% in 2005. There has also been a spectacular rise in holdings by foreign investors, who now make up the largest group of shareholders of Japanese listed companies, from being virtually the smallest in 1993. For some time, many major Japanese companies have had in excess of 50% of their outstanding share capital owned by foreign institutional investors. This movement was mirrored by the activities of foreign institutional asset management firms, who increased their presence significantly in Japan, in some cases, such as the firm for whom I worked, UBS, by acquisition, or through the establishment of offices in Japan. Increasingly through the 1990s foreign asset management firms were not just managing Japanese equity and bond portfolios for overseas pension funds, but were making rapid inroads into the Japanese domestic pension fund market.

This change in share ownership structure has undoubtedly had some impact on Japanese corporate behaviour. Japanese executives appear to be much more preoccupied with the company's share price than before and this has led to the rapid growth in investor relations activity as a core function of the finance group (Buchanan, 2006). Robinson and Shimizu (2006) show that Japanese CEOs spend a considerably greater proportion of their time on investor relations than twenty years ago and correspondingly less on their main banking relationships.

This has led Dore to conclude (2006) that there has been a "quiet shareholders' revolution" in Japan, which has seen a dramatic rise in the gap between workers' and directors' pay, as well as an unprecedented increase in dividend payments and share buybacks. The tide of reform, the passivity (or even the complicity) of the union movement and the irresistible rise of shareholder value and "global standard" discourse, promoted by the new political elite and an ever-increasing population of like-minded Japanese returning with MBAs and PhDs from US universities, many of whom are now in senior positions, all threaten the very existence of the quasi-community firm.

What I hope to show in succeeding chapters, in which I examine the component parts of the Japanese employment system and recent developments affecting them, is that it is too early to talk about the demise of the Japanese firm that Dore depicted in 1973. Certainly, it has had to adapt to a vastly different landscape than that which Hitachi faced in 1973. Many of the practices which were features of the 1973 version of the welfare corporatist organisation, particularly family allowances, have disappeared. The inequality between the haves and the have-nots is certainly greater in Japan now than it was thirty years ago. This also applies to the difference in salary between those identified in a cohort group as being destined for the top and those who are not. As Jacoby puts it: "On the market-organization continuum, Japan is moving, albeit slowly, towards the market pole" (2005, p. 158).

Many argue, however, and I would agree with them, that despite the undoubted crisis endured by the Japanese version of capitalism in the last decade and a half, there is no immediate prospect of the Japanese organisational form "converging" on the Anglo-Saxon model. Entrenched norms, severely questioned as they were during the depths of the economic slump, still appear to shape views on the role of the firm and its relationship with stakeholders. The most recent survey of newly elected directors and "corporate officers" of listed Japanese firms (JMA, 2006) shows a marked cooling off, starting in 2004, in support of the proposition that the interests of shareholders should come first in the stakeholder hierarchy and a corresponding increase in the view that the interests of employees should come first. As these were the views of tomorrow's presidents as opposed to today's (average age of respondents was 52.6 years), these represent the views of Japan's future leaders. The Ministry of Finance report into investor views on corporate governance concluded: "institutional investors take the view that companies still put stress on stakeholders that reflect the Japanese corporate system and it is suggested that they think that the corporate governance structure of Japanese companies has basically not changed" (Ministry of Finance of Japan, 2002, p. 15).

Although many commentators see significant changes in the Japanese labour market and its institutions with moves towards greater flexibility and a reliance on market mechanisms in the deter-mination of compensation, very few see a fundamental break from the past. Rebick (2005, p. 174) sums it up in the following way: "the employment system is not breaking down, just remodelling itself to cope with a new economic and demographic environment". In an in-depth study of organisational change at Hitachi, Inagami and Whittaker (2005) conclude that "the community firm will persist, but the classic model may be giving way to what may be called, for want of a better term, a *reformed model*" where "there may be a movement on the part of some top managers towards the 'enlightened share-holder value model', but hardly a conversion to shareholder financial capitalism" (p. 241).

Despite the increasing criticism of many elements of the community firm during the past two decades and the emphasis in recent Japanese corporate governance discourse on the concept of "shareholder value", which would seem to indicate that an alternative vision of legitimacy is emerging, the system has proved remarkably resilient.

The tentative conclusion of most contemporary commentators would appear to be that, despite the manifest pressures on Japanese organisations, the basic shape of the community firm has remained largely intact. This would tend to support the conclusions of Fligstein (2001) that, once the institutions of employment systems are in place, they are difficult to dislodge, given the large amount of social and political capital at stake in maintaining them. Those with a stake in the institutionalised order will coalesce to prevent the emergence of an alternative definition of reality (Berger and Luckmann, 1966, p. 107). At the level of the individual organisation there appears to be no solid evidence that the broad consensus among the various key interest groups has changed in a way to disturb what Greenwood and Hinings (1996) would call the "pattern of value commitments".

Despite changes in the legal framework that give shareholders more of a voice, opinion among corporate governance commentators (Nakamura, 2004; Patrick, 2003) appears to suggest that the underlying stakeholder-driven approach remains intact. The system is still "one of entrenched managerial autonomy and corporate governance by strong norms of managerial restraint" (Milhaupt, 2003). Any changes by traditional Japanese firms in corporate governance practices would only have occurred "because doing so could help them regain social legitimacy, not because they believe such practices necessarily improve asset efficiency or can even deliver shareholder value" (Yoshikawa and Phan, 2001).

The theme of the enduring nature of organisational forms and practices is also reflected at the level of business systems literature. Whitley (1998) argues that, while competition among national business systems may have increased, patterns of FDI will continue to be constrained by localised institutional factors. The impact of the internationalisation of capital markets and the role of foreign capital will continue to be limited: "the more cohesive is the host business system and its associated institutions, the less likely it is that the system will change just as a result of foreign firms developing a significant presence within it" (pp. 476–477).

Institutional theory and change: deinstitutionalisation and the role of outsiders and M&A

Berger and Luckmann (1966) identify institutionalisation as a "core process in the creation and perpetuation of enduring social groups". There must be, however, various circumstances that cause practices, however deeply entrenched, to change, or to become "deinstitutionalized". Oliver (1992) defines the process of deinstitutionalisation as being:

the process by which the legitimacy of an established organisational practice erodes or discontinues. Specifically, deinstitutionalisation refers to the delegitimation of an established organisational practice or procedure as a result of organisational challenges to or the failure of organisations to reproduce previously legitimated or taken-for-granted organisational actions. (p. 564)

There are social, functional and political pressures that work to cause change within organisations. Political pressure is caused by increasing problems of organisational performance, conflicting internal interests and the influence of innovation. Political responses may be to changing power distributions (e.g. change in leadership or divisional influence) or the threat of failure or obsolescence (p. 570). All of these, as we shall see, are critical in the Japanese context.

Functional pressure is brought to bear through increasing technical specificity, for example, when demands on an organisation are re-oriented so that "the organisation is rewarded less for the sustained implementation of institutionally acceptable structures and procedures and more for the technical quality or quantity of its outputs". Another important factor may be an increase in the clarity of organisational objectives, particularly if they conflict with "prevailing organisational myths, superstitions or beliefs about the appropriate or legitimate means of obtaining organisational ends". Again, these are significant in the Japanese context.

Social pressures, Oliver argues, cause "normative fragmentation", which refers to a "loss of cultural consensus or agreement among organizational members" (p. 575). A number of factors are likely to cause a fragmentation of the consensus, such as high turnover, succession, increasing workforce diversity and weakening social mechanisms. It is in the social context that Oliver discusses the destabilising effect of "culturally disparate inter-organisational relations (mergers, joint ventures, for example)", which will have an impact on the value systems of members of the organisations and possibly cause a re-evaluation of a number of taken-for-granted organisational practices and beliefs. This theme, of course, is central to our thesis and the relationship between institutional theory and mergers will be developed later in this chapter.

The pressures outlined above cause changes to take place in three broad areas: in political distributions that help to support existing practices, in functional necessity, or how the organisation perceives the value or utility of these practices, and finally in the social consensus concerning the legitimacy of these practices. Oliver outlines a number of "predictive factors" associated with each type of change that determine the possible course of deinstitutionalisation. These are outlined in Table 1.1.

Table 1.1 *Empirical predictors of deinstitutionalisation*

Intra-organisational factors

Changes in political distributions
Increasing workforce diversity
Declining performance or crises
Power reallocations
Threat of obsolescence

Changes in functional necessity
Increasing technical specification
Increasing goal clarity

Changes in social consensus
Increasing turnover or succession
Weakening socialisation mechanisms
Culturally disparate mergers and alliances
Increasing diversification, dispersion or differentiation

Source: Adapted from Oliver (1992).

It is clear that not all of Oliver's "predictors" have to be present at the same time, nor with the same degree of force, to presage the process of deinstitutionalisation. Thus, for example, the extent to which a merger is "culturally disparate", or the extent to which such a merger is combined with "power reallocations" and/or "increasing succession or turnover", will have an important bearing on the path that deinstitutionalisation takes. We will be coming back to this model to test the extent to which institutional factors can explain the organisational changes that take place in the cross-border acquisitions that I have examined for the purposes of this book.

A crucial role in the change process is played by exogenous forces. Organisations are subject to "jolts" (Greenwood *et al.*, 2002; Alan D. Meyer *et al.*, 1990), which may come about through social upheaval, technological disruption, or regulatory change. In proposing an "exogenous theory of market transformation", Fligstein (2001, p. 84) notes that forces that cause change often result from external factors outside the control of market: "shifts in demand, invasion by other firms, or actions of the state".

However, "exogenous forces" do not just refer to an event; just as important, it refers to the role of organisations or actors who enter a field to precipitate change. Greenwood and Hinings (1993) allude to the role of outsiders, in their case the marketing and HR management personnel that infiltrated accounting firms, in the precipitation of organisational change. This theme is developed by Leblebici *et al.* (1991) who, in their study of the US radio broadcasting industry, assert that "radically new practices that may evolve into conventions are most likely to be introduced by parties from the fringes of an inter-organisational field" (p. 358). These fringe players are either newer entrants or are less powerful (or, more likely, both), who have less vested interest in the established institutional order. Hirsch (1986), examining the development of the hostile takeover in the US, identifies it initially as a "deviant" or "illegitimate" innovation (p. 808) prior to the 1970s, after which it became legitimised and diffused. Early practitioners tended to be entrepreneurial individuals of "low formal education and humble background", outsiders who had little to lose in challenging established norms and practices.

This theme will recur in our investigation of Japanese firms taken over by foreign organisations, hitherto considered very much as outsiders in the Japanese established corporate order (Kang, 1991). Hirsch's analysis of the use of vocabulary to depict the hostile takeover as deviant behaviour in the public's perception has parallels in Japan as we saw in the last chapter (Debroux, 1996) although, unlike the US experience, Japanese vocabulary has not changed, suggesting that this behaviour is still not considered to be acceptable.

What role for foreign firms? The problem of "institutional distance" and overcoming the "liability of foreignness"

Given the deeply embedded nature of Japanese organisations, what are the prospects of foreign firms causing fundamental change when they take control of Japanese firms? Indeed, do foreign firms even attempt to make such changes, given the large differences that would appear to exist between their own home organisations and Japanese ones? What factors do they take into consideration when evaluating their options? Again, institutional analysis offers us some clues.

For the last thirty years, academics have tried to infer that, in one way or another, distance from a multinational company's home base is an important determinant of entry mode into foreign markets. Rather than physical distance, emphasis has been laid on national differences in cognitive/cultural make-up. Thus, investment decisions would not just be based on economic factors such as market size, growth, interest rates, and so on, but on the size of the gap in knowledge and experience that existed in a firm's management cadre of a new market. This gap was initially framed as "psychic distance", defined as "the sum of factors preventing the flow of information from and to the market ... examples are differences in language, education, business practices, culture and industrial development" (Johanson and Vahlne, 1977, p. 24). Managers seeking to reduce uncertainty would tend to take a more cautious attitude towards market entry if there was a large psychic distance from their home base.

Lack of a systematic methodology for measuring psychic distance led Kogut and Singh (1988) to develop the concept of "cultural distance" using the dimensions of national culture developed by Hofstede (1980). Kogut and Singh point out that cultural factors are likely to be of particular importance in the case of acquisitions and that the higher the cultural distance between the investing firm and the country into which it is making its investment, the more likely it is to choose the greenfield or joint venture route rather than acquisition. A number of studies of the effects of cultural distance found that greater distance was associated with negative value creation in mergers and acquisitions (Datta and Puia, 1995) and that it reduced firm valuation by impeding the creation and transfer of knowledge within firms (Antia *et al.*, 2007).

The idea of cultural distance has been widely criticised for methodological inadequacies (e.g. Shenkar, 2001) and institutional theory has stepped in to provide a new view on the issues of international expansion facing multinational corporations (MNCs) by focusing on the complex legitimacy constraints in which they operate. Westney (1993) introduces the notion that the operations of MNCs straddle a multiplicity of institutional fields, which exert isomorphic pressures that pull in different, and often opposite, directions. MNCs operate in many markets, whose societal, political and economic institutions may differ considerably from those of the MNC's home market but they must achieve organisational legitimacy in all of them

(Kostova and Zaheer, 1999). Following Scott (1995) an institutional profile of a society is developed which consists of regulative (i.e. laws and rules), cognitive (i.e. a people's widely shared social knowledge) and normative (i.e. a people's shared set of values, beliefs and norms) components (Kostova and Roth, 2002). Legitimacy accrues to organisations where the regulative, cognitive and normative "pillars" of the organisation and of society at large are in alignment. The cognitive and particularly the normative domains are the most difficult for outsiders to observe. These pose the most problems for MNCs.

The extent to which one country's institutions differ from those of another is measured as "institutional distance". MNCs thus operate under conditions of "institutional duality" (Xu and Shenkar, 2002) where an MNC subsidiary will seek to maximise legitimacy within its local institutional context, but must also conform to certain institutional expectations set by its parent company, whose organisational structures and practices tend to be developed in the specific national setting of the home market (Whitley, 2001). It needs to enhance competitive advantage by mitigating the "liability of foreignness", which means adapting to local practices and customs, but must also be mindful of its position as part of a global enterprise, which means dealing with pressure to adopt "global best practice". The greater the institutional distance of the subsidiary from the parent, the greater the impact of institutional duality. Institutional distance has a direct bearing on an MNC's entry strategy into new markets. The greater the cognitive and normative distance from the home market, the greater the likelihood that a firm will choose to enter it through greenfield operations or a joint venture, rather than through M&A (Xu and Shenkar, 2002 pp. 613–614), mirroring the findings of Kogut and Singh noted above.

Institutional distance has a direct bearing on a subsidiary's propensity to internalise and/or implement practices mandated by head office. Kostova and Roth report that there were "minimal" levels of internalisation and implementation in groups which operated in environments with particularly hostile normative and cognitive alignments towards those practices. These subsidiaries also tended to have the lowest levels of dependence on the parent, as well as low levels of trust and identity. They also point to the possibility of a "ceremonial" adoption of practices, where implementation is not necessarily underpinned with high levels of internalisation.

Morgan and Christensen (2006) link the idea of institutional distance to the varieties of capitalism literature. The MNC subsidiary's "liability of foreignness" is re-branded as it having to operate under conditions of a "legitimacy deficit" (p. 1469). Distinguishing between two broad mechanisms of transfer between head office and its subsidiaries – practices, processes and work systems which add up to a set of "best practices" on the one hand and resources (financial, knowledge and reputational) on the other – they point out that the receptiveness of overseas operations will depend on the nature of the capitalistic system in which the subsidiary is embedded (Hall and Soskice, 2001). They speculate that organisations that are part of a "coordinated market economy", characterised by cohesive employment relations, high degrees of vertical and horizontal coordination across organisational hierarchies and local institutions such as suppliers, financial institutions and so on, who tend to have high levels of skill and expectations of consultation, are likely to resist transfers if they threaten these systems.

Morgan and Christensen also add two significant insights into the relationship between head offices and subsidiaries. First, they identify the key role played by micro-political factors in determining the way in which "institutional dualities" are resolved, in particular the significance of the subsidiary to the overall profitability of the firm and the extent to which the output of the subsidiary is aimed at its local market, or whether it is integrated more fully into the firm's global production and distribution infrastructure. The emphasis on politics serves to reinforce the messages of Oliver (1992) on the importance of the political process on the trajectory of organisational change.

Second, they allude to the crucial role played by capital markets into which the parent company is embedded and the generally prevailing attitude towards ownership and the status of shareholders. Relationships between senior management and institutional investors differ across markets, particularly the level of scrutiny that managers are put under regarding the achievement of short-term financial goals, as well as the consequences of failure in achieving them. The implication is that companies who are answerable principally to capital market participants in liberal market economies such as the UK or the US are more likely to apply greater pressure to subsidiaries through extensive benchmarking and resort sooner to restructuring solutions in the event of the failure of the subsidiary to meet expectations. Managers located in institutionally distant subsidiaries must decide whether to follow a "boy scout" strategy and cooperate using measures to increase productivity in ways that may conflict with local norms, or a "subversive" strategy in which they may try to reach objectives, but within the legitimacy constraints of the local environment. This is a particularly salient point in interpreting the contrasting outcomes of our cases, as we shall see.

Mergers and acquisitions and the process of institutional change

Given the nature of our enquiry, we are particularly interested in one particular type of deinstitutionalising event: that which takes place in institutionally distant mergers. We would expect that the greater the distance of the acquiring firm from the target, the greater the extent of the "jolt" to the target organisation. However, exogenous events can work at a number of levels to contribute to the rejection of institutionalised practices or organisational forms. Fligstein (1991) shows how the appointment of a new CEO from a different functional background provided "a new view of the firm's strategy" which in turn represented a "redistribution of power dependencies" (Greenwood and Hinings, 1996), causing deinstitutionalisation pressure. Thus I am asserting that mergers and acquisitions (M&A) are just one of many phenomena that might contribute to institutional change.

Typically, organisational research in merger and acquisitions literature has focused on issues relating to cultural fit (see Haspeslagh and Jemison, 1991; Marks and Mirvis, 1992). Much has been written about the negative side of merger activity, relating to employees' feelings of conflict, tension and alienation and the deterioration of co-worker trust (Marks and Mirvis, 1985, 2001). It is evident that, at the organisational level, deeply institutionalised practices and taken-for-granted routines can be immediately called into question with the sudden entry of outsiders into an organisation. Again, the greater the institutional distance of the acquiring firm, the greater we would expect the level of questioning to be, particularly if the merger of two organisations has come about as a result of a hostile takeover.

Schneider and Dunbar (1992), extending Hirsch's textual analysis of the media in the arena of corporate takeovers, find that hostile takeovers "threaten organisational boundaries, autonomy, and control ... challenge existing forms of ownership ... question the usual notions of market mechanisms for corporate control and ... disrupt individual careers by calling into question professional competence and job security". Narratives relating to such takeovers "cause a re-evaluation of the sacred myths of the free market, humanistic philosophies, and social responsibilities" (p. 561).

According to a study by Jackson and Miyajima (2007) there is strong evidence to suggest that M&A activity is institutionally mediated and that patterns of M&A exist based on liberal markets and coordinated market varieties in Japanese, German and French companies. The link between varieties of capitalism and cross-border post-merger integration outcomes is made by Aguilera and Dencker (2004) who suggest that there are material differences in the human resource (HR) strategies of companies which are embedded at head office level in liberal market economies and coordinated market economies in such mergers. HR strategies are closely aligned to M&A strategy. Thus, firms from liberal market economies (LME), who are less institutionally constrained when it comes to downsizing, are more likely to be involved in cross-border M&A where the primary aim is to cut capacity. In product or market extension M&A, LME firms are more likely to integrate the acquired company fully than firms from coordinated market economies (CME). LME firms are more likely to impose their value systems on the acquired firm than the other way round. CME firms, on the other hand, are more likely to devote resources to training (see also Child *et al.*, 2001).

It is also clear that there are important national differences in the extent to which there is an open market for corporate control. While external influences play an important role in determining the nature of this market, particularly the country's legal framework, cultural and institutional factors also have a strong influence. Japan, for example, has a very weak market for corporate control, something that is attributed to its greater emphasis on human rights as opposed to property rights in the corporate context. Thus, Dore (2000, pp. 25–26) states: "in Japanese firms, by contrast [with Anglo-Saxon firms], nobody gives a great deal of thought to owners. Firms are not seen as anybody's 'property' ... They are more like communities."

It is this contrasting position on human as opposed to property rights that gives rise to major differences between the Japanese and Anglo-Saxon view of corporate acquisitions. Walter (1985) describes the central conflict in a merger/acquisition event to be the rights of the individual pitted against the rights of capital, human rights versus property rights. In any organisation there is a balance between these two antithetical values – a state of equilibrium that is generally acknowledged by members of the organisation, with the location of that equilibrium constituting an important part of its cultural identity. However, the effect of a merger/acquisition event is to provide a shock to the cultural status quo, as the event represents "the assertion of power in the service of property rights [and] ... a new thesis is inserted which in turn invites and perhaps even generates a new antithesis position on behalf of human rights". The pivotal human rights of freedom, self-esteem and equality are struggling against the corresponding elements of property rights: control, performance and primacy. Walter further refines the competing value expressions as security, privacy, identity, inclusion, comparable competence and self-determination representing the "human" versus flexibility, scrutiny, substitutability, segregation, superior competence and organisational direction elements of property rights. (See Table 1.2.)

Table 1.2 *Value contrasts in mergers and acquisitions*

Value basis	Human	Property
Pivotal elements	Freedom Esteem Equality	Control Performance Primacy
Value expressions	Security	Flexibility
	Privacy	Scrutiny
	Identity	Substitutability
	Inclusion	Segregation
	Comparable competence	Superior direction
	Self-determination	Organisational competence

Source: Walter (1985).

Thus, in the conflict between identity and substitutability, the sense of congruence between self and context, the sense of identification that employees may feel towards an organisation will be threatened by capital's emphasis on optimal capital utilisation, which calls for the substitutability of elements and impersonality. Employees become "human capital" upon which returns should always be calculable. The power asymmetry that develops between the acquired and acquiring company will necessarily lead to a greater emphasis on substitutability at the expense of identity.

If mergers do represent, as Walter believes, a conflict between human and property rights, it follows that the outcome of mergers will depend on the extent to which a nation's societal, political and economic institutions emphasise either of these antithetical values. Given the low value that Japanese organisations put on property rights in the context of company ownership (Dore, 2000; Itami, 1994), the position of Japanese companies would appear to be far closer to the "human rights" end of the continuum than at western firms. Therefore it could be argued that many of the value expressions that constitute the human rights-oriented firm are precisely those that are highly valued in Japanese organisations that have prevented an active market for corporate control developing and, as is indicated below, determines the way Japanese firms merge with each other.[6] Insofar as Anglo-Saxon and Japanese firms stand at opposite ends of the property vs human rights scale in the context of the meaning of corporate ownership, we would expect a merger between such firms to produce precisely the kind of "shock to the cultural status quo" to which Walter refers. As we have seen in the previous section, however, attempts by the new management to address the "legitimacy deficit" by adapting to local norms may serve to mitigate the impact of the shock.

In the case of institutionally distant mergers, however, organisational outcomes will depend to some extent on where the two organisations that are merging find themselves on the continuum between the two extremes of emphasising property versus human rights. In practice, the acquiring firm may espouse property rights to a lesser extent than a purely shareholder-driven firm might. Even if the

---

[6] It is of course questionable whether Japanese employees actually enjoy more "freedom" or "self-determination" compared with their Anglo-Saxon counterparts. However, for the purposes of this analysis, I take these expressions to mean the collective freedom and self-determination of the body of employees in relation to the desires of the owners of the company.

acquiring firm did espouse these rights, they may choose to impose them less forcefully on the acquired firm. The extent of the "shock to the cultural status quo" that Walter talks about will therefore depend on the interplay of these factors in the acquisition and integration process.

Mergers and acquisitions in Japan

There has historically been a very low level of M&A activity in Japan, and virtually no examples of hostile bids for one firm by another, other than some examples of "greenmailing" activity in the 1980s. There are of course a number of practical reasons for this: significant legal and accounting barriers must be overcome before acquiring a Japanese company; corporate disclosure has been poor; the commercial code, which has protected the rights of minority shareholders, has not until recently permitted stock-swaps as a method of taking over another firm; and there has been a lack of infrastructure (lawyers, accountants, investment bankers, etc.) to facilitate the process of takeover (Guild, 2000; Japan Investment Council, 1996; Lebrun, 2001). There have also been economic reasons: in the past, Japanese companies have been very expensive, trading on earnings multiples which are much higher than US or European firms (Debroux, 1996; Morrison and Floyd, 2000).

Underlying this, however, are more fundamental reasons: it is precisely the strong sense of cultural homogeneity in Japanese organisations that has contrived to keep the level of M&A down. Cultural homogeneity, created by the organisational framework that emphasises "employee sovereignty" (Itami, 1994), does not encourage the trading of companies which are run primarily in the long-term interest of its employees for the short-term benefit of its shareholders. A word often used in Japanese for the acquisition of one company by another is *nottoru*, which literally means "to hijack". The threat of takeover is something that simply has not existed for employees and managers of large Japanese firms: it is not something that one member of the community does to another. As Imai and Komiya (1994) explain it:

The potential threat of a takeover becomes a "final deterrent" impelling managers toward maximising share prices. American economists, especially those who see the relationship between shareholders and managers as a relationship between a principal and his agent, insist that in an efficient capital market, managers act, and indeed must act, so as to maximise share prices. By contrast, in large firms in Japan, this supplementary pressure from the market either barely functions or does not exist. (p. 33)

The care that almost all Japanese companies have taken to build up a "stable shareholder" base, and the elaborate system of cross-shareholdings that has existed in Japan, "blunts the direct influence of the stock market on the management of firms. This has given managers the autonomy to be able to distribute a proportion of the profits to the workers whom they represent and on whose support they depend."

The nature of the internal labour markets in Japan, which develop highly firm-specific skills, deters even friendly mergers between large firms on account of the difficulties in combining two firms with different firm-specific practices (Nakamura, 2004, p. 33). Moreover, for insiders who have climbed the ladder within the system, there is an implicit promise that one day, if they perform well, they will have a chance at the reins of control. These are therefore compelling reasons for Japanese managers to resist outside control (Debroux, 1996).

The result is that acquisitions are often limited to distressed companies (Guild, 2000) and, in these situations, the role of the companies' main banks can be pivotal (see Hoshi and Kashyap, 2001, for examples of bank interventions). Nakamura (2004, p. 46) goes so far as to say that "in Japan the market for corporate control has been replaced by banks' involvement in the management of troubled firms". Wherever possible mergers are arranged as a "merger of equals" (*taitō gappei*) in order to "save face", and care has been taken to respect the feelings of both parties long after the merger has taken place (Debroux, 1996; Nakamura, 2004).[7] This is done by having the two firms "coalesce" gradually over a long period. By branding such coalitions as a "merger

---

[7] Examples cited by Nakamura are the fact that, since the merger of Fuji Steel and Yawata Steel to form Nippon Steel in 1970, the president of the firm has alternated between members of the two firms, a practice which was only broken in 2008, nearly forty years after the merger, with the appointment of two successive presidents from the old Fuji Steel, and the fact that following the merger of Kangyo Bank and Dai-ichi Bank in 1971, two separate personnel departments were maintained to protect the interests of the employees of both banks for a period of ten years.

of equals" and stretching out the integration over a long period, difficult decisions about doing away with past practices can be avoided by leaving them in place until they gradually merge into a common practice for both firms.

The extent to which Japanese practices diverge from those in the US is illustrated in Table 1.3 below which shows the difference in time that elapses between the announcement date and the closure of Japanese and American mergers of financial institutions that took place in the 1990s and early 2000s. As can be seen, Japanese mergers take between five and ten times as long as US mergers and, while institutional barriers such as commercial code requirements for the approval of two-thirds of shareholders undoubtedly contributes to the delay in Japan, a more serious barrier is the cultural consideration of fusing two similar organisations while preserving the sense of balance and propriety between the two firms (or in the case of Mizuho, three firms).

Table 1.3 *Merger speed: Japan/US comparison*

Country	Firm	Time required
Japan	Mizuho Financial Group (DKB/Fuji/IBJ)	31 months
Japan	Mitsui Sumitomo Bank	19 months
Japan	Sumitomo Fire & Marine/Mitsui Fire & Marine	20 months
US	Chase/JP Morgan	4 months
US	Travelers Group/ Solomon Smith Barney	2 months
US	Morgan Stanley/Dean Witter	3 months

Source: Milhaupt and West (2002).

In recent years, there have been some noticeable changes in the functioning of the market for corporate control in Japan. As we have seen, the government, as part of the overall effort to revitalise the economy through measures that increase corporate flexibility (as well as to increase inbound FDI), has increased the ease with which Japanese companies can be acquired. This has not only been through legal changes, including a substantial revision of the securities and exchange law and company law in 2006, but also by trying to establish clearer ground rules for contested takeovers and an understanding as to the meaning of "corporate value" (see Whittaker and Hayakawa, 2007). We have seen an increasing level of domestic M&A activity which has been overtly hostile (e.g. Livedoor and Fuji TV, Rakuten and TBS, Oji Paper's bid for Hokuetsu Paper in 2006) or near-hostile, as in the case of Hoya's takeover of Pentax. The widespread adoption of defensive measures by listed Japanese firms is a clear indication that the prospect of a hostile takeover is much more in the minds of Japanese managers than was the case ten years ago.

However, while these cases are eye-catching, they represent a minis-cule proportion of M&A activity. Most Japanese chief executives are far from the mould of Hiroshi Suzuki, the US-educated CEO of Hoya.[8] Oji's bid for Hokuetsu was built on the rationale of reducing excess capacity by strengthening the Japanese paper and pulp industry against emerging Asian competition. While the bid was made by what is a very conservative company and is in that sense ground-breaking, what was equally notable was the speed with which the insiders of corporate Japan rallied around Hokuetsu which was eventually saved from acquisition by a combination of deeply discounted third-party share allocation to Mitsubishi Corporation and a white knight bid from Nippon Paper. The result, far from industrial consolidation, has been to enable Hokuetsu to expand capacity.

M&A in Japan is characterised by low valuations of the target company and low levels of share price premiums for acquired firms (Jackson and Miyajima, 2007) indicating that the impact of "share-holder value" thinking has not yet penetrated the market for corpo-rate control to any great degree. Much of the M&A in Japan has been in the form of increased stakes in existing stock-holding relationships. During the period 1999–2005, the average stake held in the target firm at the time of a bid was 10.8%, compared with 3.6% for the US and 4.8% in the UK (where the target firm was listed). The average amount by which ownership in the target was increased was 27% in the case of Japan, compared to 75% in the US, and 65% in the UK.

[8] See *Financial Times*, 12 January 2006.

During the same period, the value of M&A in Japan as a percentage of GDP was 2.2%, compared with 12.8% in the US and 23.2% in the UK (Miyajima, 2007).

Foreign M&A in Japan

Although foreign firms have been established in Japan for about 150 years, they have generally been regarded as being fundamentally different from Japanese firms, in a way that, say, a French firm in the UK would not. The reputation of foreign firms has had a significant impact on their hiring policies. T. W. Kang, in a study of foreign firms in Japan (1991), observed:

Given the strong cultural cohesion of the Japanese, it is not surprising that people who work for *gaishi*s[9] are considered maverick Japanese. It is assumed that they either have misplaced loyalties or could not cope with the Japanese environment. Even employees of Japanese firms who come back to Japan from overseas assignments suffer from a weaker version of this stigma. (p. 126)

Their hiring practices are quite different; relying much more heavily on mid-career hires it has historically proved difficult to attract good quality graduates from universities, unless they are the mavericks about whom Kang writes. Their employment practices are also much closer to those of their head offices: compensation practices are meritocratic, and seniority plays a much less significant role than in Japanese organisations. Hierarchies are flatter and the decision-making process less consensual (Kang, 1991).[10]

Foreign firms looking to start or expand an existing Japanese business have in the past been left with no alternative but to go

---

[9] *Gaishi* literally means "foreign capital" and is shorthand for a foreign firm.

[10] Two further points should be made. First, there are examples of foreign firms, such as IBM, who have been present in Japan for decades, which operate "hybrid" employment systems, which closely resemble the Japanese systems in a number of respects. Second, during the last ten years, the stigma attached to joining a foreign firm has greatly dissipated, thanks to the success of some of these firms' Japanese operations (Yashiro, 1998).

the "greenfield" route, because the alternative – buying an existing Japanese firm – has been so difficult. For Japanese firms, the prospect of merging with another Japanese company was bad enough: "being bought by foreigners is the greatest fear because they might disrupt the old culture and systems completely, as well as indulging in large lay-offs" (Rafferty, 2000, p. 82).

Typically, transactions involving foreign firms purchasing Japanese companies have been cases of the foreign firm buying out a joint venture partner and have entailed a "long gestation period" (Abegglen and Stalk, 1984; Cooke, 1991) during many years of trust-building in the operation of the joint venture. Most transactions have been small. Where they have been large, they have usually involved distressed firms (Nakamura, 2004) and the main bank playing a critical brokerage role, such as in the case of Mazda and Ford (see Hoshi and Kashyap, 2001).

In the past, the bureaucracy, and in particular the Ministry of Finance, has actively intervened to block attempts by foreign firms to buy Japanese companies (Cooke, 1991). In the case of the scandal-ridden Snow Brand Milk Products, the Ministry of Agriculture and Fisheries effectively vetoed the intervention of foreign firms in 2004, prompting the *Nihon Keizai Shimbun* to comment:

While the government recites the mantra of increasing the level of M&A activity, when it comes to the reality of actual transactions, you find situations such as the intervention of the Ministry of Agriculture and Fisheries opposing the involvement of foreign firms in the reconstruction of Snow Brand Group. What we thought was the departed spirit of the anti-foreign control measures of the 1960s such as the maximum foreign ownership rules seem still to be with us. (*Nihon Keizai Shimbun*, 2004)

In parallel with developments in domestic M&A, there has been an increasing level of foreigners attempting to acquire Japanese firms. Japan has not been immune from the large increase in M&A activity carried out by private equity firms. Many of the major private equity firms have representatives in Japan scouring the landscape for investment opportunities. Some foreign funds have resorted to overtly hostile activity – the attempt in 2007 of the US-based Steel Partners to take over Bulldog Sauce being the most high-profile example. Indeed, the rapid adoption of "poison pill" defences by listed Japanese firms is widely seen as a measure against just this kind of acquirer. One Japan-based fund, Ichigo Asset Management, has succeeded for the first time in leading a victorious proxy fight to thwart a friendly merger by one steel firm, Tokyo Kohtetsu, with another, Osaka Steel, on the grounds that the premium being offered by Osaka Steel in exchange for Tokyo Kohtetsu shares was too low (in fact, it was non-existent) and was therefore against the interests of Tokyo Kohtetsu's minority shareholders. However, while these transactions have received a great deal of publicity, they are still rare occurrences and do not represent in any way a turning point in the history of the market for corporate control.

The strong underlying message of the admittedly sparse academic literature on the Japanese market for corporate control is that it is mediated strongly by local institutional factors. Hostile mergers are still seen as highly illegitimate – even M&A of a friendly nature is constrained by a system of "implicit, personalised contracts which unite their long-term constituents, namely managers, employees and corporate shareholders" (Morrison and Floyd, 2000, p. 270). Where mergers do take place, there seems to be an implicit communitarian template at work that governs the merger process. The perceptions of all of these key participants in the system, including the government, the bureaucracy and the banks, of their role in the functioning of the Japanese economy, have helped to perpetuate this.

Increasing levels of Japanese M&A: signs of change?

There are signs that attitudes in Japan towards M&A are changing. The legal and tax frameworks have undergone extensive revision to facilitate acquisition and disposals. In addition to the evidence of a rise in the volume of transactions, the support infrastructure (i.e. lawyers, bankers, accountants, etc.) that is required to support an active market in corporate control is growing rapidly (*International Herald Tribune*, 2007). There was even a time when the prevailing negative attitude towards hostile takeovers appeared to be changing when the young CEO and founder of Livedoor, Takafumi Horie, made a bold attempt to take control of a major television network, Fuji TV, in 2005 – a move which seemed to have widespread popular support. Although the Livedoor/Fuji TV saga ended in ignominy for Horie, who was prosecuted for insider dealing and given a prison sentence, many argue (e.g. Whittaker and Hayakawa, 2007) that this, and other hostile takeover bids, such as Rakuten's attempt to take over another broadcaster, TBS, have fundamentally altered the landscape for listed Japanese firms, with clear implications for the future of the "community firm".

This is also evidenced in the behaviour of Japanese CEOs. A number of studies have shown that they are more preoccupied than before with enhancing shareholder value, indicating a shift in stakeholder priorities away from employee and banking relationships to institutional shareholders. They spend more time pondering issues relating to M&A, either to grow their own businesses, or to defend them from predators (Robinson and Shimizu, 2006). Amongst employees there is a greater sense that their company's share price is important and that the company should be run for the benefit of shareholders. There was a significant difference in perception between employees of listed companies versus those of unlisted companies in this regard (Miyamoto, 2006).

One significant consequence of the decade and a half of economic decline, however, is that, notwithstanding attempts by bureaucrats to maintain the status quo as seen in the Snow Brand case, the acquisition of major Japanese companies by foreigners has become a possibility. It is true that, in most cases, purchases have been made of distressed or bankrupt companies (e.g. Nissan, Shinsei Bank, a number of life insurance companies) and that the fall in value of Japanese companies during the 1990s increased their relative attraction to foreign firms. However, it is also the case that the weakness of the Japanese banks has meant that the traditional "Japanese" solution of either a bail out or a marriage to a suitable Japanese partner has not been possible.[11] Furthermore, the weakness of the financial institutions has hastened the unwinding of cross-shareholdings that made the acquisition of Japanese companies difficult in the first place.

However, it is also clear that the pressing economic situation was starting to cause a fundamental change in the perception of legitimacy

---

[11] In 1989 there were twelve "city banks" and three long-term credit banks, all of whom were, in one form or another, acting in a "main bank" capacity. These are now down to three. This has undoubtedly affected the long-standing main bank relationships, and the feeling of responsibility towards clients may have dissipated somewhat.

in the notion of a foreign firm taking over a major Japanese corporation, and an acceptance of the possible consequences. This is vividly illustrated by the lack of opposition to the acquisition of Nissan by Renault in 1998, despite Renault's declared intention to shut significant manufacturing capacity in Japan, and the non-intervention of the government in the semi-hostile takeover by Cable & Wireless of the telecommunications company IDC when a domestic solution (through NTT, who had also bid for the company) was available. The evident success of Nissan since Renault took control and the mythical status of the company's CEO Carlos Ghosn have undoubtedly helped the legitimation process.

We will now explore the component parts of the employment system to see whether the assertion that the quasi-community firm is still "alive and kicking" is borne out by actual corporate practice.

References

Abegglen, J.C. (1958) *The Japanese Factory: Aspects of its Social Organisation*. Boston, MA: Massachusetts Institute of Technology Press

and Stalk, G. (1984) "The Role of Foreign Companies in Japanese Acquisitions", *Journal of Business Strategy*, 4: 3–10

(1985) *Kaisha, the Japanese Corporation*. New York, NY: Basic Books

Aguilera, R.V. and Dencker, J.C. (2004) "The Role of Human Resource Management in Cross-Border Mergers and Acquisitions", *International Journal of Human Resource Management*, 15: 1355–1370

Antia, M., Lin, J.B. and Pantzalis, C. (2007) "Cultural Distance and Valuation of Multinational Corporations", *Journal of Multinational Financial Management*, 17: 365–383

Aoki, M. (1988) *Information, Incentives, and Bargaining in the Japanese Economy*. Cambridge: Cambridge University Press

(1990) "Towards an Economic Model of the Japanese Firm", *Journal of Economic Literature*, 28: 1–27

(1994) "The Japanese Firm as a System of Attributes: A Survey and Research Agenda". In M. Aoki and R. Dore (eds.) *The Japanese Firm: Sources of Competitive Strength*. Oxford: Oxford University Press

Barron, D.N. (1998) "Pathways to Legitimacy among Consumer Loan Providers in New York City, 1914–1934", *Organization Studies*, 19: 207–233

Benedict, R. (1967) *The Chrysanthemum and the Sword*. Cleveland, OH: Meridian Books

Berger, P. L. and Luckmann, T. (1966) *The Social Construction of Reality*. New York, NY: Doubleday

Besser, T. L. (1995) "Reward and Organizational Goal Achievement: A Case Study of Toyota Motor Manufacturing in Kentucky", *Journal of Management Studies*, 32: 383–399

Buchanan, J. S. (2007) "Japanese Corporate Governance and the Principle of 'Internalism'", *Corporate Governance*, 15: 27–35

Business Labor Trend (2006) "Kabunushi Juushi No Kouporeeto Gabanansu Wo Nihon No Juugyouin Wa Dono You Ni Kangaete Irunoka?" ("What Do Japanese Employees Think about Shareholder Value-Based Corporate Governance?"). 7–11

Chalmers, N. (1989) *Industrial Relations in Japan: The Peripheral Workforce*. London: Routledge

Child, J., Faulkner, D. and Pitkethly, R. (2001) *The Management of International Acquisitions*. New York, NY: Oxford University Press

Clark, R. (1979) *The Japanese Company*. New Haven, CT: Yale University Press

Cole, R. E. (1971) *Japanese Blue Collar: The Changing Tradition*. Berkeley, CA: University of California Press

Cooke, T. E. (1991) "Environmental Factors Influencing Mergers and Acquisitions in Japan", *Journal of International Financial Management*, 3: 160–188

Datta, D. K. and Puia, G. (1995) "Cross-Border Acquisitions: An Examination of the Influence of Relatedness and Cultural Fit on Shareholder Value Creation in U.S. Acquiring Firms", *Management International Review*, 35: 337–359

Debroux, P. (1996) "Japanese Mergers and Acquisitions: Overcoming Obstacles to Improved Systemic Efficiency", *Atlantic Economic Journal*, 24: 244–256

Dedoussis, V. (2001) "Keiretsu and Management Practices in Japan – Resilience Amid Change", *Journal of Managerial Psychology*, 16: 173–188

DiMaggio, P. J. and Powell, W. W. (1983) "The Iron Cage Revisited: Institutional Isomorphism and Collective Rationality in Organizational Fields", *American Sociological Review*, 48: 147–160

Dore, R. (1973) *British Factory – Japanese Factory: The Origins of National Diversity in Industrial Relations*. Berkeley, CA: University of California Press

—— (1997) "Good Jobs, Bad Jobs and No Jobs", *Industrial Relations Journal*, 24: 262–268

(2000) *Stock Market Capitalism: Welfare Capitalism. Japan and Germany versus the Anglo-Saxons*. Oxford: Oxford University Press

(2006) *Dare No Tame No Kaisha Ni Suru Ka? (For Whose Benefit the Corporation?)*. Tokyo: Iwanami Shoten

Bounine-Cabale, J. and Tapiola, K. (1989) *Japan at Work: Markets, Management and Flexibility*. Paris: OECD

Euromoney (2000) "Some Signs of an Urge to Merge". October, pp. 82–85

Fliaster, A. and Marr, R. (2001) "Change in the Insider-Oriented Corporate Governance in Japan and Germany: Between Americanisation and Tradition", *Journal of Change Management*, 1: 242–256

Fligstein, N. (1991) "The Structural Transformation of American Industry: An Institutional Account of the Causes of Diversification in the Largest Firms, 1919–1979". In W. W. Powell and P. J. DiMaggio (eds.) *The New Institutionalism in Organizational Analysis*. Chicago, IL: University of Chicago Press

(2001) *The Architecture of Markets: An Economic Sociology of Twenty-First Century Capitalist Societies*. Princeton, NJ: Princeton University Press

Gordon, A. (1998) *The Wages of Affluence: Labor and Management in Postwar Japan*. Cambridge, MA: Harvard University Press

Granovetter, M. (1985) "Economic Action and Social Structure: The Problem of Embeddedness", *American Sociological Review*, 91: 481–510

Greenwood, R. and Hinings, C. R. (1993) "Understanding Strategic Change: The Contribution of Archetypes", *Academy of Management Journal*, 36: 1052–1081

(1996) "Understanding Radical Organizational Change: Bringing Together the Old and the New Institutionalism", *Academy of Management Review*, 21: 1022–1054

Suddaby, R. and Hinings, C. R. (2002) "Theorizing Change: The Role of Professional Associations in the Transformation of Institutionalized Fields", *Academy of Management Journal*, 45: 58–80

Guild, T. (2000) "Making M&A Work in Japan", *McKinsey Quarterly*, 87–93

Hamada, K. and Kurosaka, Y. (1986) "Trends in Unemployment, Wages and Productivity", *Economica*, 53: 275–296

Haspeslagh, P. C. and Jemison, D. B. (1991) *Managing Acquisitions: Creating Value through Corporate Renewal*. New York, NY: Free Press

Hirakubo, N. (1999) "The End of Lifetime Employment in Japan", *Business Horizons*, November–December: 41–44

Hirsch, P.M. (1986) "From Ambush to Golden Parachute: Corporate Takeovers as an Instance of Cultural Framing and Institutional Integration", *American Journal of Sociology*, 91: 800–837

Hofstede, G. (1980) *Culture's Consequences: International Differences in Work-Related Values.* Beverly Hills, CA: Sage

Hori, S. (1993) "Fixing Japan's White-Collar Economy: A Personal View", *Harvard Business Review*, November–December: 157–172

Hoshi, T. (1994) "The Economic Role of Corporate Grouping and the Main Bank System". In M. Aoki and R. Dore (eds.) *The Japanese Firm: Sources of Competitive Strength.* Oxford: Oxford University Press
   and Kashyap, A. (2001) *Corporate Financing and Governance in Japan: The Road to the Future.* Cambridge, MA: MIT Press

Imai, K. and Komiya, R. (1994) "Characteristics of Japanese Firms". In K. Imai and R. Komiya (eds.) *Business Enterprise in Japan.* Cambridge, MA: MIT Press

Inagami, T. and Whittaker, D.H. (2005) *The New Community Firm: Employment, Governance and Management Reform in Japan.* Cambridge: Cambridge University Press

International Herald Tribune (2007) "Japan Merger Culture: An Investor's Guide". 4 May

Itami, H. (1994) "The 'Human-Capital-Ism' of the Japanese Firm as an Integrated System". In K. Imai and R. Komiya (eds.) *Business Enterprise in Japan.* Cambridge, MA: MIT Press

Itoh, H. (1994) "Japanese Human Resource Management from the Viewpoint of Incentive Theory". In M. Aoki and R. Dore (eds.) *The Japanese Firm: Sources of Competitive Strength.* Oxford: Oxford University Press

Jacoby, S. (1979) "The Origins of Internal Labor Markets in Japan", *Industrial Relations*, 18: 184–196
   (2005) *The Embedded Corporation: Corporate Governance and Employment Relations in Japan and the United States.* Princeton, NJ: Princeton University Press

Johanson, J. and Vahlne, J.-E. (1977) "The Internationalization Process of the Firm – a Model of Knowledge Development and Increasing Foreign Market Commitments", *Journal of International Business Studies*, 8: 23–32

Johnson, C. (1982) *MITI and the Japanese Miracle – the Growth of Industrial Policy 1925–1975.* Stanford, CA: Stanford University Press

Kamata, S. (1982) *Japan in the Passing Lane: An Insider's Account of Life in a Japanese Auto Factory.* New York, NY: Random House

Kang, T. W. (1991) *Gaishi: The Foreign Company in Japan*. Tokyo: Tuttle

Kogut, B. and Singh, H. (1988) "The Effect of National Culture on the Choice of Entry Mode", *Journal of International Business Studies*, 19: 411–432

Koike, K. (1994) "Learning and Incentive Systems in Japanese Industry". In M. Aoki and R. Dore (eds.) *The Japanese Firm: Sources of Competitive Strength*. Oxford: Oxford University Press

Kostova, T. and Roth, K. (2002) "Adoption of Organizational Practice by Subsidiaries of Multi-national Corporations: Institutional and Relational Effects", *Academy of Management Review*, 45: 215–233

and Zaheer, S. (1999) "Organizational Legitimacy under Conditions of Complexity: The Case of the Multinational Enterprise", *Academy of Management Journal*, 24: 64–81

Leblebici, H., Salancik, G. R., Copay, A. and King, T. (1991) "Institutional Change and the Transformation of Interorganizational Fields: An Organizational History of the U.S. Radio Broadcasting Industry", *Administrative Science Quarterly*, 36: 333–363

Lebrun, L. N. (2001) "Recent Amendments to the Commercial Code of Japan: Impact on Mergers & Acquisitions", *Law & Policy in International Business*, 32: 811–823

Levine, S. B. (1958) *Industrial Relations in Postwar Japan*. Urbana, IL: University of Illinois Press

Lincoln, J. R. (1997) "The Transformation of the Japanese Employment System: Nature, Depth and Origins", *Work and Occupations*, 24

and Kalleberg, A. L. (1990) *Culture, Control, and Commitment: A Study of Work Organization and Work Attitudes in the United States and Japan*. Cambridge: Cambridge University Press

Marks, M. and Mirvis, P. H. (1985) "Merger Syndrome: Stress and Uncertainty", *Mergers and Acquisitions*, Summer: 50–55

(1992) "The Human Side of Merger Planning: Assessing and Analysing 'Fit'", *Human Resource Planning*, 15: 69–92

(2001) "Making Acquisitions Work: Strategic and Psychological Preparation", *Academy of Management Executive*, 15: 80–84

Marsh, R. and Mannari, H. (1976) *Modernisation and the Japanese Factory*. Princeton, NJ: Princeton University Press

Meyer, A. D., Brooks, G. R. and Goes, J. B. (1990) "Environmental Jolts and Industry Revolutions: Organizational Responses to Discontinuous Change", *Strategic Management Journal*, 11: 93–110

Meyer, J. W. and Rowan, B. (1977) "Institutionalized Organizations: Formal Structure as Myth and Ceremony", *American Journal of Sociology*, 83: 340–363

Morgan, G. and Kristensen, P.H. (2006) "The Contested Space of Multinationals: Varieties of Institutionalism, Varieties of Capitalism", *Human Relations*, 59: 1467–1490

and Takahashi, Y. (2002) "Shareholder Value in the Japanese Context", *Competition and Change*, 6: 169–191

Morishima, M. (1995) "Embedding HRM in a Social Context", *British Journal of Industrial Relations*, 33: 617–640

Morris, J., Wilkinson, B. and Munday, M. (2000) "Farewell to HRM? Personnel Practices in Japanese Manufacturing Plants in the UK", *International Journal of Human Resource Management*, 11: 1047–1060

Morrison, J. and Floyd, D. (2000) "Merger Activity: Solutions to Japan's Economic Downturn?" *Management Decision*, 38: 263–271

Mroczkowski, T. and Hanaoka, M. (1998) "The End of Japanese Management: How Soon?" *Human Resource Planning*, 21: 20–30

Nakamura, M. (2004) "Corporate Governance and Management Practices in Japan: Current Issues", *Corporate Ownership & Control*, 1: 38–52

Nakane, C. (1970) *Japanese Society*. London: Weidenfeld & Nicolson

Nihon Keizai Shimbun (2004) "Tainichi Chokusetsu Toushi Wo Fuyasu Koizumi Kaikaku Wo" ("The Koizumi Reforms and the Increase of Inbound FDI"). 4 April, p. 1

Okabe, Y. (2002) "Culture or Employment Systems? Accounting for the Attitudinal Differences between British and Japanese Managers", *International Journal of Human Resource Management*, 13: 285–301

Okazaki, T. (1994) "The Japanese Firm under the Wartime Planned Economy". In M. Aoki and R. Dore (eds.) *The Japanese Firm: Sources of Competitive Strength*. Oxford: Oxford University Press

Oliver, C. (1992) "The Antecedents of Deinstitutionalization", *Organization Studies*, 13: 563–588

Ornatowski, G.K. (1998) "The End of Japanese-Style Human Resource Management?" *Sloane Management Review*, 73–84

Orrù, M., Biggart, N. and Hamilton, G.H. (1991) "Organizational Isomorphism in East Asia". In W.W. Powell and P.J. DiMaggio (eds.) *The New Institutionalism in Organizational Analysis*. Chicago: University of Chicago Press

Ouchi, W. (1981) *Theory Z: How American Business Can Meet the Japanese Challenge*. Reading, MA: Addison-Wesley

Pascale, R.T. and Athos, A.G. (1981) *The Art of Japanese Management*. New York: Simon & Schuster

Rafferty, K. (2000) "Some Signs of an Urge to Merge", *Euromoney*, 82–5

Rebick, M. (2005) *The Japanese Employment System.* Oxford: Oxford University Press

Robinson, P. and Shimizu, N. (2006) "Japanese Corporate Restructuring: CEO Priorities as a Window on Environmental and Organizational Change", *Academy of Management Perspectives*, 20: 44–75

Rohlen, T.P. (1974) *For Harmony and Strength: Japanese White-Collar Organization in Anthropological Perspective.* Berkeley, CA: University of California Press

Scher, M.J. (1997) *Japanese Interfirm Networks and their Main Banks.* Basingstoke: Macmillan Press

Schneider, S.C. and Dunbar, R.L.M. (1992) "A Psychoanalytical Reading of Hostile Takeover Events", *Academy of Management Review*, 17: 537–567

Scott, W.R. (1995) *Institutions and Organizations.* Thousand Oaks, CA: Sage

and Meyer, J.W. (1991) "The Organization of Societal Sectors: Propositions and Early Evidence". In W.W. Powell and P.J. DiMaggio (eds.) *The New Institutionalism in Organizational Analysis.* Chicago, IL: University of Chicago Press

Selznick, P. (1957) *Leadership in Administration.* New York, NY: Harper and Row

Sheard, P. (1994) "Interlocking Shareholdings and Corporate Governance in Japan'. In M. Aoki and R. Dore (eds.) *The Japanese Firm: Sources of Competitive Strength.* Oxford: Oxford University Press

Shenkar, O. (2001) "Cultural Distance Revisited: Towards a More Rigorous Conceptualization and Measurement of Cultural Differences", *Journal of International Business Studies*, 32: 519–535

Suchman, M.C. (1995) "Managing Legitimacy: Strategic and Institutional Approaches", *Academy of Management Review*, 20: 571–610

Sugayama, S. (1995) "Work Rules, Wages, and Single Status: The Shaping of the 'Japanese Employment System'", *Business History*, 37: 120–140

Sullivan, J.J. and Peterson, R.B. (1991) "A Test of Theories Underlying the Japanese Lifetime Employment System", *Journal of International Business Studies*, First Quarter: 79–97

Tolbert, P.S. and Zucker, L.G. (1983) "Institutional Sources of Change in the Femoral Structure of Organizations: The Diffusion of Civil Service Reform, 1880–1935", *Administrative Science Quarterly*, 28: 22–39

van Wolferen, K. (1993) *The Enigma of Japanese Power.* Tokyo: Tuttle

Vogel, E.F. (1979) *Japan as Number One.* Cambridge, MA: Harvard University Press

Walter, G. A. (1985) "Culture Collisions in Mergers and Acquisitions". In P. J. Frost (ed.) *Organizational Culture*. Beverly Hills, CA: Sage

Watanabe, T. and Sato, Y. (2000) "Analysis of Labor Markets in Postwar Japan", *International Journal of Sociology*, 30: 3–33

Westney, D. E. (1987) *Imitation and Innovation: The Transfer of Western Organizational Patterns in Meiji Japan*. Cambridge, MA: Harvard University Press

(1993) "Institutionalization Theory and the Multinational Corporation". In S. Ghoshal and D. E. Westney (eds.) *Organization Theory and the Multinational Corporation*. New York, NY: St. Martin's Press

Whitley, R. (1990) "East Asian Enterprise Structures and the Comparative Analysis of Forms of Business Organization", *Organization Studies*, 11: 47–74

(1991) "The Social Construction of Business Systems in East Asia", *Organization Studies*, 12: 1–28

(1998) "Internationalization and Varieties of Capitalism: The Limited Effects of Cross-National Coordination of Economic Activities on the Nature of Business Systems", *Review of International Political Economy*, 5: 445–481

(2001) "How and Why are International Firms Different? The Consequences of Cross-Border Managerial Coordination for Firm Characteristics and Behaviour". In G. Morgan, P. H. Kristensen and R. Whitley (eds.) *The Multinational Firm: Organizing Across Institutional and National Divides*. Oxford: Oxford University Press

Whittaker, D. H. (1994) "SMEs, Entry Barriers and 'Strategic Alliances'". In M. Aoki and R. Dore (eds.) *The Japanese Firm: Sources of Competitive Strength*. Oxford: Oxford University Press

and Hayakawa, M. (2007) 'Contesting "Corporate Value" through Takeover Bids in Japan', *Corporate Governance*, 15: 16–26

Xu, D. and Shenkar, O. (2002) 'Institutional Distance and the Multinational Enterprise', *Academy of Management Review*, 27: 608–618

Yashiro, N. (1998) *Jinjibu Wa Mou Iranai (Who Needs an HR Department Any More?)*. Tokyo: Kodansha

Yoshikawa, T. and Phan, P. H. (2001) 'Alternative Corporate Governance Systems in Japanese Firms: Implications for a Shift to Stockholder-Centred Corporate Governance', *Asia Pacific Journal of Management*, 18: 183–205

Yoshimori, M. (1995) 'Whose Company Is It? The Concept of the Corporation in Japan and the West', *Long Range Planning*, 28: 33–44

Zucker, L. G. (1977) 'The Role of Institutionalization in Cultural Persistence', *American Sociological Review*, 42: 726–743

2 | *The study: overview and methodology*

T HE TENTATIVE conclusion from the previous chapter in which the literature on Japanese organisations and institutional theory was reviewed is that, despite enormous pressure for change, most commentators observe that the Japanese system of employment has been remarkably resilient. An institutional interpretation would be that deeply institutionalised and socially embedded organisational practices are resistant to change. This conclusion, albeit tentative and subject to verification, has enabled us to establish a "baseline", or context, from which we can measure the extent that practices diverge from the communitarian template when Japanese companies are taken over by foreign firms.

We now return to the main theme of this book, namely the investigation of the impact of foreign ownership and control on the HR and other organisational practices at Japanese organisations. The questions we laid out in the Introduction were: does a "institutionally distant" merger cause organisational change and deinstitutionalisation of communitarian practices? How are these changes perceived and internalised by employees? Finally, what are the contextual factors that affect the outcomes? In this and subsequent chapters I describe, based on the most recent literature, each of the main "domains" of the Japanese employment system, such as recruitment, training, reward system, and so on. Having examined both Japanese firms that were taken over by foreign firms (the "case companies") as well as Japanese firms in similar industries that were not taken over (the "comparator companies"), I lay out my findings from these investigations categorised by domain so that the impact of foreign control can be more easily assessed.

First, however, I will briefly describe the methodology, which will include a brief description of the case and comparator companies.

Qualitative case-based research: guiding framework

My objective was to investigate and describe what changes took place in traditional HR practices and organisational forms at Japanese companies that were taken over by foreign companies. Using institutional theory as my conceptual framework, I was looking for evidence that deeply institutionalised organisational routines and the values that underpinned them would, under foreign ownership, be delegitimated, leading to their eventual "deinstitutionalisation" (Oliver, 1992). Clearly, an examination of the organisation and work practices before and after the takeover would have provided verification of change having occurred, as well as evidence of the type of change that had taken place. However, in addition to the process of verification, I also needed to gain insights into the cause of the changes and, if possible, to identify them as a common feature in Japanese companies taken over by foreign firms, but which were absent, or at least not so prevalent, in other Japanese companies. If these changes were not common to all companies taken over by foreigners, I wanted to know why.

As I outlined in Chapter 1, I have drawn heavily on Dore's idea of the "welfare corporatist" organisation (1973). We have seen that most commentators conclude that, despite pressure for change, many aspects of welfare corporatism are still present in large Japanese organisations today. In the following chapters I seek to determine what changes take place in the event of an "institutionally distant" merger between a welfare corporatist, employee-favouring, organisation and a western, shareholder-oriented, firm. I focus particularly on the distinguishing features of the Japanese organisation, broken down into two broad categories, HR practices and organisation and decision making, which were further broken down into more detailed "domains", such as recruitment, training, reward systems, board composition and so on.

My line of enquiry would be to establish what changes were occurring in each of the above domains and to try to reach some conclusion, if indeed changes were found, as to whether they amounted to a deinstitutionalisation of corporatist welfare practices, as well as to try to understand why some companies changed in different ways to others.

The aim therefore was to collect the necessary empirical evidence to show, first, what happened at Japanese firms when they were taken over by foreign firms (called hereinafter the "case companies") and, second, to observe whether comparable Japanese companies (hereinafter "comparator companies" or "comparators") were changing in a similar way. The objective of the underlying methodology was the collection of data that could be shown to have, as Eisenhardt (1989, p. 532) puts it, an "intimate connection with empirical reality that permits the development of a testable, relevant and valid theory". The case method seemed a particularly good way to investigate the impact of foreign acquisitions of Japanese organisations, which had been a rare occurrence before this. Again to quote Eisenhardt, case studies were particularly appropriate "when little is known about a phenomenon [and] current perspectives seem inadequate because they have little empirical substantiation ..." and reliance on incremental empirical testing or past literature are insufficient (p. 548).

Case design: sampling decisions

Case study companies

In terms of case selection, I felt it was important to try and adhere to the precept that sampling was "based on selecting a portion of a population to represent the entire population to which one wants to generalise" (Strauss and Corbin, 1998, p. 214).

While there are some advantages to the single-case format, particularly in the unusual or rare, the revelatory, or critical case, and/or where the resources of the researcher are extremely limited (Dyer and Wilkins, 1991), the advantage of the multiple format is that it offers more compelling evidence and it is considered more robust (Yin, 1994, p. 45). Although there appears to be a large degree of homogeneity in Japanese organisational design and routine, there are significant sectoral differences. In addition, the dynamics, in particular the relative strengths of the parties in a merger, are very different in each case and it seemed important to get a wider variety of responses than was available from just a single case. It therefore appeared to make sense to adopt a multiple-case design where the objective would be replication, or at least where contrasting results would be exposed, but where the contrasts came about for predictable reasons.

In terms of the number of cases and the nature of the companies to be studied, I felt that I would need a sufficient number to give coverage of the range of industries where Japanese companies had been acquired by foreigners. There are severe limits to random selection in qualitative research (King *et al.*, 1994). Eisenhardt (1989, p. 537) states that the goal of theoretical sampling "is to choose cases which are likely to replicate or extend the emergent theory" and concludes that a random approach to sampling is "neither necessary, nor even preferable". I therefore decided on a "purposive" strategy (Patton, 2002), focusing on variation (e.g. to avoid biases that might come from sectoral idiosyncrasies), criticality (where, according to experts in the field, relationships to be studied become especially clear) and, to a certain extent, convenience (both in terms of location and access).

The first decision related to choosing the number of companies to act as case studies, and which companies to select. In the study I was proposing, however, the universe of potential case studies was limited by the number of large acquisitions made of Japanese companies by foreign firms. Prior to the late 1990s, as I pointed out in the Introduction, there were very few instances of large Japanese companies being taken over by foreign firms. Large transactions that had occurred in the 1980s consisted almost entirely of foreign companies merging with local firms with whom they had had a long relationship (as in the merger of Shell Sekiyu KK and Showa Oil in 1985) or the acquisition of a controlling interest by a foreign company of a Japanese firm with whom they had had an existing relationship (as in the case of BOC's acquisition of Osaka Sanso in 1982 or Merck's acquisition of Banyu Pharmaceutical in 1984). While there was, as we saw in Figure 0.1 in the Introduction, a large increase in the number of "out-in" transactions during the second half of the 1990s, there were not yet a sufficient number to adopt a "gradual selection" approach. Thus, while the "theoretical sampling" approach developed by Glaser and Strauss (1967) decrees that there is no *a priori* definition of sample structure, and notwithstanding the limitations imposed by such an approach to sampling upon the "developmental space of theory" (Flick, 1998), it was unavoidable for the purposes of this study.

Out-in transactions (i.e. cases of Japanese companies being acquired by foreign firms) were concentrated in certain key sectors (e.g. the automotive and finance sectors) and this had a bearing on case selection. As for the companies themselves, I developed a number of criteria for selection. First, as I mentioned in the Introduction, there has historically been a distinction between the employment practices of large Japanese companies and SMEs (Cole, 1971; Whittaker, 1994). My research is focused on large companies, where the traits of the welfare corporatist organisation were most likely to be present. Thus, size was an important criterion. I decided that companies should have over 1,000 employees, as this was the cut-off point in research by the Japan Institute of Labour between medium and large-size companies.

Second, in order to study the impact of foreign control, a certain amount of time needed to have elapsed since the merger was completed. I therefore set a minimum of one year between completion and the start of the interviewing process.

Finally, as I would be making fairly serious demands on the management of the case study companies, the issue of access would be of critical importance. I wanted to interview both senior management and a number of other executives. In addition, they would be required to disclose extensive data on employment practices, including sensitive data regarding salaries and HR issues. In other words, the likely level of cooperation from the company's management was a vital factor.

As for the comparator companies, the same criteria applied. They would need to be similar companies operating in the same sector and under Japanese control. Access was also crucial, as I would doubtless be making demands on the time of senior management and the HR department.

Access

I made a pilot visit to Japan in March 2002. It was evident from this visit that the area I wanted to research was one of increasing interest, not just among the academic community, but also the business community at large. The success of the Renault–Nissan relationship and the high visibility of the CEO, Carlos Ghosn, were clearly contributory factors.

As a result of this visit, I drew up a list of four priority companies from a diverse range of industries and contacted them to request cooperation in my research. Fortunately, all four agreed to cooperate and undertook to arrange an interview schedule and provide data along the lines that I had requested (see below). One further company was added to the list, making a total of five.

Having obtained permission from the case companies, I decided on four Japanese-controlled firms that could act as suitable control companies and made contact with them. Again, I was fortunate in that all four accepted and agreed to let me interview senior figures in the firm, as well as provide HR data, and grant access to working-level HR managers. There is a brief description of the case and comparator companies later in this chapter.

In addition to the nine companies who were the focus of my research, I approached a number of other Japanese companies. The purpose of this was to try and get as broad a view of the Japanese organisations as possible. As we saw in Chapter 1, there is considerable debate as to whether change is actually taking place at Japanese companies and the extent to which the communitarian model is now an extinct mode of organising. I therefore felt it was important to get as broad a view of Japanese organisations as possible, beyond just the four comparator companies. One company in particular, a large utility company, was helpful in granting access to senior figures and extensive data. Although this did not constitute a "comparator company" insofar as it operated in quite a different sector to the case study companies, it was a company run on very traditional Japanese lines and would provide useful evidence as to the continued existence of communitarian features in Japanese organisations.

Company profiles

Three out of the five case companies gave me permission to reveal the identities of their firms; two declined. For the two companies that declined, I have invented code names, and have as far as possible disguised their identity to respect their wish for anonymity. Referring to some of the case companies by name and others by their code names has inevitably made the data chapters somewhat messy, but I hope that it will not detract from the flow. As for the comparator companies, I had permission from the majority of them to reveal their identities, but ultimately decided that the main focus of the book should be the case companies, and that the comparators should remain anonymous. Again, I hope that this does not reduce interest in the subject matter.

I lay out below a brief description of each case study company, along with the Japanese company with which it is to be compared ("comparator").

Case company 1: Nissan

Nissan is a major Japanese automotive manufacturing company with a long history, stretching back before World War II. It has a global manufacturing and sales organisation, and employs more than 120,000 people worldwide. It ran into financial difficulties in the late 1990s to the extent that doubts were expressed as to its viability. After abortive merger discussions with Daimler, discussions were initiated with Renault, who took a 36.8% share of the company, which has subsequently been raised to 44%. While this does not give Renault outright control, it gives them sufficient rights over Nissan so that virtual control is assured. Renault sent a small number of expatriates to Nissan, including Carlos Ghosn, who first took the position of COO, but quickly became CEO. Other than Ghosn, Renault started with two further employees on the Nissan board: Thierry Moulonguet, who was Executive Vice President and Chief Financial Officer, and Patrick Pélata, Executive Vice President in charge of product planning, design and strategy. The two firms have not merged their respective operations. They have preserved their separate identities and have termed their relationship as an "alliance". Since its establishment, however, they have extensively shared research and development, technology, manufacturing facilities and purchasing with an emphasis on shared platforms. There are also a number of Japanese Nissan employees who are seconded to Renault, mostly working at Renault's headquarters.

The alliance is run by the Global Alliance Committee, which is chaired jointly by the two CEOs of Renault and Nissan (initially Schweitzer of Renault and Hanawa of Nissan, but currently by Ghosn, in his capacity as CEO of both companies) and meets monthly. An "Alliance Charter" was drawn up to promote common values, based on "a shared ambition, mutual trust, a respect for differences and a balance between the two partners".

Ghosn, in an article for the *Harvard Business Review* (2002), identified cultural issues as being Nissan's "fundamental challenge", with the traditional reward system based on seniority and the organisation's inability to assign and take responsibility (a "culture of blame") being major impediments to improved corporate performance. A series of cross-functional and cross-company teams creating stronger intra-company and intra-alliance links, breaking down divisional barriers, have been set up and have been credited with playing a major role in the improvements that Nissan has seen since 2000.

Since the acquisition, the new management of Nissan has virtually disbanded the old network of supplier relationships and associated cross-shareholdings, and has realigned its key banking relationships.

It is notable that the Japanese media, initially sceptical of Renault's chances of success and fearful for the fate of Nissan's employees, soon became enthusiastic supporters, emphasising the personal role of Ghosn himself and building something of a cult around his personality. With a slow-down in performance over the past two years, there has been a noticeable cooling in the media attitude towards the company, although this would appear to be as exaggerated a reaction as the highly sycophantic reaction was in the wake of the company's initial remarkable turnaround.

Comparator company 1: J-Mfg Co
J-Mfg Co ("J" standing for "Japanese" and "Mfg" standing for "manufacturing") operates in the same industrial sector as Nissan and has historically been considered a key competitor. It is a significant participant in the global automotive field and has had a good record of sales growth and profitability. Like Nissan, it has a global manufacturing and sales operation and employs in excess of 200,000 people.

Case company 2: Chugai Pharmaceutical ("Chugai")
Chugai is a significant manufacturer of pharmaceuticals focusing on prescription medicines for central nervous, cardiovascular, respiratory, gastrointestinal and metabolic systems, hormones and diagnostic products and OTC drugs. It was founded early in 1925 as a family concern, and the family maintain significant links with the firm to this day. The company has been consistently profitable and has not suffered financial difficulties in the same way as Nissan. However, the management of the company decided that, in view of a shrinking domestic market and increasing international competition, an alliance with a major global firm with whom Chugai could derive synergies in R&D and distribution was the way forward in the long term. The company therefore entered into negotiations with Roche, the Swiss multinational pharmaceutical firm, with a view to Roche taking a controlling stake in the company, which they duly did in 2001. Roche

themselves had been operating in Japan (through their subsidiary Nippon Roche) for many decades and had built up a substantial operation, including a research and development capability. As part of the transaction, the assets and employees of Nippon Roche were merged with those of Chugai. The management of Chugai has remained virtually intact. Other than some non-executive directors from Roche, the composition of the board did not change after the acquisition. At the outset, no expatriate managers were sent from Roche to work at Chugai and Chugai is still run by Osamu Nagayama, who has been CEO of the company since 1992. Like Nissan, Chugai has kept its original company name and independent corporate identity and its operations have been relatively undisrupted, other than absorbing the operations of Nippon Roche.

Comparator company 2: J-Pharma Co

J-Pharma Co is a large Japanese pharmaceutical company just outside of the top rank. It focused on ethical drugs, but had a presence in the OTC business as well as in medical supplies and chemicals. It was started at the end of the nineteenth century as a family concern and is not dissimilar in size to Chugai. However, as with many Japanese pharmaceutical firms, it has been the subject of a merger and no longer exists in the form it did at the time of my research.

Case company 3: Shinsei Bank ("Shinsei")

The history of Shinsei Bank goes back to 1952, the year its predecessor organisation, the Long Term Credit Bank of Japan ("LTCB"), was founded. LTCB was one of three "long term credit banks" (the others being the Industrial Bank of Japan ("IBJ") and the Nippon Credit Bank ("NCB")) which were authorised to extend long-term fixed-rate loans to Japanese corporations and therefore occupied a privileged position in the hierarchy of Japanese financial institutions in post-war Japan. With demand for long-term credit in decline, LTCB aggressively expanded lending to real estate and consumer finance companies during the 1980s. As economic conditions deteriorated in the 1990s, LTCB's position became increasingly precarious and the bank eventually collapsed in 1998. It was quickly nationalised.

The bank was sold in December 1999 to a US private equity firm, Ripplewood, who paid ¥1 billion in cash and in addition injected ¥120 billion in new equity. Ripplewood also extracted various guarantees from the Japanese government, such as the right to "put" existing loans to the government under certain circumstances. A new CEO was hired, Masamoto Yashiro, a veteran in successfully managing operations of foreign firms in Japan. The new bank, named "Shinsei", commenced operations in March 2000. Preferring to leave management to Yashiro and the management team, Ripplewood did not send any executives to manage the company, although it was represented on the board through a number of non-executive positions. One individual, Christopher Flowers, was particularly involved in strategic and senior-level recruitment issues (Tett, 2004). There are no former LTCB board members left in the company and a large number of employees left the firm during the bank's two years as a nationalised entity.

The company has altered its business model considerably since it was acquired by Ripplewood, offering a very different product line. It has de-emphasised traditional low-margin lending business and focuses on more profitable, fee-based transactional business, giving it more of a feel of an investment bank. This was not traditionally an area of expertise for Japanese banks and Shinsei recruited extensively from outside, particularly foreign investment banks. Once a senior person was hired in this way, he would often bring in parts of, or in some cases the entire, team from his original employers.

In its existing lending business, Shinsei started to take the creditworthiness of the borrowers into account in the pricing of its loans than was hitherto the practice for major Japanese banks. This hard-nosed approach caused controversy when, in the summer of 2000, shortly after it commenced operations, Sogo, a large financially troubled Japanese retailer, requested debt forgiveness for ¥100 billion of loans. Shinsei, eschewing the tradition of Japanese banks supporting its borrowing clients, even if it were to result in losses for themselves, declined. This precipitated one of Japan's largest ever corporate failures.

Another important pillar of Shinsei's business model is retail banking, where management has introduced a number of innovative products and services (such as 24-hour ATM machines) and has succeeded in attracting a large number of new depositors (1.2 million by December 2004). However, in both institutional and retail operations, Shinsei's new business model demanded many skills that the old LTCB employees did not have, so the company has hired a large number of mid-career employees, including a number of foreigners with expertise in these areas, to build these new business lines. While a large proportion of the senior management of the old LTCB had left the firm during the period of nationalisation, quite a large number of junior and middle-ranking managers remained and three years into the new firm's existence, in 2003, 55% of Shinsei's employees were from the former LTCB.

In February 2004, Shinsei was listed on the Tokyo Stock Exchange in a secondary sale in which Ripplewood substantially sold down its holding in the company through a sale of 35% of its issued share capital. The government, through the Deposit Insurance Corporation, remains a significant shareholder.

Comparator company 3: J-Financial Co
Choosing a comparator company for Shinsei was perhaps the most difficult challenge in the case selection process, because there are no Japanese companies with the same business model as the new Shinsei. I have selected a large Japanese financial institution, J-Financial Co, which is itself the result of a merger of domestic financial institutions. While there are businesses within J-Financial Co that resemble those of Shinsei, and there are many executives within the company that would be drawn from the same pool of elite university-educated graduates as at LTCB, giving rise to similar cultural traits, the two firms only overlap in a limited way, so it is hard to draw definitive conclusions from the comparison.

Case companies 4 and 5: F-Services Co 1 and F-Services Co 2
As stated above, two firms were reluctant to have their identity revealed in this book, and I will refer to them simply as F-Services Co 1 and F-Services Co 2. As I am trying to disguise the identity of the firms as far as possible, I will only be able to give a brief outline of the firms, as well as the comparator company.

F-Services Co 1 is a relatively young, hitherto fast growing and relatively successful company that was set up only in the last twenty years. It was bought towards the end of the 1990s by a foreign firm whose head office was located in a liberal market economy. The new parent, F-Parent Co 1, sent a number of expatriate managers to the company, including the CEO, CFO and other board members.

As explained above, although I originally expected only to have four case companies, a fifth company, F-Services Co 2, was added at a late stage. F-Services Co 2 is in the same industrial grouping as F-Services Co 1 but does not compete directly with it. The company was set up in the late 1980s by a number of large Japanese corporations who were its principal shareholders and who had seconded a large number of staff to the company. It was taken over by a foreign firm, F-Parent Co 2, in the late 1990s which had had a long relationship with, including an equity stake in, the company. The head office of F-Parent Co 2, like F-Parent Co 1, is located in a liberal market economy. Since coming under the control of F-Parent Co 2, the company has absorbed a number of local subsidiaries of other foreign firms which were acquired by F-Parent Co 2 as part of its global expansion strategy. The employees of F-Services Co 2 therefore comprise the former employees of these subsidiaries, former employees of one of the Japanese corporate shareholders, a large number of mid-career hires who joined the company in its early stages and university graduates that have joined the company. F-Services Co 2 sent a number of expatriate managers to the firm, including the CEO, CFO and the head of HR. It should be pointed out that, although I was given extensive access to employees and management at F-Services Co 2, I was not given the extensive HR data that I was given from the other case companies. Nevertheless, as the interview data was rich and informative, I decided to include the company as part of this study.

Since I carried out my study, both F-Services Co 1 and F-Services Co 2 have been sold by their respective acquirers and are now back in Japanese hands.

Comparator company 4: J-Services Co
J-Services Co is a major Japanese corporation that competes directly with F-Services Co 1. It is a leading player in its field in Japan, with advanced technology, a strong brand and a dominant market position.

Other Japanese companies
As mentioned above, I visited a number of other Japanese companies. I was given particularly good access to a major regional utility company, and evidence from this company ("J-Utility Co") will be referred to extensively. I also interviewed senior management at other firms, including a major steel company, a securities firm and a

trading company. Where appropriate, evidence from these firms will also be referred to.

Data collection and analysis

As far as sources of data were concerned, the chosen starting place was the management of the companies. Hirsch (1986) points out that pressure for organisational change often starts from outsiders and fringe players who do not suffer the same legitimacy constraints as insiders. There were a number of issues that warranted investigation. First, to what extent did the new controlling shareholders wish to impose control on their new subsidiary by sending its own management to run it? Second, to what extent would the management,[1] as representatives of the new shareholders, judge existing employment and organisational practices to be flawed and requiring change? If changes were made, then to what extent was this based on a perception that *Japanese* practices were the problem and that importing practices commonly associated with western, and in particular Anglo-Saxon, firms was the answer? The extent to which the new management consisted of outsiders might also have some bearing on the extent to which changes were seen. I therefore interviewed members of the management to ascertain their intentions towards organisational change.

   The next step was to examine the changes that were actually taking place. I therefore looked for signs that the traditional elements of the communitarian firm were being altered. This in turn consisted of two elements. First, I examined HR and organisational data that showed what the pre-merger organisation looked like and how it now appeared. I did this qualitatively, through interviews with members of the HR department, and by obtaining quantitative data that might indicate the extent to which change had taken place. For example, one of the cornerstones of the welfare corporatist system is seniority-based pay. Second, interviewing employees at the HR department, especially those who were familiar with pre-merger practices, shed light on aspects of the new reward system and how it compared with the pre-merger system. Quantitative data on the speed at which employees used to

---

[1] In referring to "management", I refer to the very senior management of the company, being the CEO and the senior directors of the firm, who are in a position to determine its overall strategy.

reach, and now reach, a key management rank, or the gap that used to exist, and now exists, between the lowest- and highest-paid members of a cohort[2] of employees, provided some numerical evidence of the actual impact of changes in the reward structure.

The third step was to collect the views of the employees themselves. It was one thing for the management or HR department officials to assert that the reward structure was, for example, more meritocratic, or that there were now greater career opportunities for women, or that there was more accountability in the decision-making process. But if the perception of the employees differed significantly from the pronouncements of the management or HR department officials on exactly what had changed, then this would have considerable bearing as to whether the legitimacy of existing organisational practices was actually being eroded. Interviewing employees also enabled me to gauge the impact of any changes on different employee groups. This gave me important insights into the rate at which the legitimacy of existing organisational practices were eroding among different groups of employees. For example, even if management and male employees felt that career opportunities for female employees had increased, if the female employees themselves did not perceive this, the claim that change had taken place could legitimately be challenged. I also spoke to former employees, as they provided insight into pre-merger practices.

There were, however, further steps to take. Assuming that I were to find extensive signs of change at the case study companies and that these findings were borne out by HR data and employee perception, it was another matter to establish that these changes were associated with an "institutionally distant" merger. It might be that Japan as a whole is changing, so the changes that were occurring at the case study companies would have taken place anyway. As a fourth step, therefore, I visited Japanese companies, competitors of roughly the same size and in the same industrial sectors (the comparator companies), to investigate how, if at all, those companies were changing.

Finally, I obtained observations from an array of other experts, industry leaders, academics, journalists, government officials, and so on.

As I have indicated above, I tentatively decided to focus on a dual approach to data collection, qualitative data from (mostly)

---

[2] By "cohort" I mean a group of university graduate employees who joined the firm in the same year.

structured interviews and quantitative data from the HR departments illustrating what changes had taken place in HR policies during the last five years.

Qualitative data: interview strategy

I decided to use a variety of interview techniques, tailored to the nature of the data I wished to extract and the type of interviewees. There were, broadly speaking, four types of interview, which I list below.

(i) Company management: case study companies/comparators

Much of the conversation with management of the case companies would touch on issues of some sensitivity: what was, or had been, "wrong" with the pre-acquisition organisation and what was their vision "to put it right"? It seemed to me that this open and "conversational" style was the most suitable method for interviews with senior executives. These interviews were therefore unstructured, with only broad themes outlined in advance and they were not always recorded.[3]

(ii) HR department: case study companies/comparators

Interviews with HR department officials took on a more structured format and I sent them in advance a list of the broad areas of the employment system and the individual domains that I wished to discuss with them. However, in addition to factual information, I also wanted the officials' own interpretations of the changes, so I was keen to keep the interviews as conversational as possible.

(iii) Employees: case study companies only

The third, and most time-consuming, data-gathering interviews were those with case company employees. These were an important source of information, not only yielding factual information about the actual changes that had occurred at the firms, but also the employees' interpretation of the changes. The interviews were therefore carried out in a systematic manner, in a much more focused style. A list of twenty

---

[3] I made a judgement as to whether to record the meeting at the very beginning of each meeting. The atmosphere was not always conducive to making this request, in which case I desisted and made interview notes instead.

questions, submitted to interviewees in advance, was drawn up to gauge employee perception of change in the domains of the welfare corporatist organisation. Most of the questions were structured to elicit observations about what had changed and what the impact of that change was on the employee and the organisation. Some questions, however, were designed to elicit subjective feelings on the changes. I wanted to know, for example, what employees thought about the fairness of the new remuneration system.

In order to obtain feedback from as broad a range of employees as possible I requested that the companies schedule the interviews with employees in the following way:

- Age:
  - one-third in the "young" pre-manager grades (aged up to 35)
  - one-third in the "middle management" grades (aged 35–45)
  - one-third in the "senior management" grade (aged 45 and over)
- Functions: representatives from at least three functions; for example, marketing, sales, finance, HR
- Sex: at least one female employee
- Career: at least one mid-career hire.

With three age groups and three functions to see, I felt that a minimum of three employees in each of the groups would give me a reasonable spread of opinion and that a total of somewhere between ten and fifteen employees per company would be the appropriate number.

I did not replicate the comprehensive employee interview programme at the comparator firms as, first the main thrust of the project was to obtain feedback from employees of Japanese firms taken over by foreign ones and, second, the enormous amount of time that such interviews would have taken to carry out and to transcribe.

Given these factors, and the limited extra insights that I felt the interviews would give me, I decided to stick with my plan to limit the scope of my interviews at the comparator companies to the senior management and members of the HR department.

(iv) Other interviews

The fourth and final type of interview was with the employees of other Japanese companies, including people in leadership positions, HR officials and other managers, plus industry experts and other informed sources (i.e. bankers, government officials, a senior union official, journalists and academics). These interviews were generally not recorded, but notes were taken and written up as memos summarising the main points.

In total I completed 224 interviews during my fieldwork, a breakdown of which is contained in Table 2.1.

Table 2.1 *Fieldwork interviews*

Case study and comparator company interviews		
CEOs/EVPs	29	
Employees	81	
HR dept	34	
Former employees	13	
Sub-total		157
Other interviews		
Industry leaders	18	
Other co. employees	19	
Journalists	3	
Academics	13	
Industry experts	14	
Sub-total	67	
Total interviews		224

The fieldwork for the research was carried out in three major phases, with extended visits to Japan in April and May 2003, October 2003 and March to May 2004, when I was stationed at the Policy Research Institute of the Ministry of Finance. A lot of data has been gathered by telephone calls and e-mail in the follow-up process. The interviews at the foreign companies were carried out in the first two visits, the last visit being used mainly to gather company data and interview key personnel at the Japanese comparators. Since carrying out these interviews, I have had a limited number of follow-up meetings with senior management at the case companies.

Qualitative data analysis

After transcriptions were completed, I initially reviewed them in their entirety to get a sense of the whole (Cresswell, 2003) and get a preliminary sense of sub-themes. Then, following Strauss and Corbin (1998), I went through them line-by-line to search for patterns of response in greater detail and gradually developed a series of categories within the preset domains that I had developed, to which labels were attached, manually, in the margins of the text. This manual process was important in the initial theme-building process (Miles and Huberman, 1994, p. 67) as I felt it enabled me to develop a deeper and richer insight into the data than had I transferred it straight onto a computer database for analysis. I went through the transcripts several times and, through each iteration, patterns gradually emerged. I then transferred the coded interview data onto a spreadsheet for ease of analysis and sorting. The data were cross-referenced and linkages developed between intra-case and inter-case data, as well as between different subsets, such as employee type.

Quantitative interview data

My original intention was to obtain only quantitative verbal data from the interview process. However, while studying the data it struck me that much of the coded information was open to numeric scaling. I was particularly searching for insights into employee perceptions of change and the way in which interviewees had responded to my questions on the whole enabled me to "grade" their responses to reveal the extent to which they had perceived change in various aspects of the companies' employment systems or organisational structures. This would enable me to see more clearly differences between the process and perception of change in the different organisations I was studying, as well as seeing differences in perceptions of the various groups I was interviewing (e.g. male vs female; career workers vs mid-career hires; young vs old, etc.). Miles and Huberman (1994, p. 42) discuss this process in terms of "quantising" of text and recommend three-to five-point scales as being the easiest and most reliable method. I selected a three-point scale, where a score of three represented "great change" to a work routine or an organisational feature (e.g. employee evaluation methodology) and one represented "no change".

Thus, for example, in answer to the question "has the recruitment system changed, and how?", it was fairly clear from the interview transcripts the extent to which interviewees felt the process had changed. Thus, the responses generally fell into the "yes, it's changed a great deal ..." and the "no, it hasn't really changed at all ..." types, with a middle category of "yes, it has changed, but ...", and these would be categorised accordingly. There were, of course, a number of responses that were initially difficult to grade; for example, where interviewees appeared to voice contradictory opinions when answering the same question. Where this ambiguity existed, I listened to the tapes of interview again to ensure that my perception of the interviewee's response was as accurate as possible.

Problems associated with the interviewing process

There were, however, a number of problems associated with the process. Three in particular stood out.

Employee categorisation

There were some employee categorisations that were not as homogeneous as I thought they would be. The best example was the mid-career hire category. I had expected that these employees would have a different outlook on the process of change at a Japanese company taken over by a foreign organisation compared to an employee who had joined the company on graduation from university, and indeed this proved to be the case. However, on closer examination, there were a number of definitional problems associated with this category. First of all, F-Services Co 1 and F-Services Co 2 were relatively new companies that had been set up originally with employees who were seconded from the then principal shareholders. Many of them eventually severed ties with their previous employers to join the new companies as full-time employees. Was it reasonable to classify these employees, who had been with the company since its inception, as "mid-career hires", whereas graduates, who had joined subsequently, were "career employees"? Second, in the case of Shinsei there had been widespread recruitment of mid-career hires after its purchase by Ripplewood. However, some had been hired from Japanese firms, whereas others had been hired from other foreign firms. Their perspectives on work routines and organisational structure were quite often diametrically opposed. Given this situation, the "mid-career hire perspective" is not necessarily a homogeneous one.

Employee perception of change

As I mentioned above, most of my questions concerned employee perceptions of change. However, in performing the analysis,

I recognised very quickly that employees' starting points were very different and that it was important to incorporate into the analysis some reference point which indicated the change "from what, to what" in order to produce any data that was useful. The most important split in perspectives was again between career employees and mid-career hires. While there was a striking homogeneity in the opinions of employees who had been at the firm all their lives in the way they perceived the "old practices", it was a different matter when it came to the mid-career hires, a number of whom had joined the case study companies from other foreign firms. Many of these observed that the company they had joined, although it was now under foreign control, had many organisational features that were typically found in large Japanese corporations. They would have perceived great change in their new surroundings, but it would have been in the opposite sense from the change observed by career employees when foreigners took over, or by a mid-career hire who had joined from another Japanese firm. In the analysis, therefore, I reinterpreted the responses of these mid-career hires to be answers to the question "what changes have you noted in this organisation from what you perceive to be typical of a Japanese organisation?" rather than just "what changes have you noted?". Fortunately, there appeared to be a sufficiently strong sense of what constituted a typical Japanese organisation among interviewees and this, I believe, makes the data quite relevant.

Low n

While the total size of the sample was reasonable (60 employees), the number of interviewees from some of the sub-groups (e.g. female employees, of whom there were eleven) would ideally have been larger. This has had an impact on the statistical significance of the inter-employee group analysis.

Quantitative HR data

I sent questionnaires to all nine case companies asking them to lay out what changes had been made to HR practices (e.g. employee evaluation procedures, salary dispersion among cohorts) during the past five years. I requested data at two historic points: one as of 31 March 1998, which for all case study companies preceded the takeover, and 31 March 2003, which for all case study companies represented at least a one-year interval from the completion of the merger (in the case of Chugai, exactly one year). In all five cases of Japanese companies taken over by foreign firms, this would give me a picture of pre-takeover practices and how they had changed post-takeover, as well as a comparison with Japanese companies.

As I have mentioned I did not receive any quantitative HR data from F-Services Co 2 despite repeated requests. This did not overly concern me, as I had originally not intended to include it as a case study company. Therefore, I have qualitative and quantitative interview data from F-Services Co 2, but not quantitative HR data.

The findings

Turning now to the findings themselves, we will attempt to determine the actual impact of foreign ownership and control on Japanese organisations.

Management view: the shareholder's voice

There was considerable evidence that, for new owners, institutional distance was a major factor in the way they were intending to handle the integration of their acquisition. Some of this stemmed from the fact that major acquisitions of Japanese companies by foreign firms had hitherto been uncommon, causing their acquisitions to be more in the spotlight than would have been the case in other countries. For Roche, the apparent difference with which foreign companies are perceived compared to their Japanese counterparts was a major factor in deciding to build through acquisition. Franz Humer, Chairman of Roche, commented:

I am absolutely sure that in Japan if you are regarded as a Japanese company and not as a foreign company you have a different status, a different relationship with government, different access to government, different access to universities, different access to opinion leaders, and I think that was one of the strong underlying reasons for [acquiring Chugai]: to tap into the different potential of knowledge science and know-how.

Thierry Moulonguet, Nissan's Chief Financial Officer from 1999 to 2003 who subsequently returned to Renault to take up the position of Chief Financial Officer there, commented on the difficulties facing foreign firms in Japan:

> the Japanese environment is different ... Carlos Ghosn was saying that "to be recognised as achieving one, I must achieve 3 in Japan!" I still sense that we are not exactly viewed as a normal Japanese company even though we have respected everything: Nissan's corporate entity, corporate identity, brand identity, a majority of the management committee and the board are Japanese. Even with the success of the initial years, which was good news for Japan to have this big company reviving, they still question our credibility. The Japanese media and financial analysts are much more demanding of Nissan than other companies like Toyota, Honda, etc.

It was apparent from discussions with the senior management of the case companies that they had a different idea of the company's "new conceptual destination" (Greenwood and Hinings, 1996) and that the "institutionalised definition of success" (Oliver, 1992) had changed from what they perceived it to have been under the old regime. We saw in Chapter 1 that most Japanese CEOs felt the support of the company's employees was far more important to them than that of the company's shareholders (Yoshimori, 1995). By implication, the most important constituency to whom the CEO must appeal is that of the employees, and it is their perception of success that is key. To this extent, the measurement of the "performance" is different at a communitarian firm and has to be seen in the context of the employee-favouring company, as opposed to a shareholder-oriented one.

The considerable "institutional distance" between the new head offices and the Japanese subsidiary would suggest that the parent would try to maximise control through CEO and board appointments. While this was generally the case, there was in practice a significant variation in the way in which the new shareholders exercised control.

- *Nissan*: the CEO, Carlos Ghosn, was sent by Renault. The board consisted of a mixture of Renault secondees and original directors of Nissan.
- *Chugai*: the CEO, Osamu Nagayama, was the original CEO of Chugai. Other than non-executive directors, Roche did not initially send any directors.

- *Shinsei*: the CEO, Masamoto Yashiro, was appointed by Ripplewood. At the outset, there were only two other executive directors, both former LTCB employees (but who were not on the LTCB board).
- *F-Services Co 1*: the CEO and all members of the drastically reduced board were appointed by the parent company.
- *F-Services Co 2*: the CEO was appointed by the parent, but the board consisted of a mixture of parent appointees and former directors of the pre-acquisition firm.

There was also considerable variation in the way the acquired company was referred to by the new management. The words "alliance" and "partnership" were often used at Nissan and the fact that the Nissan and Chugai brands were very much in existence post-acquisition contributed to a stronger sense of independence and continuity of the original identity of the company. Although Ripplewood effectively controlled Shinsei, as it was an institutional investor, Shinsei was in no sense a "subsidiary".

Management interviews

Common to all leaders of the five firms was the feeling that a transformation of the culture of the company was a vital part of the process of reaching the destination outlined in the new vision. There was in particular a stress on instilling a stronger "performance culture" and a clear message that shareholders' interests had in the past not been sufficiently understood by employees. Emphasis on "performance" implied a much greater degree of focus on the rational, the efficient, the bottom line.

It was not just that shareholders' interests were insufficiently understood or considered: there was some suggestion that excessive consideration of shareholders' interest transgressed norms of acceptable behaviour. One senior expatriate manager, contemplating a headcount reduction to reduce costs, observed:

Some people will interpret that as negative. Externally it'll be viewed as greedy ... And that's the fundamental perception that's hard to challenge, that to do something that makes shareholders money, that's not worthy, that is playing to your lowest, your basest elements. We have to take that out and say: "No guys, we are here because shareholders have given us money that we have to give a return on." You have to help people feel good about having those feelings.

In the case of Japanese financial institutions, transforming the culture of the firm into one that was more performance-driven was complicated further by the perceived special status of financial institutions in Japan. A manager at Shinsei noted that:

in Japan, companies like ours are semi-public institutions and our mission is thus also in some ways to serve the public. The profit motive is there as we are after all a limited liability company, but it has to work alongside the need to serve the public good ... So when one of our large corporate clients got into serious difficulties, our first reaction is not just to think about the economic issues but the wider issues affecting Japan and the economy if a company like that went bust ... Public opinion also wanted us to behave in a typical Japanese fashion in this situation.

The lack of a "performance culture" at the case companies manifested itself in a number of ways. First, the new management commented that the employees had no real concept of "returns", and how they were achieved. Thus, one expatriate head of HR observed: "I don't think anyone thinks about this sort of thing. An expression like ROI never comes up in discussions. We get the company's numbers, profit and loss, and so on, but I don't think anyone is aware of what the shareholder thinks or wants from us."

At Nissan, Thierry Moulonguet, the CFO, said that one of his main tasks was:

to put financial criteria back at the centre of the decision-making process. Before, for decisions on matters like expansion, development, purchasing, criteria were fuzzy, not shared and it depended on who was in charge. We have established clear criteria and financial hurdles. We have laid down consistent exchange rate references, discount rates for all our profitability studies and methodology to go from operating profit for one product to how it contributes to the overall profitability of the company. We also stick to the budget rigidly through the year whereas before it was quite easy if something changed to work within some new framework. The budget was considered to be quite flexible. Now the annual budget is the main frame of reference for people to work off and they know it's not going to change every three months.

Second, there was no direct linkage between company performance and its human resource (HR) strategy. The approach to HR development was characterised by a strong sense of routine and "taken-for-granted-ness". The expatriate head of the International Human Resources Department at Nissan used the evocative term "automatism" to describe the state of affairs on his arrival:

The first thing that shocked me on getting here was the automatism in the management, in career appraisals, salary review, and even bonus which was a fixed "second salary" and not a variable part. We had to fight against this automatism.

Third, there was a suggestion that, in order to improve performance, the decision-making process had to change. One expatriate case company manager, who was trying to convince the employees to focus less on market share as an indicator of performance, said:

You need to reorganise decision making so it's less on the old emotional bonds and more fact based. Get the facts on the table, then base decisions on factors such as positive cash flow, earnings. You have practical shareholder expectations that you need to balance against what everyone here organically wants to do which is gain market share.

Another senior expatriate manager expressed the opinion that the consensual approach of Japanese decision making was not appropriate for organisations trying to make radical change:

The fact is that Japan doesn't champion a "Jack Welch" style of management and all the management at the top of Japanese companies lead by consensus: they are not the kind of leaders that you want when you want to make radical change. The challenge is at the leadership level and there is an argument that more foreigners should be brought in or that younger people should be brought through.

The role of emotional bonds in decision making and the role of outsiders are important themes to which we will be returning.

The new leadership of the case companies, then, appear determined to transform the cultures of the firms that have been taken over and introduce a much stronger orientation towards "performance".

Osamu Nagayama of Chugai stood out in his emphasis of the need for stability, meaning that extreme caution needed to be used before making fundamental alterations in the company's employment practices:

> It's a matter of common sense and we just don't do it [i.e. fire employees]. It's important for Chugai's profile that it is a company that you can stay at, so long as you want to. That gives a lot of comfort to employees ... the fact is that people from good universities still want stability and that means lifetime employment. If we move too quickly, we will lose people.

He noted, however, that some form of cultural transformation was necessary and acknowledged that, in order to transform Chugai, our staff and our culture, it requires changing our human resource development programme".

Franz Humer, the Chairman of Roche, emphasised that the acquisition of Chugai and the decision to let it operate on an arm's-length basis was as a result of many decades of frustration for Roche as it tried to manage its own subsidiary in Japan:

> We realised having been in Japan for over 100 years that despite all these efforts we were number 33 in the market and did not feel we would make the progress that we should, or attain the ranking that we needed in that important market through our own strength despite new products ...

It was also clear in the case of Chugai that Nagayama had prepared the ground at an early stage for the merger, recognising that, as a mid-ranking Japanese pharmaceutical company, his strategic options were limited:

> When it came to our merger, for several years prior to the merger, I gathered our people together very often to talk to them about how I perceived the environment in which we were operating, and what was necessary for Chugai to survive. Unless you take these steps, when it comes to the major change, no one will follow you.

This was clearly an advantage that not all the CEOs in the case companies had.

The tone set by the CEO of the various companies regarding the degree of change that he perceived as being required is closely reflected by the perceptions of the employees of the company, as we shall see.

Employee reaction

Let us now examine what changes were made and how the employees perceived these changes.

I asked the case company employees two general questions. First, their perception of their company's new orientation towards shareholders and, second, the perception of overall change since acquisition. Significantly, among all twenty questions that were posed, the question regarding the firm's shareholder orientation was the one that elicited the highest and most consistent indication of change (see Table 2.2).

Table 2.2 *Case company employees' shareholder orientation*

Shareholder orientation						
Q: Do you feel the company is more/less shareholder-oriented since the merger? 1 = no change 2 = changed somewhat 3 = changed a great deal						
Nissan	Chugai	Shinsei	F-Svcs Co 1	F-Svcs Co 2	Total	
2.73	2.69	2.67	2.90	2.45	2.68	
Male	Female	Career	MCH	20–35 yrs	35–45 yrs	45 yrs +
2.71	2.55	2.70	2.62	2.63	2.71	2.67

There was a remarkable consistency of response across companies and across employee groups, suggesting that all the case companies started off, so to speak, "on a level playing field". They recognised that the company would henceforth be managed and decisions made according to benefits that accrued to shareholders, rather than employees. This meant a shifting concept of "ownership" and a rebalancing of stakeholder priorities, away from a company managed for the sake of employees, and this has obvious implications for employees. A senior manager at one case company put it as follows:

The meaning of "ownership" is different in western firms. Ownership is a much more short-term concept than that in Japan, or at least it has been in the past. So [we now have new owners] but you don't know for how long they will continue to be the owners. The staff understand that but it affects their mentality: it becomes more short term.

Table 2.3 *Employee interviews: overall impressions of change:*
quantitative data

			Change		

Q: Overall, how great has the change been since the merger?
1 = no change
2 = changed somewhat
3 = changed a great deal

Nissan	Chugai	Shinsei	F-Svcs Co 1	F-Svcs Co 2	Total	
2.73	1.85	2.67	2.74	2.36	2.47	
Male	Female	Career	MCH	20–35 yrs	35–45 yrs	45 yrs +
2.57	2.00	2.70	1.62	2.50	2.35	2.67

n = 60

I asked the employees of case companies what their overall impression of change was after the shareholding of the company changed hands (see Table 2.3). As can be seen, there was generally a perception of great change at the case study companies. In particular, the employees of Nissan, Shinsei and F-Services Co 1 were mostly under the impression that life had changed considerably. However, response was not uniform by any means, with a very low perception of change at Chugai, with F-Services Co 2 lying between Chugai and the "extreme change" group. The data are fairly consistent with the views expressed by interviewees on change within the individual domains: thus, high scores for overall change were generally associated with strong indications for change in areas such as recruitment, reward systems, and so on. The possible exception, as we shall see, is Nissan where, despite the perception of great change overall, key institutions such as lifetime employment and reward according to seniority had not been severely undermined in employees' minds.

There were sharp differences in perception between male and female employees. We will explore the issue of the treatment of female employees below, but at least from these data it would appear that becoming a foreign firm has not made a significant difference to the lives of female employees, or at least their perception of it.

The gap is even greater between career employees and mid-career hires. This was expected to a certain extent, as many of the mid-career hires themselves came from other foreign firms. However, the sharpness of the difference was surprising. As will become clear from the interview data, career employees perceived great change to their organisation as consistently as mid-career hires saw many traditional elements of the Japanese organisation still remaining.

I was also expecting a greater perception of change among older employees than younger ones and to a certain extent this was borne out, but not to the extent expected.

We will now explore each of the domains of the communitarian firm in the format followed in Chapters 1 and 4, and analyse what has changed and how employees reacted to these changes.

References

Cole, R.E. (1971) *Japanese Blue Collar: The Changing Tradition*. Berkeley, CA: University of California Press

Cresswell, J.W. (2003) *Research Design: Qualitative, Quantitative, and Mixed Methods Approaches*. Thousand Oaks, CA: Sage Publications

Dore, R. (1973) *British Factory – Japanese Factory: The Origins of National Diversity in Industrial Relations*. Berkeley, CA: University of California Press

Dyer, W.G. and Wilkins, A.L. (1991) "Better Stories, Not Better Constructs, to Generate Better Theory: A Rejoinder to Eisenhardt", *Academy of Management Review*, 16: 613–619

Eisenhardt, K.M. (1989) "Building Theories from Case Study Research", *Academy of Management Journal*, 14: 532–550

Flick, U. (1998) *An Introduction to Qualitative Research*. London: Sage Publications

Ghosn, C. (2002) "Saving the Business without Losing the Company", *Harvard Business Review*, 37–45

Glaser, B.G. and Strauss, A.L. (1967) *The Discovery of Grounded Theory: Strategies for Qualitative Research*. Hawthorne, NY: Aldine de Gruyter

Greenwood, R. and Hinings, C.R. (1996) "Understanding Radical Organizational Change: Bringing Together the Old and the New Institutionalism", *Academy of Management Review*, 21: 1022–1054

Hirsch, P.M. (1986) "From Ambush to Golden Parachute: Corporate Takeovers as an Instance of Cultural Framing and Institutional Integration", *American Journal of Sociology*, 91: 800–837

King, G., Keohane, R.O. and Verba, S. (1994) *Designing Social Inquiry.* Princeton, NJ: Princeton University Press

Miles, M.B. and Huberman, A.M. (1994) *Qualitative Data Analysis.* Thousand Oaks, CA: Sage Publications

Oliver, C. (1992) "The Antecedents of Deinstitutionalization", *Organization Studies*, 13: 563–588

Patton, M.Q. (2002) *Qualitative Evaluation and Research Methods.* Thousand Oaks, CA: Sage Publications

Strauss, A.L. and Corbin, J.M. (1998) *Basics of Qualitative Research.* Thousand Oaks, CA: Sage Publications

Tett, G. (2004) *Saving the Sun: Shinsei and the Battle for Japan's Future.* London: Random House

Whittaker, D.H. (1994) "SMEs, Entry Barriers and 'Strategic Alliances' ". In M. Aoki and R. Dore (eds.) *The Japanese Firm: Sources of Competitive Strength.* Oxford: Oxford University Press

Yin, R.K. (1994) *Case Study Research: Design and Methods, 2nd edn.* Thousand Oaks, CA: Sage

Yoshimori, M. (1995) "Whose Company Is It? The Concept of the Corporation in Japan and the West", *Long Range Planning*, 28: 33–44.

3 | *Entering the firm: recruitment and training*

IVEN THE "insiderist" nature of Japanese organisations and the propensity for Japanese employees to stay at the firm they join on leaving university, it is difficult to overstate the importance of the recruitment process in Japanese firms. In terms of selection, the company is obliged to take extraordinary care to ensure that they are getting the right people, as the consequences of hiring the wrong person are much greater than in an environment where there is an active external labour market. For the student, the price of picking the wrong company is similarly great, as it will be all the more difficult to change track later in his or her career. In practice, this means extensive use of examinations, a lengthy interview process, heavy reliance on introductions and personal background checks (Beck and Beck, 1994; Rohlen, 1974). Traditionally there has been a great deal of involvement of young alumni who are one or two years into the company. At some firms they have formed teams to identify potential talent at their former universities, called the "*rikurūtā seido*" or "recruiter system".

The focus on graduate recruitment and training employees up internally means that, for the company, there is little incentive to hire people mid-career. Indeed, there has been an implicit code of restraint on the part of larger firms in the hiring of employees, particularly skilled ones, from other firms (Aoki, 1988). Itoh (1994, pp. 248–249) gives three other reasons why firms may lack the incentive to hire people mid-career: first, the possibility that outsiders will not be as productive as insiders due to "the latter's accumulation of firm-specific human capital"; second, because hiring outsiders will have a negative impact on existing employees' motivation; and third, firms "may infer that a job-changer is of low ability or a 'bad' type".

For students about to embark on a career with his or her chosen company, the implications of "insiderism" are serious. In referring to the phenomenon of "*uchi* (insider) versus *soto* (outsider)" Beck and Beck comment as follows:

> The pervasive sense in Japanese society is that when a man has spent a number of years with one firm (especially in his early, formative years), he absorbs that organisation and can never be changed ... Related to the problem of cultural labelling is the company's fear that a mid-career recruit would not understand the subtle cultural aspects of communication in his new firm after having been "trained" in a very different system. (1994, pp. 107–108)

For employees, changing jobs incurs substantial income penalties. The worker has also made a significant investment in firm-specific human capital. The penalty increases with age and by the time an employee who has stayed at the same company his entire career reaches his mid-forties he will be paid double what a mid-career hire of the same age is paid (Bank of Tokyo-Mitsubishi, 1998).

The legal and regulatory framework has also been a barrier to the development of an external labour market, with the lack of pension portability being a significant factor (Ono and Rebick, 2002). The government introduced a defined benefit pension framework in 2001 with one objective being to increase labour mobility through pension mobility. While there has been a steady take-up of these plans by Japanese companies, their impact does not yet appear to have been felt (Conrad and Heindorf, 2006).

Training

On entering the firm, the new employee undergoes a period of intense socialisation within the firm, starting off with a highly formalised induction ceremony invariably presided over by the President. The President makes a speech, in which he welcomes the new recruits into the corporate "family" and hands over letters of appointment to each of the employees in turn, mirroring the graduation ceremony they have just attended (e.g. Kasai, 2003).

The socialisation process continues throughout the careers of the employees, and a strong bond develops among cohorts, reinforced by the training programme, which is predominantly handled in-house and is strongly cohort-based, at least for the first ten to fifteen years, as the group moves slowly up through the hierarchy.

The training system is aligned to the incentive system, designed to give all employees an equal opportunity to demonstrate his or her potential and to keep competition among employees "tight" for as long as possible (Itoh, 1994). In addition to the formal cohort-based programmes, there are a large number of specialist training courses open to employees. However, more important than the formal training employees undergo is the programme based on "broad on-the-job training" (Aoki, 1990; Koike, 1994), or "informal" OJT (JIL, 2004), an important element of which is rotation through a number of different areas of the firm's operations. The subject of rotation will be covered below.

The process of recruitment, socialisation and training is handled centrally and is controlled by the HR department (Dore, 1973; Yashiro, 1998). The career paths that they will follow are also completely out of their hands: "new recruits have traditionally had little or no input into the decision-making process that assigns hundreds of new employees to rather small and unimportant jobs around the company" (Beck and Beck, 1994, p. 76).

While the highly internal nature of employee training at large Japanese firms brings undoubted benefits in terms of increased cohesiveness and cohort solidarity, one drawback is that its very firm-specific nature does not enhance the attractiveness of the employee to other firms. This firm-focused, rather than craft-focused, training inhibits the development of the external labour market and reduces the flexibility of the HR department to reduce headcount.

Changes in recruitment and training

There are some signs of change in attitudes towards recruitment and training. In line with the emphasis on more transparency, many large companies (94% of companies of more than 5,000 employees) have introduced web-based recruitment systems (JIL, 2004). However, "introduction or recommendation by teachers" was still the most common method of recruitment (38.4%) by firms of college students according to a Japan Institute of Labor survey in 2001 (JIL, 2004). In recent years, there has evidently been less emphasis on a formal joining ceremony for incoming graduates, with firms like Fujitsu, Mitsubishi Corporation and Sony settling for either no ceremony or an informal glass of beer with the President (JIL, 2002).

There is certainly a great deal of discussion about the larger role that mid-career hires are playing, or will play, in the recruiting process. In a survey published in the *Nihon Keizai Shimbun* in October 2003, large companies were found to be planning a 7% reduction in the hiring of graduates, while increasing employment of mid-career hires by more than 9%.[1] However, when one actually looks at the statistics, it would not appear that much has changed in the last decade: in 2002, the rate of new hires due to job changes (i.e. percentage among all hired workers of mid-career hires) was 8.8% – exactly the same percentage as in 1992.

There is also some indication of a shift in emphasis away from the company taking complete responsibility for employees' careers towards a greater degree of autonomy and "self-development". In a Ministry of Labour survey carried out in 2001–2002, a decrease was noted in firms providing off-the-job training. Two important attitudinal shifts appeared to be occurring: first that training expenditure would be shifting towards "selected employees" and that, in future, training would be increasingly the responsibility of the individual employee (JIL, 2003). This trend was also noted in research into recruitment trends in the banking sector (Watanabe, 2003). This ties in with the increased consideration companies appear to be giving to employees when making staff-move decisions and the setting up of the "multiple-track personnel management system" which will be discussed below.

To summarise, therefore, the communitarian template consists of the following features:

• recruitment and training planned on the assumption of long-term commitment by employees;
• focus on elite universities;
• strong cohort socialisation process;
• ceremony and symbolism attached to entry to firm: "initiation rites";
• use of cohort-based training.

Summary of findings from the literature:

• more web-based recruiting, but introductions still important (JIL, 2004);

---

[1] A related development is the explosive growth of temporary workers (called "dispatched workers") sent from manpower agencies. This has tripled in the period from 1992 and reached 1.45 million in 2001.

- only limited evidence of increased mid-career hiring: legal framework still a barrier to mobility (Hanami, 2004);
- slightly more emphasis on individual responsibility for career planning (JIL, 2003);
- central control of recruitment and training by HR department (Yashiro, 1998).

At the case companies we would expect that part of the new management's efforts to enhance the "performance culture" would be to alter the recruitment and training regime. In particular we would expect that in recruitment there would be:

- a greater emphasis on recruitment of mid-career hires with specialist skills;
- reduced dependence on university graduates;
- more involvement of the operating divisions in the recruitment process;
- less emphasis on the socialisation of new employees, preparing them for a "lifetime with the company".

In the domain of training, we would expect:

- greater emphasis on developing specialist skills;
- less emphasis on solidarity-building, cohort-based training;
- more emphasis on individual choice.

Findings at comparator and case companies

At the comparator companies, there is some evidence, in line with the findings above, of change in these areas, predominantly in recruitment where there appears to be a greater emphasis on transparency. All companies handle graduate recruitment through the web and have put an end to the "recruiter system" where recently hired employees take charge of recruiting graduates from their former universities.

I took the company's record in hiring mid-career hires as a "proxy" for changing recruitment practices. As we have discussed, the communitarian firm does not promote mid-career job moves and, as a consequence, the external labour market is under-developed. Thus, the extent to which companies increased mid-career hiring indicates an undermining of communitarian recruitment practices.

Table 3.1 *Comparator and case mid-career hires*

	Mid-career hires			
	Total mid-career hires employed during year		Mid-career hires as percentage of total employees	
	1998	*2003*	*1998*	*2003*
J-M'facturing Co	40	110	0.1%	0.2%
Nissan	240	545	0.6%	1.8%
J-Pharma Co	20	80	0.4%	1.7%
Chugai	62	34	1.7%	0.7%
J-Financial Co	N/A	140	N/A	0.5%
Shinsei	21	186	0.6%	9.1%
J-Services Co	59	29	1.7%	0.5%
F-Services Co	174	80	7.3%	2.6%

We can see from Table 3.1 that, while the number of mid-career hires at the comparator companies has generally increased, as a percentage of total employees it is still limited. J-Pharma Co and J-Manufacturing Co have increased the hiring of such employees, while at J-Services Co, the number has decreased from five years ago. At J-Manufacturing Co, a middle-management employee said in answer to a question about mid-career hires, making a specific reference to Nissan:

Yes we are taking them, especially in the specialist functions like engineering, but I have never worked with one myself. There are probably quite a lot in areas like finance but not so many in HR. Maybe our head of HR would say that compared with Nissan we have sufficient resources internally to progress without hiring too many MCHs. Maybe Nissan couldn't have changed without taking people from the outside. That's not the case here. We can change things ourselves. That's the pride we have.

The reference to the role of outsiders in the changes taking place at Nissan is noteworthy. At J-Utility Co, mid-career hires only made up 0.8% of the total workforce in 2004 and their recruitment policy is geared almost exclusively towards universities and high schools, with mid-career recruitment exclusively focused on jobs with a high degree of specialisation, such as IT.

The recruitment system at J-Financial Co has changed in two respects. First, J-Financial Co has created a new category of employee – *"professional shoku"* ("professional employees") – distinguished from the normal management grade employees who operate under the lifetime employment system. The "professional employees" are all on the *nenpōsei* salary structure where their salaries are reviewed on an annual basis and are based on a combination of factors relating to rank, performance and competency. Although in theory anyone within the J-Financial Co can be on this type of contract, in practice the vast majority are in the securities area, where competition with foreign firms is most intense and where there is the highest degree of labour mobility. Significantly, however, it was pointed out that, while, again theoretically, these employees are operating on the same "high risk, high return" employment philosophy as their counterparts in the foreign securities firms, in practice the underlying assumption is that they are "long-term" employees and that this is reflected, in reality, in lower pay for "professional employees" than those working at foreign firms.

The second change is in the area of graduate recruitment, where new employees can elect either to be generalists in the traditional way, or to specialise from the outset in one of three specialist areas: securities and investment banking, trust banking, and financial engineering. In 2004, slightly more chose the generalist course than the specialist courses. Even the generalists, however, are eventually expected to develop specialist skills, or what the company calls a "franchise". Understanding that in many cases graduates will not know what field suits them best initially, the firm has deemed the first ten years of an employee's career to be the "skills development period" towards the end of which generalist employees are encouraged to select a "franchise".

In training, there is still a great deal of emphasis on cohort-based programmes. At J-Utility Co, enormous effort is put into training, and 65,000 employees go through the extensive training centre annually (i.e. each employee does an average of three courses every year). The graduate will go through four cohort-based training programmes prior to becoming a manager – twelve years into the firm. In addition, there are a large number of specialist courses, from engineering, construction and other technical courses, plus others focusing on accountancy, leadership, etc.

At all comparator companies, recruitment and training is still strictly controlled by the HR department.

Case companies: recruitment

Measured in terms of recruitment of mid-career hires, there has been some widening of the gap between the case companies and the comparators. The evidence is not entirely conclusive, however, as the absolute numbers are still fairly low except at Shinsei. The contrast between Shinsei and J-Finance Co is very dramatic, with Shinsei increasing mid-career hire intake nine-fold. It should be pointed out, however, that 1998 was the year of LTCB's collapse, therefore hiring of any kind would have been very limited. Nissan has more than doubled its mid-career hire intake. J-Manufacturing Co, too, has seen significant increases, although from a smaller base. F-Services Co 1 had in fact decreased its mid-career hire intake in 2003 compared to 1998, but the manager of the HR department explained that considerable hiring had taken place in 2001 and 2002, when the company had filled most of its vacancies, which had led to a decline in hiring in 2003. J-Services Co also decreased their mid-career hire intake, at a slightly faster rate, and mid-career hire intake as a percentage of total employees is substantially lower than at F-Services Co 1. The figure for J-Pharma Co, although relatively high, may not be totally representative, as PhD hires, which are quite substantial in the industry, are counted as mid-career hires. A breakdown between PhD hires and the rest was not available. Chugai actually reduced mid-career intake in 2003 because of the large influx of personnel from Nippon Roche.

Case companies: employee perception

There was a significant perception of change in the recruitment process, especially at Nissan, Shinsei and F-Services Co 1. There were no particularly substantial differences in the employee groups, although career employees were inclined to perceive greater change than mid-career hires and older employees were inclined to see more change than younger ones, both of which are quite predictable findings.

Prior to acquisition, all the five firms engaged to a greater or lesser extent in traditional Japanese recruiting practices. All recruited graduates directly from university. The longer-established firms, Nissan, Chugai and LTCB until quite recently had used the *"rikurūtā seido"* or "recruiter system" that was referred to earlier.

As with the comparator companies, the role of the HR department had been central in the recruiting process. Doubt was expressed by a number of interviewees as to the extent to which the recruiting process had been coordinated in any strategic way with management of the company or of the individual divisions as a response to future human resource requirements. According to a young executive at Nissan:

The old Nissan didn't pay too much attention to recruitment and didn't have a long-term or strategic perspective, just hiring a lot of graduates when times were good and holding back when they weren't. When I entered the company in the mid-1990s, the entry was 170 people but three years before that it was about 1,000. That was the peak of the bubble. People didn't think Nissan was so popular and not so many people would apply but they did and we ended up taking that many!

The apparent lack of a coordinated strategic perspective in the recruiting process is puzzling, especially in the context of lifetime employment, as, once hired, the employee was likely to stay with the firm for the long term. This had a significant impact on corporate strategy formation and constrained flexibility. According to a deputy general manager at Shinsei, "companies built businesses around the staff and the human resources they had. If you wanted to pursue a new strategy or change the direction of the firm, it took a really long time."

Employees perceived that the new recruitment policy was much more tied to the company's overall strategy. This means, first, that recruitment decisions are taken out of the hands of the HR department and given to the operating divisions and, second, that the focus of recruitment shifts from university graduates to professional mid-career hires. In the words of the head of HR at Shinsei:

It has changed a great deal. The overwhelming proportion of recruitment has been mid-career hires and they are professionals, for whom there is a market price. When it comes to recruiting professionals, you can't rely on the HR department because we don't necessarily grasp the needs of the business, so the divisions do all of this. They are the ones who know best what resources are required to get the job done. There is a role for HR in recruiting university graduates, visiting the schools, creating internship programmes, making presentations, turning the attention of the students towards us. But even for them, the final decision lies with the divisions.

In the case of Shinsei the situation was exacerbated by the fact that there had been signficant changes in the basic business model. Internal resources were not deemed adequate to lead the bank in the new direction identified by the management and external resources were therefore necessary, and in large quantities.

There was a marked shift in the career employees' attitudes towards mid-career hires, or at least a recognition that they would have to change. One executive at Nissan noted that there were still difficulties in the process of absorbing mid-career hires: "This is partly a cultural issue; we simply aren't used to dealing with them. The concept of the seniority system is still strong and we identify people by the year of their intake." There was a strong belief that, even in highly specialised functions, there were overriding institutional contexts that made the job difficult if not impossible for an outsider to perform. A Nissan Finance Manager noted: "The hiring of people mid-career rarely took place as we believed that even specialist functions like finance and accounting took place within a very specific Nissan context and this could not be carried out by outsiders." Both F-Services Co 1 and F-Services Co 2 were fairly new companies that had grown quickly in a short space of time, so they had had to rely on mid-career hires to fill the ranks of middle management. The way these companies had developed had led to a less homogeneous culture and an easier environment for mid-career hires to operate in.

Other significant changes to the recruiting system were, first, to make the process more transparent and competitive. Nissan and Chugai no longer use the "recruiter system" and Shinsei had stopped using it prior to acquisition. All companies now use a web-based system through which all applications are processed. Nissan and F-Services Co 1 have devised a system where interviewers are not permitted to see the name of the interviewee's university to prevent deeply embedded views on university hierarchy and prestige from interfering with the decision-making process.

Second, the process was now far less ritualistic. Under the previous management, the process of graduate recruitment was heavy with symbolism, with all the new employees joining the firm with great fanfare on 1 April (and only on that day), the inevitable presidential address in a large arena or hall welcoming the new employees into their "new family". There was an inflexibility and a formality about the recruitment process, a "taken-for-granted-ness" that reminds us of the "automatism" referred to by the expatriate head of HR at Nissan. The symbolism that accompanied that recruitment process undoubtedly had great meaning in the context of the Japanese firm which entirely changed with the entry of foreign capital. According to a senior figure at Nissan:

In the old days graduate entry was on one day only, the 1 April … Now we [individual departments] are given a headcount budget and it's up to us when and what kind of staff we recruit. There is no need to stick to bureaucratic procedures like recruiting graduates only on 1 April. We are told to act in a timely manner when the need arises. After all, the objective here is not hiring staff. We are gathering resources to get a job done, to sell our products, to increase profitability, and that needs flexibility. This flexibility is a great change.

Third, the time within which recruits were expected to start contributing was much shorter. Generally graduate recruitment was sharply reduced at these firms, not only because there was more emphasis on mid-career hires, but also because the long-term approach of building up employee experience through job rotation and slow but regular promotion had changed. There was a much shorter time horizon for assimilating new employees, and this had a particular impact on the graduate intake. In the words of the head of recruitment at F-Services Co 1:

In this type of company in a rapidly changing environment we simply don't have the time to train up people. We can only really look to hire the best, people who can make an immediate contribution. We used to be able to tolerate hiring a mixed bag and giving them ten years to prove themselves, but not any more.

Finally, we see the company handing a much greater degree of responsibility for career design to the employees. For newly hired graduates at Shinsei, this meant making a selection prior to the interviews of the division in which he or she wanted to work. The interviewing process would then take place within that division, and the ultimate decision as to whether to hire that person would lie with that division's management. Those that did not have a clear idea of where they wanted to work would still be able to use the HR department to fix up interviews with people of various divisions so that they could make a more informed choice. However, in this situation it was also the division's ultimate responsibility as to whom they did and did not take. The pattern of recruitment was similar at Nissan and F-Services Co 1.

There has not been a substantial shift in Chugai's recruitment policy and this was reflected in the low level of perceived change by interviewees. A major role is still played by the HR department both in the selection and deployment of new recruits. A number of interviewees commented, however, that the number and the quality of applicants had increased after its merger with Roche, principally because the new Chugai was seen to be a more dynamic and international place to work than the traditional Japanese firm and was a firm with a more secure future, with a giant multinational firm behind it. At F-Services Co 2, poor business performance meant that graduate recruitment had been frozen, although recruitment of mid-career professionals was taking place. This may explain the low level of perceived change by interviewees. The change in recruitment is summarised in Table 3.2.

Table 3.2 *Change in recruitment*

Recruitment						
Q: To what extent has the process of recruitment changed?						
1 = no change						
2 = changed somewhat						
3 = changed a great deal						
Nissan	Chugai	Shinsei	F-Svcs Co 1	F-Svcs Co 2	Total	
2.91	1.69	2.87	2.70	2.27	2.48	
Male	Female	Career	MCH	20–35 yrs	35–45 yrs	45 yrs +
2.53	2.27	2.55	2.23	2.38	2.47	2.56

n = 60

Case companies: training

Grading the responses to the questions on changes to the training regime was quite difficult. Generally, interviewees responded that there had only been limited change, but when they developed on this, it was apparent that there had been a marked shift away from the egalitarian cohort-based training of old, but that there had not been a coherent training strategy to replace it. There was in fact general disappointment with the new owners' training philosophy, with the possible exception of employees at F-Services Co 1. Thus, the scores seem to imply a low degree of change, but that may not reflect the true situation.

The biggest change to the training regime was, first, that the socialisation process was virtually non-existent compared to large Japanese firms and, second, there was a greater emphasis on using resources for smaller groups of high potential employees, rather than more equally across the whole cohort group.

As would be expected in an environment that demands greater specialisation, the focus of training is the development of technical skills. Other than the induction programme for university graduates on entry to the firm, cohort-based training has ceased at all firms except Chugai. For Shinsei, greater emphasis on specialisation seen in recruitment was reflected in the new training regime. There has been a strong focus on product-based training, as many of the former bank employees had no experience in selling financial products to retail clients, whereas there was now a wide range on offer such as mutual funds, foreign currency denominated deposits, insurance products, and so on. At F-Services Co 1, where there was already some emphasis on specialised training, there was a progression towards developing a greater degree of professionalism. According to the head of training:

Up until now, if you were able to do the routine jobs, you were able to get on in the company. That was OK when the market was growing so fast but now it's not good enough. We all have to act as professionals to keep the company on top in a maturing market. The common training is now focused on specific skills such as presentations, negotiations and so on, which individuals can develop. There is less emphasis on cohort-based training, which is all we had when I joined the company.

In line with the theme of self-responsibility that has entered the recruiting process, employees are now expected to be far more active in planning their own training programmes. At Chugai, a young employee observed: "Now we have to take the initiative completely by looking at the training home page. We now have to focus on developing ourselves. We were rather more passive before."

At some firms, however, there was a feeling of disappointment about the quality of training in the new organisation and a view that the emphasis on "self-responsibility" was just an excuse to cut the training budget. This was felt most keenly at F-Services Co 2, where business conditions were quite severe. Many interviewees indicated that there was no training at all and that the system had "fallen apart". There were also complaints that training had been "globalised" and centralised at headquarters, which meant that local requirements were not taken into consideration.

The exceptions were Chugai and F-Services Co 1. F-Services Co 1 was the company that put the most stress on a consistent, new style of training. The company was in the process of building a "learning centre" in Tokyo for training purposes. Employees by and large had detected and were able to articulate a new philosophy on training and there was a sense that training was a priority for the new management.

Chugai retained their traditional cohort-based training programmes. The former employees of Nippon Roche, which had merged with Chugai, observed the difference in philosophy regarding training. For example, a middle-ranking manager remarked:

Chugai seems to spend a lot more money on training. Nippon Roche had a simple way of looking at things. I don't think they thought too much about employee development. Chugai's philosophy is basically that employees are here for life and the company will look after you, including of course in the area of developing the necessary skills to contribute to the firm.

For the staff at some of the case companies, used to the training philosophy geared towards a long-term, seniority and generalist-based career, the new training regime seemed very inadequate. While it was acknowledged that the old cohort-based training scheme had its drawbacks, it was at least seen as fair and inclusive, while the new regime, being targeted at high-fliers, was not. At Nissan, the inadequacies of the new training regime appear to have been recognised, and during the two-year period that I visited the company (2002–2004), Nissan appointed one of their brightest Japanese HR executives to take charge. There was a substantial reorganisation of the training department and the training programmes to make them more effective.

From the average scores of perceived change, 2.20 for training and 2.48 for recruitment, the actual changes being implemented by the case companies and the interview data, the picture that seems to be emerging is one of change. However, it is also one of unevenness. The figures for mid-career recruiting comparing 2003 with 1998 would suggest that the comparator companies are not generally moving at great speed from the communitarian template. At some of the case companies, particularly those such as Shinsei where a new business model has necessitated a substantial refocusing of the training effort, there appears to have been a dramatic move away from the traditional Japanese model. At Chugai, however, where there have not been substantial changes in the business model, but which more importantly continue to emphasise a longer-term commitment between employees and the company, the opposite is the case.

The change in training is summarised in Table 3.3.

Table 3.3 *Change in training*

Training						
Q: To what extent has the process of training changed?						
1 = no change						
2 = changed somewhat						
3 = changed a great deal						
Nissan	Chugai	Shinsei	F-Svcs Co 1	F-Svcs Co 2	Total	
2.18	2.00	2.47	2.50	1.82	2.20	
Male	Female	Career	MCH	20–35 yrs	35–45 yrs	45 yrs +
2.29	1.82	2.23	2.08	2.13	2.15	2.33

n = 60

Summary

The increased emphasis at the case companies on responsibility and accountability is mirrored in changing HR practices with evidence that many "taken-for-granted organisational actions" (Oliver, 1992) are being questioned by both employers and employees. In the recruitment and training domains, there is now generally greater flexibility in recruiting and employees are being asked to take more initiative in designing training regimes for themselves. There is a trend towards greater specialisation. Equality is less important: training resources are being concentrated on individuals who have clearly been identified as high achievers. Time horizons appear to have become shorter and employees are expected to make a contribution sooner. This, combined with the need for greater levels of specialisation, has led to a greater intake of mid-career hires, particularly at Nissan and Shinsei.

References

Aoki, M. (1988) *Information, Incentives, and Bargaining in the Japanese Economy*. Cambridge: Cambridge University Press
   (1990) "Towards an Economic Model of the Japanese Firm", *Journal of Economic Literature*, 28: 1–27
Bank of Tokyo-Mitsubishi (1998) "How to Provide the Japanese Economy with More Room for Growth", *Tokyo-Mitsubishi Review*, 3: 1–8
Beck, J. C. and Beck, M. N. (1994) *The Change of a Lifetime: Employment Patterns among Japan's Managerial Elite*. Honolulu, HI: University of Hawaii Press
Conrad, H. and Heindorf, V. (2006) "Recent Changes in Compensation Practices in Large Japanese Companies: Wages, Bonuses and Corporate Pensions". In P. Matanle and W. Lunsing (eds.) *Perspectives on Work, Employment and Society in Japan*. Basingstoke: Palgrave Macmillan
Dore, R. (1973) *British Factory–Japanese Factory: The Origins of National Diversity in Industrial Relations*. Berkeley, CA: University of California Press
Hanami, T. (2004) "The Changing Labour Market, Industrial Relations and Labour Policy", *Japan Labour Review*, 1: 4–16
Itoh, H. (1994) "Japanese Human Resource Management from the Viewpoint of Incentive Theory". In M. Aoki and R. Dore (eds.) *The Japanese Firm: Sources of Competitive Strength*. Oxford: Oxford University Press
JIL (2003) "Firms Reduce Opportunities for Off-the-Job Training", *Japan Labor Bulletin*, 42: 3–4
Kasai, Y. (2003) *Japanese National Railways: Its Break-up and Privatisation*. Folkestone: Global Oriental

Koike, K. (1994) "Learning and Incentive Systems in Japanese Industry". In M. Aoki and R. Dore (eds.) *The Japanese Firm: Sources of Competitive Strength*. Oxford: Oxford University Press

Oliver, C. (1992) "The Antecedents of Deinstitutionalization", *Organization Studies*, 13: 563–588

Rohlen, T. P. (1974) *For Harmony and Strength: Japanese White-Collar Organization in Anthropological Perspective*. Berkeley, CA: University of California Press

Watanabe, T. (2003) "Recent Trends in Japanese Human Resource Management: The Introduction of a System of Individual and Independent Career Choice", *Asian Business and Management*, 2: 111–141

Yashiro, N. (1998) *Jinjibu Wa Mou Iranai (Who Needs a HR Department Any More?)*. Tokyo: Kodansha

4 | *Lifetime employment and career patterns*

Lifetime employment

Cole (1971) notes that one of the official criteria for dismissal at Takei Diecast, one of the Japanese firms he studies, is "strikingly ... similar to what one might expect in an industrially advanced Western country":

> when there are superfluous personnel because of readjustment and curtailment of business, rationalisation of operations and other unavoidable reasons, and these personnel are not absorbed through personnel realignment, changes in type of work or other means. (p. 117)

But, he adds, in reality, "the management's dismissal rights at the Takei firm was far more limited and not necessarily because of worker pressures" (p. 118), hinting at the long-term mutual commitment between the employee and the company that forms the cornerstone of Japanese labour relations. Thus, Abegglen (1958, p. 72) notes:

> It is family-like. When a man enters the large Japanese company it is for his entire life. Entrance is a function of personal qualities, background, and character. Membership is revocable only in extraordinary circumstances and with extraordinary difficulty. As in a family, the incompetent or inefficient member of the group is cared for, a place is found for him, and he is not expelled from the group because he is judged inadequate ... Fidelity and tenure bring the highest rewards and, should the group encounter financial difficulty, it is expected that all members will suffer these difficulties together.

The concept of lifetime employment is fundamental to the community firm and the functioning of the internal labour market. It is variously referred to as "permanent employment", "continuous employment" or "long-term employment" to reflect the fact that the employee is not necessarily employed by the same firm until the moment of retirement. Indeed, it is normal for white-collar employees in their late forties and onwards who have been left behind in the promotion race to be forced to move to subsidiaries and affiliates of the parent company, often at substantially lower salaries (although this is sometimes compensated with a later retirement age), thus producing a substantial cost saving (Beck and Beck, 1994; Sato, 1997).

The practice of lifetime employment has become deeply embedded at large Japanese firms since 1945 and with it the entire interdependent system of recruitment, socialisation, training, assessment and rewards that are associated with it. The system is underpinned by an implicit contract between employers and workers. According to Dore (1973), there is both a cultural pre-disposition to "stay" reinforced by rational economic factors to do so on the part of employees, mirrored by a sense of obligation on the part of the employers to keep him, reinforced by union pressure.

Numerous studies, including early comparative work such as those of Dore (1973) and Cole (1971), found lower turnover rates and longer tenure at Japanese firms. Despite widespread belief that the recessions of the 1970s would cause either an end to, or at least a major readjustment of, the system, studies in the 1980s (Hashimoto and Raisian, 1985, 1992) confirmed a continuation of the trend. During the 1990s, pressure again built up in the Japanese employment system and predictions of the demise of lifetime employment resurfaced. By the turn of the decade, however, the system was still holding up. As can be seen from Figure 4.1, which shows the tenure of male graduates at Japanese companies with over 1,000 employees, taken from the Ministry of Health, Labour and Welfare's regular "Statistical Report on the Structure of Wages", tenure continued to rise until the mid-2000s. For the years 1990, 1995, 2000 and 2003 average tenure for this group rose, from 15.8, to 16.2, 16.8 and 17.0 years respectively. By 2007, it had fallen back to the level it was in 1995 – 16.2 years.[1] Tenure of Japanese employees is longer than that of employees

---

[1] It is interesting to note that, while tenure at the younger years (mid-20s to mid-40s) has trended generally downwards, in 1990 there was a distinct flattening of the tenure curve in the 40s while the recent trend has been for tenure to continue to climb steeply until a much later age. One possible interpretation of this phenomenon has been that companies are

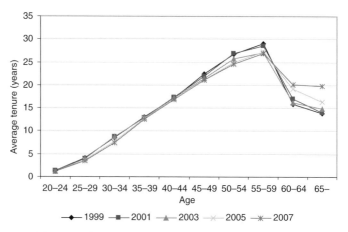

Figure 4.1 Tenure at large Japanese companies
Source: Ministry of Health, Labour and Welfare

in France and Germany and considerably longer than that of the US, Canada and the UK (Hattori and Maeda, 2000, p. 20). Between 1990 and 2003, the number of employees working at large Japanese companies fell from 5.17 million to 4.92 million (Oh, 2002).

The persistence of the lifetime employment phenomenon is attributable to at least three factors. First, employment security is a matter of explicit government policy, reinforced by the legal framework and precedent. In addition to a raft of measures to incentivise companies to keep workers on the payroll during economic downturns such as "adjustment subsidies" (Hirakubo, 1999; Rohlen, 1979), government policy has historically been to insulate Japanese firms from competition. This in turn has enabled firms in sectors such as construction, retail and agriculture to maintain high levels of employment (Weinstein, 2001).

While we can see from the Takei Diecast example above that companies have the theoretical right to fire workers, the courts have played an active role in protecting the labour rights (Komiyo, 1991), sticking rigidly to the four criteria emphasising financial necessity for such action, a reasonable effort on the part of the employer to avoid

forced to keep employees on as the dissolution of cross-shareholdings and general restructuring has reduced the number of places to which older employees can be "outplaced".

dismissals, to consult and bargain with unions during the process and to ensure that the standards for selecting employees for dismissal were fair. While this has been attributed to the judiciary following the government line, it also reflects a desire to reflect the broad social consensus as to where the boundary lies between legitimate and illegitimate managerial action. As a recent ILO paper put it:

Current practices reflect social norms as embedded in judicial decisions. And the judicial decisions, in turn, are the result of the social definition of acceptable corporate behaviour. The prevalent philosophy is that private sector employers bear a major responsibility for maintaining low levels of unemployment. (Evans-Klock *et al.*, 1998, p. 6)

Opinion is divided as to whether the legal framework is shifting to allow a greater degree of flexibility for employers to reduce headcounts. Hanami (2004) argues that, if anything, the legal framework is becoming even more restrictive. It has been generally acknowledged that the amendment to the Labour Standards Law in 2003 has made it more difficult to dismiss workers. According to the Fraser Institute, which campares levels of economic freedom across a range of countries (e.g. property rights, freedom to trade internationally, etc.), regulations made it more restrictive in Japan between 1995 and 2005. Dore argues (2005) that, in the intricate discussions over the wording of the "right to fire" clauses of the new Labour Standards Law in 2006, there was a subtle shift in the balance of power from labour to management, with subsequent judicial interpretations suggesting a less rigid adherence to the "four criteria".[2] In addition, the revised law conferred discretionary powers on the judiciary to interpret the articles in the context of "prevailing social norms" (*shakai tsūnen*) when passing judgment on the fairness of non-disciplinary dismissals.

This links in with the second factor that has sustained the lifetime system: the attitude of the managers themselves. Thus far, these have been strongly and consistently supportive of a lifetime commitment

---

[2] It should also be noted that, according to statistics from the Fraser Institute, the ability to hire and fire workers had fallen by an even greater margin than Japan's in the UK, France and Germany between 1995 and 2005. Furthermore, Japan was adjudged to have a much easier climate to hire and fire (4.6 out of a scale of 10) than Germany and France (both 2.4 out of 10, with the UK and the US being 5.8 and 7.0 respectively).

to employees (see Morishima, 1995). In a 2003 managerial survey, only 20% of companies stated that they either did not have lifetime practices (5.2%) or saw fundamental change as necessary (15.3%). The vast majority (76%) saw no need for change (36.1%) or the need for only partial adjustment (40.0%). This caused the Japan Institute of Labour to conclude:

> not many companies are implementing major reviews of their lifetime employment systems and changing to fluid employment practices. There is instead an increasing trend for companies to restrict the number of regular employees that are subject to lifetime employment and to increase the number of non-regular employees such as part-time employees for whom employment adjustment is relatively easy. (JIL, 2004, p. 28)

In continuing to guarantee lifetime employment at Canon, the President, Fujio Mitarai, criticised the "American system" where employees routinely switch jobs between companies: "Worker mobility has not taken root in Japan. Our society has no system to support it, either. Bringing in the American system will not work" (JIL, 2004).

The third factor is union opposition to the ending of lifetime employment. Having originally traded concessions in workplace flexibility for job security in the bitter and often violent industrial action of the 1950s (Gordon, 1998), the unions' bargaining strategy has centred on preserving employment stability for its members, even at the expense of wage issues (Morishima, 1995; Watanabe, 2003), as manifested by the disappearance of the "base-up" as an item of negotiation during the "spring offensive" in recent years.

During the last fifteen years, there has been increasing focus on the negative aspects of lifetime employment. It has been criticised for preventing Japanese companies from making the necessary adjustments during downturns, and for breeding complacency rather than acting as a motivating factor for employees. From a strategic perspective, the lifetime commitment to employees limits the options available to Japanese managers. Hitachi's President in the late 1990s, Dr Tsutomu Kanai, told *Fortune* magazine in 1998: "Jack Welch (of GE) was able to get out of computers and light bulbs. For us to get out of a business would involve firing people, and that can't be done easily in Japan" (quoted in Inagami and Whittaker, 2005, p. 114).

One way that Japanese firms have been able to increase flexibility, while preserving the lifetime commitment to core employees, has been to increase non-standard employees. The last decade has seen the growth in such employment as an overall component of the labour market (Inagami and Whittaker, 2005; Jacoby, 2005; Vogel, 2006). The percentage of non-regular employees doubled from 16.6% of the total labour force in 1986 to over 32.6% in 2005. The majority of these are part-time workers, although there has been a sharp increase in the proportion of dispatched workers, the proportion of the total workforce more than doubling in just three years from 0.9% in 2002 to 2.1% in 2005 (JIL, 2006).[3]

Job rotation and career patterns

A much greater tendency to rotate through a number of different roles, especially at the early stages of their careers, is a distinctive characteristic of the Japanese employment system. Employees generally start in fairly lowly positions, ensuring, as Dore (1973) puts it, that, "later in their careers, managers have a reasonably intimate knowledge of the actual work of those whom they supervise".

The pursuit of generalist, rather than specialist, careers is supplemented by a lack of clear definition of job boundaries.

Japanese organisations … tend not to use detailed job and occupational classifications, and in both blue- and white-collar strata, promote job rotation and generalist careers. A common characterisation is that Americans tend to pursue careers within occupations that cut across firms, which the opposite pattern holds in Japan. (Lincoln and Kalleberg, 1990, p. 172)

In addition to providing Japanese organisations with much greater flexibility, the system of job rotation and the lack of detailed job demarcation and job descriptions have the effect of putting greater emphasis on work groups. This in turn diffuses responsibility from the individual to the group – from higher up to lower down in the organisational hierarchy (Itoh, 1994). "It is this collective sharing of responsibility and

---

[3] Indeed, while Mitarai of Canon has strongly defended the virtues of lifetime employment, the company has dramatically increased the number of irregular employees on its payroll.

accountability that motivates and complements the absence of functional and authority role assignments to individuals and their positions" (Lincoln and Kalleberg, 1990). Regular rotation "also prevents workers from identifying strongly with specific jobs, workshop, plants, and offices so that the development and assertion of local interest inconsistent with the organisational goals are restrained" (Aoki, 1990, p. 11).[4]

However, this system has also been criticised, first, for leading to a proliferation of organisational sub-units at Japanese companies (Yoshino, 1968); second, for not enabling an organisation to establish clear accountability when failures occur;[5] and third, for not developing sufficient specialist skills in workers in an increasingly specialised world. Yashiro (1998) characterises graduates' first few years of work experience as "latrine duty" and questions the fundamental value of the learning experience.

Recently companies have put greater emphasis on employee responsibility and there is evidence that they are giving more serious consideration to employees' wishes when making assignments and transfers. Many companies, for example, have introduced a "double-track" personnel system, whereby employees may opt out of being part of the *sōgōshoku* or management stream to become specialists in a certain field. By 2003, over 40% of companies with more than 5,000 employees had implemented the multi-track personnel management system (JIL, 2004).

To summarise, therefore, the communitarian template consists of the following features:

- a strong commitment to long-term employment security;
- career development based on a generalist track, rather than developing specialisations, especially early in the career.

Conclusions from the literature:

- Attitudes of the key participants, managers, unions and government, are still strongly supportive of long-term employment security (JIL, 2004; Morishima, 1995).

---

[4] The "control" perspective would be that rotation prevents employees from developing too much solidarity by keeping the workplace fluid, thereby reducing union strength. See Gordon (1998).

[5] Koike (1994), however, notes that, for blue-collar workers, problems on the factory floor are often (in four out of the six factories he studied) noted in writing to assign individual responsibility in the event of customer complaints, and to provide a clear factual basis for employee evaluation.

- Judicial interpretations are not supportive of increased management flexibility (Hanami, 2004).
- Tenure of white-collar university graduates at large Japanese companies is increasing, rather than decreasing (Oh, 2002; Rebick, 2001).
- Japanese companies are increasing flexibility by gradually shrinking the size of the core employee group and increasing part-timers (Oh, 2002).
- There appears to be a greater emphasis on flexible career structures and the promotion of specialists as witnessed by the "double-track career" and the "in-house recruiting" systems (JIL, 2004).

At the case companies we would expect:

- the new management might take the view that an implicit guarantee was not something that is inherent in a "performance culture" and is detrimental to shareholders, especially given that lifetime employment comes with seniority-based rewards, making older workers particularly expensive;
- the strong emphasis on generalist careers might give way to greater focus on specialisation.

As we will see in the next chapter on rewards, there is some evidence to suggest that the tradition of lifetime employment and seniority-based rewards as an inextricably woven "set" is eroding. However, there are few signs that the fundamental philosophy towards lifetime employment is changing at large Japanese firms. I witnessed at one firm a discussion between the head of the HR department and his subordinate as to whether there were grounds for dismissal of an employee for "poor performance". The head of HR believed that there was no provision for this according to the company's employment rules, but was proved wrong by his subordinate. However, the discussion was concluded by the head of HR saying that "it wouldn't make any difference anyway, as it would be inconceivable for anyone to be dismissed for poor performance". This recalls the findings of Cole (1971) at Takei Diecast that we highlighted in Chapter 1.

According to the HR representatives of J-Utility Co, the company requires approximately 14,000 employees to maintain its utility operations, compared with its current headcount of nearly 21,000.

This means that it is approximately 50% over-manned in its core operations. This does not mean, of course, that surplus employees are sitting idle. Most of the 7,000 surplus staff are older workers (45 and over) and are seconded to subsidiaries, affiliates or related companies (on full pay – where pay is lower than at the J-Utility Co, the difference is made up by the company). The company emphasises that its key mission is safety. It considers that loyal and motivated employees are critical to the creation of sufficient levels of "safety consciousness", and that the key ingredient for this is a stable workplace, which in turn depends on employees being able to work secure in the knowledge that they can do so until retirement. The company also believes that seniority pay is vital to this sense of security so, for them, lifetime employment and seniority pay still come as a set.

At J-Manufacturing Co too, this sense of the long term and the ability of employees to see the future only in the context of the company are fundamental to the company's key competitive strengths. The head of the company's HR department described "respect for people" and "continuous improvement" (also called "*kaizen*") as the two main pillars of the "J-Manufacturing Co way". However, these two concepts are inextricably linked. The "respect for people" that underpins J-Manufacturing Co's HR policy is an essential component of *kaizen*. Without a long-term commitment on the part of the company to its employees and vice versa, *kaizen* would not function properly. The director of HR explained this link in the following way:

[*Kaizen* is the process] where each individual worker responds to the changing environment by making tiny incremental changes to his work routine. Somewhere there has to be an expectation that some of the benefit derived from this system flows back to the employee. However, this has to be seen as a very long-term process, and it means that for *kaizen* to work it requires a very long period of study by the employees. It's not the case that just because you study how machines work at some vocational school you can put that learning to work straightaway with us. That's not the characteristic of the company. The balance between contribution and reward in the J-Manufacturing Co context has to be seen as a very long-term prospect. So for the workers on the frontline, the concept of long-term employment is in a sense an integral part of the arrangement and without it we couldn't produce the kind of products for our customers that we do.

The clear implication is that the absence of the long-term commitment makes it difficult to enable the *kaizen* philosophy to become embedded in employee consciousness and to have an impact on behaviour. Thus, *kaizen* is difficult to implement in countries with different employment characteristics:

In some countries there is a very fluid external labour market where it is very difficult to secure long-term commitment from employees and for those overseas affiliates the power of *kaizen* just doesn't take root. So we really understand that we've got to work at it in those areas. But we can't just say: "Well these markets are different. Let's just not bother to try and do there what we do in Japan." We simply can't give up. So for this element of our HR philosophy, we simply have to keep at it and introduce it everywhere we have a presence.

There is a considerable body of literature which attempts to establish a direct link between the employment system at firms such as Toyota, the effectiveness of *kaizen*, and superior company performance (e.g. Fujimoto, 1999; Womack *et al.*, 1990). However, even if one were to have a cynical attitude to the series of miniscule improvements amounting to anything, what is fairly clear is that the process produces the general attitude of conscientiousness towards the work that employees have to perform. As Dore points out, "latrine duty is important not just for learning about latrines, but forming the attitudes of commitment and earnestness that contribute to efficiency".[6]

At J-Services Co, there is increased emphasis on creating a more flexible labour environment, one that takes into account the possibility that employees may desire a change in career and makes it easier for them to leave. Greater flexibility and labour mobility would enable the company to enter new businesses, although the company does stretch the meaning of "mobility" to include the possibility of laying staff off if a business does not work. A senior member of the HR department at the company observed:

---

[6] Private correspondence with author (2007).

I think we need to consider more carefully those that want to leave mid-career, as the company may not suit everyone all the time. For example, if we want to go into a new area of business and de-emphasise another, we need labour mobility. So we need a market from which we can hire good people and we need people within the organisation to think more openly about a career outside the firm and have that on their list of options going forward. It's only something we are thinking about. But we've got to be careful ... we are still in the process of feeling our way towards a new equilibrium.

He seems to be suggesting that the company can intervene more actively through the recruitment process to match strategy with resources, whereas it has traditionally been the case for Japanese companies that the resources (in particular human resources) available to the company have determined strategy. However, the words of caution ("we've got to be careful ...") also suggest that the path to institutionalisation of a new alignment of HR and corporate strategy will be a difficult one. Japanese firms may be enjoying a greater level of labour mobility *into* the company, with slightly greater emphasis on hiring mid-career, but not yet *out of* the company, through the laying off of workers in difficult economic circumstances or getting out of businesses that have not worked out.

To the extent that downsizing is possible, it is very much along the traditional lines of voluntary retirement programmes with the company taking an active role in finding alternative employment, often with no financial penalty to the employee. J-Pharma Co introduced an early retirement programme during 2001–2002 (called the "second career" system) through which some 200 employees left the company. J-Steel Co reduced its labour force by 75% in the ten years from 1985 through natural attrition and by placing surplus employees with clients, suppliers and affiliated companies. Even now, as a former CFO explained:

It's very difficult for us to institute an early retirement programme as this causes quite a lot of reputational risk for us. There is the problem of the terms and conditions of the programme, the problem of social acceptance, the problem of the courts. We won't do it unless we are in really serious trouble.

It is instructive that, despite more than a decade of operating in a poor domestic economic environment, a company like J-Steel Co is sensitive to societal norms, which are perceived still not to legitim-ise headcount reduction even by using early retirement programmes. There are signs, particularly in the last decade, that early retirement programmes are gaining social acceptability, with firms such as Matsushita and Kansai Electric Power implementing them. During the period 2000–2002, nearly 25% of large Japanese companies (over 1,000 employees) were found to have announced such programmes (JIL, 2003).

As has been mentioned, one source of flexibility for Japanese com-panies to reduce headcount is the elaborate mechanism for ensuring that, despite the fact that the official retirement age at most firms is 60, very few employees actually remain on the company's books at that age. From the age of 50, they are gradually placed in subsid-iaries, affiliated companies, or third-party companies such as cli-ents or non-affiliated suppliers. At J-Utility Co, for example, about 12% of those aged 50 in 2002 had been transferred in this way. In the 55+ age group, however, the number had risen to more than 50% and, by 59, it was nearly 90%. In the case of J-Utility Co, employees transferred in this way are paid the same wage, with the company making up any shortfall if necessary. At J-Financial Co, however, there is also a well-organised out-placement system that places many hundreds of employees at affiliates and other related firms annually (total number of "outplaced" employees as of March 2003 accounted for nearly 30% of total headcount). Those who are assigned to other companies are paid the market rate, which tends to be lower than their final wage at the parent company, thus saving the parent a considerable amount – even for those who go to con-solidated subsidiaries.

To a certain degree career patterns are changing at Japanese firms, with a greater emphasis on individual employee responsibility for career management and a greater degree of specialisation. This is par-ticularly in evidence at J-Financial Co, which has divided its businesses clearly into separate companies, utilising the holding company struc-ture, permitted under the new legislation. With intensifying competi-tion in the domestic market from overseas firms, particularly in the securities business, we have already seen in the recruitment process how the company is adapting its strategy towards the development of increased specialisation by recruiting more specialists mid-career. In this environment, it is not surprising that inter-divisional transfers are more limited than before. Indeed, the company has identified thirty-nine job groups within the J-Financial Co Group characterised by "high levels of specialisation and increasing labour mobility". Employees of over six years' standing may elect, subject to approval by the HR department, to convert to "professional employee" status. A great many have already done so, with the majority coming from the securities arm.

Case companies: lifetime employment

The change in lifetime employment is summarised in Table 4.1.

Table 4.1 *Change in lifetime employment*

Lifetime employment						
Q: Has the attitude towards lifetime employment changed since the merger?						
1 = no change						
2 = changed somewhat						
3 = changed a great deal						
Nissan	Chugai	Shinsei	F-Svcs Co 1	F-Svcs Co 2	Total	
1.73	1.54	2.80	2.70	2.64	2.28	
Male	Female	Career	MCH	20–35 yrs	35–45 yrs	45 yrs +
2.31	2.18	2.34	2.08	1.75	2.41	2.28

n = 60

There was significant inter-company variation in the perception of change in the practice of lifetime employment. The greatest changes were noted at Shinsei, F-Services Co 1 and F-Services Co 2. Again Chugai employees were inclined to perceive the least change, but this feeling was also shared by a number of Nissan employees. The Nissan finding is a notable one and is consistent with the lower-than-expected perception of change in the seniority system, but is inconsistent with responses to changes in other areas, which are much higher, as we will see later. I will discuss the possible factors behind this in Chapter 8. Among employee groups, not surprisingly, male, career, middle-aged and older employees were more sensitive to change than younger, female and mid-career hires.

We did generally find strong evidence that, prior to acquisition, a lifetime commitment to the company had been a deeply embedded attitude among employees at the case study companies, especially at Nissan, Chugai and Shinsei. At Shinsei, for example, a number of interviewees referred to the strong sense of lifetime commitment felt by employees of the old LTCB. A former senior executive of the old LTCB summed up what was a basic philosophy of the institution:

In Japan, companies build their human resources from the inside whereas, in the west, the external labour market is large and you can bring people in, make them do what you want them to do, and pay them accordingly. What we need to do therefore is to give each individual employee power and we do this by developing in each of them a particular skill. Because we have lifetime employment, there is the scope for people to build this up over a long period.

To many employees, remuneration based on the concept of the consumption cycle still had some appeal. A highly regarded and relatively young employee of F-Services Co 2 said:

The thing about lifetime employment is that earnings peak at 50. This generally fits into the consumption cycle, as that is the age when your children are starting university and that's when you need the most money. You work hard in your 30s and 40s but your children are still young so you don't need the money so much. You are also working really hard so there's no time to spend the money.

There was little doubt in the minds of many at the case companies that the level of employment security had reduced considerably, although the new management had evidently been careful not to make explicit statements concerning lifetime employment. The first and most obvious manifestation was the actions of the new management to reduce employee costs in times of difficulty. At F-Services Co 2, an employee contrasted what would have been a legitimate means of reducing employment costs under the old regime with what was now deemed acceptable:

Under the old regime, the first thing that would have happened would have been that the directors' or the senior management's remuneration would have been cut. The first priority would have been to preserve employment. [New controlling shareholders] have a different attitude and their first priority is to reduce headcount. They do not cut the directors' or the senior management's salaries. They do not behave in the way of the typical Japanese firm in that respect.

These statements remind us strongly of Dore's observations (1997) that, in Anglo-Saxon firms, it is employees who are expected to show flexibility in downturns, whereas in Japanese companies it is the shareholders. If the employees had to suffer, it was across the board, with the management expected to display their responsibilities for the company's plight by making a suitable sacrifice. In other words, the pain would have been shared equally among the employees for the sake of preserving employment, but with senior employees – directors in particular – symbolically shouldering a larger share.

At Shinsei in particular, there was very strong consensus that the implicit guarantee which had manifestly existed under the old LTCB regime was now gone. A middle-ranking manager in the HR department commented on the close link between lifetime employment and seniority-based pay and that changes in one inevitably affected the other:

The seniority system is disappearing. This has important implications, as in the old days, even if you were not very capable and not doing a very responsible job, your salary would generally keep on going up. It was therefore not attractive to leave the firm. Now, if your performance is poor, or if you are no longer able to use your skills, your salary can go down so there is a much greater incentive to leave. That calculation has changed, and will continue to do so. So while you can theoretically stay if you really want to, lifetime employment has effectively ended. I'm sure that if you carried out a questionnaire among the staff their message would be the same.

The early retirement programmes undertaken by the firms were nominally "voluntary". However, it is clear in some cases that strong pressure was put on some employees to sign up. At one case company, employees were graded in terms of ability and potential and strong pressure was put on employees who were low on both counts to take early retirement. At another, the worse the company's performance was, the stronger the pressure. A senior manager in sales observed:

When I moved over here from my previous [Japanese] employer, I intended to stay here for life. When [the new controlling shareholders] first came in they said that job security was guaranteed and that they wouldn't lay anyone off. But they've had a number of early retirement programmes and quite a few senior people have left. I think there were some people who were given no alternative. I think it really was voluntary the first time, but by the third time I think people were told straight that the company wanted them to quit.

The impact of several early retirement programmes and the fact that there were so many mid-career hires in the organisation had sent a strong message to the employees that the organisation was "easy to join, easy to leave". This had fundamentally altered the career calculations of employees. With the promise of security gone, there was less incentive to think about things from the company's perspective. This was a critical issue for employees in their 40s who, in a Japanese firm, would be approaching the peak of their earning power. The same employee that had discussed the virtues of consumption cycle-related pay went on:

Now, unless you're a GM or a VP, and most people can't make it to that level, your pay actually goes down in the second half of your 40s. So it's safer to leave and find something that gives you a stable job in your 50s. It's OK if they give you the money when your output is high in your 30s or 40s but it doesn't necessarily work like that. We were used to receiving less early on because we knew it would be made up for later even if our output wasn't so high. It doesn't work like that any more …

The second factor contributing to a change in employee attitudes was the increased focus on specialisation. This had contributed to an awareness among employees that the less firm-specific their skills were, the more likely it was that the market would be able to assign a value to them. Hence, an ex-LTCB senior manager noted:

But the employees are being told to become professionals within their own narrow fields and by extension, if the market assigns a higher value to that expertise than we do, then you would be rational in leaving. The labour market in the financial field has also become much more fluid in the last few years.

However, notwithstanding the concern of many employees, some questioned the value of lifetime employment and the premise on which it is founded. A senior HR figure at F-Services Co 1 thought that over-emphasis on job security stifled the dynamism of the company and that the introduction of outsiders into the organisation enhanced internal competition:

In an environment where you look after people from the cradle to the grave, people feel very safe and secure; people stop competing with each other and trying to better themselves. But if you make people take responsibility for their own careers, they start paying attention to these things. If people can sell their skills outside, it's OK if they leave. It's also OK if people want to stay, but they have to compete. That's why we are so keen to recruit professionals from the outside even if they cost a bit more. They provide competition to our employees.

While F-Services Co 1 was not as forceful as F-Services Co 2 (who were under greater financial pressure) in pushing under-performing employees out, it was clear that pressure was nevertheless applied. A younger employee in sales observed:

The way some general managers who were pretty useless could hang on to their posts like they did in the old days is no longer possible. They are removed and put "close to the window". I would imagine that the company is quietly trying to get these people to quit ...

Not surprisingly, the employees of Chugai felt the least break with the past. Most employees felt there had been no decrease on the company's part to the implicit long-term employment commitment. Certainly, the observations of the former employees of Nippon Roche were that the old Chugai employees operated under the assumption that they were there for the long term. One remarked:

Although Nippon Roche was a bit of an old-fashioned company and some people who joined years ago from university did actually stay until retirement age, there was still an underlying assumption that you could really leave at any time, and many people did. There isn't that feeling at all here. It's quite amazing. I'd be panicking about some problem or other and the people from Chugai are so relaxed, because they have the ability to see things in the perspective of a lifelong career.

If employees of the old Chugai detected any change, it was through observing the behaviours of former Nippon Roche employees. Thus, a middle-ranking lifelong employee of Chugai noted that:

I see a lot of people from Nippon Roche leaving. I expect that's because they don't feel the Chugai style or culture is for them but anyway they are making choices for themselves about their careers and I think that rubs off on people around them.

The contrasting testimony of the former Nippon Roche employees and the career Chugai employees may serve as a pointer to the process by which the legitimacy of entrenched attitudes starts to be questioned. On the one hand, we see a clear gulf existing between the pure foreign firms and Japanese firms; at least in the short term the fact of coming under the control of a foreign firm does not necessarily lead to change. On the other hand, however, it is also apparent that the entry of "alien elements" provides the jolts that cause disruption of the "taken-for-granted" routines and cognitive processes of existing employees, possibly establishing a platform for future deinstitutionalisation to take place.

As we saw from the words of Chugai's CEO, Osamu Nagayama, in Chapter 2, the importance he perceived of a stable working environment will mean little change for the company in this area, at least in the short term. His reference to the "company's profile" in relation to the provision of lifetime employment also indicates a sensitivity to societal norms and a belief that the company's reputation would suffer if the company moved away too rapidly from the traditional HR system and resorted to illegitimate practices.

It is important to note, however, that there was no explicit message on the termination of the lifetime employment principle at *any* of the case companies. Rather, the way the message was conveyed to employees again appeared to be based on the creation of an atmosphere where employees understood implicitly that they could not be guaranteed a permanent home. Nissan appeared to take a cautious approach. Thierry Moulonguet, Executive Vice President of Nissan, had discussed the subject with the CEO just the day before the interview:

I couldn't say there is a guarantee of lifetime employment here, especially for top-ranking people. I was at a meeting yesterday when the CEO reaffirmed this principle: there is no job belonging to anyone. The process by which we measure the performance of people and their value-added is very serious indeed, especially for those at the senior levels. If they don't measure up then we have to consider what to do with them. It doesn't mean that we throw them out; we need to give them a second chance and this is where we need to strike the right balance.

It was not clear where this new balance was. The strength of the nuance in the implicit message varied among the case companies, with a more powerful message apparently seen by employees of Shinsei, F-Services Co 1 and F-Services Co 2 than at Nissan and Chugai. At Nissan, many felt that, while lifetime employment was not an issue the new management had chosen to tackle explicitly, it might have to do so in the future. A senior finance official articulated this sentiment most vividly, pointing to the need for greater specialist skills:

Now, though, there are very few subsidiaries and affiliates to go to so in a way lifetime employment has become much more important and one can anticipate staying at Nissan even longer than before. At the age of 55 unless you have some sort of specialist knowledge, you are removed from a line job although you don't have to retire until you are 60. This means that you do not represent a blockage to younger staff coming up. This does leave a body of people in their late 50s with little to do. This does represent a problem for the company.

None of the five companies had resorted to compulsory redundancies yet, although it appeared to be on the mind of one senior executive at a case company:

So far the message has been "your advancement in this company is not guaranteed and if your performance isn't good your employment isn't guaranteed" but we haven't gone so far as to make people worried as to whether they have a job or not. I think that's probably where we're going next.

He saw the ability of foreign firms to take this kind of drastic action to cut costs as being potentially a significant competitive advantage. He warned of a much more "rational" approach to costs in the future, and thought that the Japanese competitors would be hurt in mature businesses where cost competitiveness was key. However, there appeared to be a general consensus among the new management of the case companies that compulsory redundancies still did not constitute a legitimate strategic option that was open to them: societal norms simply did not permit it.

Case companies: career patterns

The change in job rotation is summarised in Table 4.2.

Table 4.2 *Change in job rotation*

Job rotation						
Q: Do employees tend to stay longer/shorter in a job function after the merger?						
1 = no change[7]						
2 = somewhat longer						
3 = much longer						
Nissan	Chugai	Shinsei	F-Svcs Co 1	F-Svcs Co 2	Total	
2.82	1.69	2.93	2.90	2.64	2.58	
Male	Female	Career	MCH	20–35 yrs	35–45 yrs	45 yrs +
2.57	2.64	2.57	2.62	2.50	2.62	2.56

n = 60

While the messages from the management of the case firms about the actuality, and even desirability, of the termination of lifetime employment were highly nuanced, there was a clearer consensus that, in order to progress in the new organisation, employees had to develop specialist expertise and that the generalist career track was no longer either the taken-for-granted route to the top or even the safe option in a world where specialisation was increasingly called for and which would have a value attached to it. Reflecting the earlier comments by the head of HR at Shinsei, the increased emphasis on specialisation would serve to solidify the concept of a "market price" for employees' skills, thus further undermining the idea of the lifetime commitment in the minds of both employees and employers. It is interesting, therefore, that employees of Nissan, many of whom saw only moderate change to the lifetime

---

[7] There were no responses indicating an increased rate of rotation. Hence, I have differentiated between grades of perceived increased specialisation.

employment commitment, did see a much greater value being placed by the new management on specialisation, implying that increased specialisation and job security were not necessarily incompatible ideas. Consistent with our findings so far, Chugai employees were least likely to have noticed drastic changes in their career patterns.

The first and most obvious outcome was a different mechanism for staff moves, with a diminished role for HR and more responsibility on the individual for career design. This was reinforced at F-Services Co 1 and F-Services Co 2 by the importation of the "*rikurūto seido*" or the "internal recruiting system" whereby openings for positions are posted publicly within the company and virtually the only way for an employee to make an inter-divisional move is to apply for such an opening. An employee within F-Services Co 1's HR department explained:

> In my case I went from customer services to HR so I've experienced some rotation but, before, it was very much a matter of you moving in accordance with the company's orders. Now, we have something called the "internal recruiting system" and it's now more up to you and the boss who is looking to fill a new post as to whether you move or not. This internal recruitment is in principle the only way you can move from one department to another. So in theory, I would be in the HR department unless I apply for a change of my own volition. Your career is your own responsibility.

While there was recognition that these developments were an inevitable part of the process of change, and a number welcomed it on the grounds that it would be linked to greater rewards, some employees questioned the motives and benefits. For them, it was another manifestation of short-termism, a feeling that the employees had to make an immediate contribution and that the company would not tolerate the disruption that came with frequent inter-divisional moves. Power had shifted significantly from HR to the divisions and the divisions were not prepared to release employees, particularly productive ones. With little mobility between divisions, communication suffered and there was less sense of cohesion. One negative outcome of the internal recruitment system was that it became very difficult for divisions that were deemed unattractive to recruit and retain employees. A particularly bitter head of one such division at F-Services Co 2 complained:

Instead of rotation we now have a system called "internal recruitment" which depends on a position being available and individuals wanting to move to that position. But it seems more a system to "steal" staff than anything else. It's quite difficult. Last year the problem was recognised and there are some attempts to change it and create something in between the old rotation system and the new internal recruitment system.

A second outcome was that there was an attempt to give a far higher degree of clarity to job definition through job descriptions, which were largely absent in Japanese firms. An employee in F-Services Co 1's HR department observed: "There are clear guidelines in the job description as to what kind of qualifications or experience is required for each position. Before the merger there were no job descriptions at all."

At Nissan, while there was a slightly lower emphasis on specialisation, clarity of responsibility and personal objectives were heavily stressed. Job descriptions, where they didn't exist before, were made mandatory. A senior sales executive offered an interpretation as to why they are not prevalent in Japanese organisations:

Clear job descriptions were quite rare. With almost all employees hired straight out of university, what a job involves is passed on by word of mouth and is understood intuitively. Nothing is written down or formalized. This makes it difficult for someone coming in from the outside to take on a job. It takes them a lot of time to learn.

In other words, job descriptions are not perceived to be necessary in a highly homogeneous environment where an organisation consists almost entirely of insiders: all employees instinctively know what they are supposed to do and there is no need for a clear demarcation of responsibility. If there is any ambiguity, employees would, at least in theory, spontaneously ensure that nothing falls through the gaps and would be evaluated accordingly. In a more heterogeneous environment emphasising individualism, however, where employees join the firm mid-career, this will no longer be the case, and the unwritten job descriptions handed down orally from generation to generation are of no use.

At Chugai, there was a strong sense of continuity. While some former Chugai employees noted that lower rates of rotation were a particular phenomenon of their industry, the following remark by a supervisor in the sales department was more typical:

I think it's true that generalists are more valued at Japanese firms, and at Chugai, at least on the sales side, a wide range of experiences is valued so we rotate more than they did at Nippon Roche. I don't feel that it's changing here and we're encouraged to keep our more generalist attitude.

Summary

We have seen that "lifetime" employment at even the largest companies does not literally mean that they are employed by the company for their entire careers. However, at the comparator firms, there is a clear understanding that, barring unforeseen events of an extreme nature, employees who want to work in the organisation (loosely defined to include subsidiaries, affiliates and so on) can do so. With the exception of Chugai, the explicit promise of lifetime employment had effectively ended at the case companies. Any implicit suggestion that there would be no compulsory redundancies was affected by such factors as voluntary early retirement systems implemented at their firms (with doubt expressed by some as to how "voluntary" the retirements were) and the fact that employees would often see former colleagues struggling to find new employment on leaving the firm. Under the old regime, when the firm was still under Japanese control, the company would have first taken other measures to cut costs, such as a salary or bonus cut, which would have been applied equally across the board, or applied to senior management first. Furthermore, increased specialisation, reinforced by strict job descriptions, introduced the notion in employees' minds that they now had some kind of "trade" for which there was a market price, and this had made employees more aware of their value to other firms.

References

Abegglen, J.C. (1958) *The Japanese Factory: Aspects of Its Social Organisation*. Boston, MA: Massachusetts Institute of Technology Press

Aoki, M. (1990) "Towards an Economic Model of the Japanese Firm", *Journal of Economic Literature*, 28: 1–27

Beck, J. C. and Beck, M. N. (1994) *The Change of a Lifetime: Employment Patterns among Japan's Managerial Elite*. Honolulu, HI: University of Hawaii Press

Cole, R. E. (1971) *Japanese Blue Collar: The Changing Tradition*. Berkeley, CA: University of California Press

Dore, R. (1973) *British Factory – Japanese Factory: The Origins of National Diversity in Industrial Relations*. Berkeley, CA: University of California Press

(1997) "Good Jobs, Bad Jobs and No Jobs", *Industrial Relations Journal*, 24: 262–268

(2005) *Hataraku to Iu Koto (What It Is to Work)*. Tokyo: Chuo Koron Shinsha

Fujimoto, T. (1999) *The Evolution of a Manufacturing System at Toyota*. Oxford: Oxford University Press

Gordon, A. (1998) *The Wages of Affluence: Labor and Management in Postwar Japan*. Cambridge, MA: Harvard University Press

Hanami, T. (2004) "The Changing Labour Market, Industrial Relations and Labour Policy", *Japan Labour Review*, 1: 4–16

Hashimoto, M. and Raisian, J. (1985) "Employment Tenure and Earnings Profiles in Japan and the United States", *The American Economic Review*, 75: 721–735

(1992) "Employment Tenure and Earnings Profiles in Japan and the United States: Reply", *American Economic Review*, 82: 346–355

Hirakubo, N. (1999) "The End of Lifetime Employment in Japan", *Business Horizons*, November–December: 41–44

Inagami, T. and Whittaker, D. H. (2005) *The New Community Firm: Employment, Governance and Management Reform in Japan*. Cambridge: Cambridge University Press

Itoh, H. (1994) "Japanese Human Resource Management from the Viewpoint of Incentive Theory". In M. Aoki and R. Dore (eds.) *The Japanese Firm: Sources of Competitive Strength*. Oxford: Oxford University Press

Jacoby, S. (2005) *The Embedded Corporation: Corporate Governance and Employment Relations in Japan and the United States*. Princeton, NJ: Princeton University Press

JIL (2003) "One-Quarter of Large Firms Call for Voluntary Retirement: Ministry Survey", *Japan Labor Bulletin*, 42: 4

Japan Labor Flash (2004) "Canon Spearheads an Original "New Japanese-Style" Labor System". 1 April

Komiyo, F. (1991) "Law of Dismissal and Employment Practices in Japan", *Industrial Relations Journal*, 22: 59–66

Lincoln, J.R. and Kalleberg, A.L. (1990) *Culture, Control, and Commitment: A Study of Work Organization and Work Attitudes in the United States and Japan.* Cambridge: Cambridge University Press

Morishima, M. (1995) "Embedding HRM in a Social Context", *British Journal of Industrial Relations*, 33: 617–640

Oh, H.-S. (2002) "Nihongata Koyou Kankou No Ikikata" ("The Future Course of Japanese Employment Customs"), *Nihon Rodo Kenkyu Zasshi*, 2002: 109–114

Rebick, M. (2001) "Japanese Labor Markets: Can We Expect Significant Change?" In M. Blomstrom, B. Gangnes and S. La Croix (eds.) *Japan's New Economy: Continuity and Change in the Twenty-First Century.* Oxford: Oxford University Press

Rohlen, T.P. (1979) ' "Permanent Employment" Faces Recession, Slow Growth, and an Aging Work Force", *Journal of Japanese Studies*, 5: 235–272

Sato, H. (1997) "Human Resource Management Systems in Large Firms". In M. Sako (ed.) *Japanese Labour and Management in Transition.* London: Routledge

Vogel, S.K. (2006) *Japan Remodeled: How Government and Industry Are Reforming Japanese Capitalism.* Ithaca, NY: Cornell University Press

Watanabe, T. (2003) "Recent Trends in Japanese Human Resource Management: The Introduction of a System of Individual and Independent Career Choice", *Asian Business and Management*, 2: 111–141

Weinstein, D. (2001) "Historical, Structural, and Macroeconomic Perspectives on the Japanese Economic Crisis". In M. Blomstrom, B. Gangnes and S. La Croix (eds.) *Japan's New Economy: Continuity and Change in the Twenty-First Century.* Oxford: Oxford University Press

Womack, J.P., Jones, D.T. and Roos, D. (1990) *The Machine That Changed the World.* New York, NY: Simon & Schuster

Yashiro, N. (1998) *Jinjibu Wa Mou Iranai (Who Needs an HR Department Any More?).* Tokyo: Kodansha

Yoshino, M. (1968) *Japan's Managerial System: Tradition and Innovation.* Cambridge, MA: MIT Press

5 | *Reward systems*

A
S WAS indicated in the Introduction, the role of market forces in the determination of rewards for Japanese employees is less evident than in other countries. Dore (1973) found that, apart from complexity, the Japanese wage system had nothing in common with the British system:

Just as the lifelong contract implicit in the employment relation involves looking at that relation as a good deal more than a temporary arrangement for the purchase of a particular type of skill, so the wages paid in Japanese factories take account of many factors – a man's age, seniority, education, demonstrated "cooperativeness" and so on – which have little to do with the notion of a "market price" for skills determined by a balance between supply and demand. (p. 74)

While there is a view that the reward system is just another element of a unique cultural tradition that emphasises equality and stability – Abegglen (1958) calls the system "indirect and paternalistic" – most commentators see strong rational foundations. An important element of the rationalist explanation is the development of the "lifecycle" wage system, which we mentioned earlier. However, as this practice became institutionalised during the decades following the end of the war, the importance of the experience that comes with tenure was emphasised to give seniority wages the sense of legitimacy that has sustained it until the present day. Thus, although economic growth rendered the concept of the livelihood wage less meaningful, and technological progress theoretically eroded the relationship between seniority and skill, the influence of seniority has been remarkably persistent in the modern Japanese employment system. There was, of course, never a period when seniority accounted for 100% of the reward structure – indeed the Japanese expression for the seniority system, *nenkō chingin*, also incorporates the meaning of "merit".

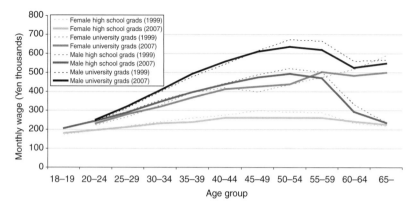

Figure 5.1 Seniority effect on wages 1999 vs 2007
Source: Ministry of Health, Labour and Welfare

However, it would appear that most Japanese use the word *nenkō* as shorthand for "seniority" and conceive it to mean age = merit. Comparisons with wage structures of other countries indicate clearly that age plays a much greater role in wage determination in Japan. A study by the Bank of Japan (Hattori and Maeda, 2000, pp. 21–22) has shown that the seniority curve rises more steeply in Japan than in the US, the UK, France or Germany.

In a Japanese firm the principal beneficiaries of the seniority-based wage system are male, middle-aged university graduates, as can be seen from the wage profile broken down by age and sex in Figure 5.1. It is noteworthy that the female university graduate only overtakes the male high school graduate in her mid-50s (at which age there are in fact so few women in this category as to make the figure meaningless). Note also that there has been a slight decline in the seniority effect across all four groups between 1999 and 2007.

The continuously upward sloping Japanese wage curve between the early 20s to the late 40s indicates that Japanese workers are paid less than the value of their marginal productivity during the early part of their careers with the reverse being true later on in their careers. Mincer and Higuchi (1987) attribute this to conscious human capital development, and propose that:

intensive formation of human capital on the job is the basic proximate reason for the strong degree of worker attachment to the firm in Japan. The greater emphasis on training and retraining, much of it specific to the firm, results also in steeper wage trajectories, due to growth of skills in the firm. (p. 24)

The system also has the advantage of not giving rise to agency problems of workers "shirking" as their stake in the fortunes of the company are significantly enhanced. There is a considerably greater degree of equality in Japanese wage structures than in the US, with a smaller, and more even, gap between workers, supervisors and managers (Itami, 1994; Lincoln and Kalleberg, 1990).

The system of promotion in Japanese firms has been referred to as "late-promotion" (Aoki, 1990; Koike, 1994). Under this system, "some clearly inadequate workers may of course drop out of competition, but most stay to compete, maintaining their morale, through their initial 10 to 15 years" (Koike, 1994, p. 263). The advantage of this system, according to Koike, is that it promotes long-term competition among workers and is also seen as fair and objective. The fairness comes from the relatively longer period of time in which employees are able to prove themselves, with a larger number of evaluators, which in turn promotes objectivity.

Thus, in the case of the Japanese system of promotion and pay, its legitimacy stems from both a sense of equity, being based on the objective criteria of age underpinned by the norm that age should be respected, as well as being "rational" in the sense that, over a lifetime of work, it represents a decent cash return for skill accumulation and effort expended, even if the returns are low in the initial years. It is not difficult to understand why employees might resist the goal posts being moved in the middle of their careers.

Evaluation and promotion

Under the slow promotion system, it is not until a very late stage, ten to fifteen years into one's career depending on the firm, that the "tournament winners" and "losers" are clearly established. Small differences do appear before the key promotion to the rank of manager. Pay grade scales are highly refined and within one rank there may be dozens of small salary bands giving the management the opportunity to send messages about relative performance fairly early on, without causing visible gaps within the cohort. After approximately seven years, a group among the cohort will pull slightly ahead of the others to reach the rank of group manager (*kakarichō*), but until the decisive promotion to manager, it is still possible to close this gap. Also at the seven-year point, the very weakest candidates will drop out of the race (Sato, 1997). This does not mean a threat to job security; it is a signal to a small proportion of the cohort that, by missing automatic promotion for the first time, their chance of eventually attaining senior management positions has effectively ended. Eventually, most of the cohort will make it to manager (again, depending on the company; at some it may not be a majority), although it is fairly clear to those who attain the position late that their chances of going beyond manager are slim. According to Sato (1997), the JIL reported in 1993 that over 70% of firms with over 5,000 employees practised late selection, or "simultaneous promotion" as the JIL report calls it. However, the selection procedure starts in earnest after this and promotion rates to divisional manager (*buchō*) are generally very low.

Criteria for success

What kinds of people are successful in the communitarian organisation? Given the strength of the internal labour market in Japan, it is not surprising that the qualities and skills the people who progress in Japanese firms should possess are specific to that organisation, as opposed to skills, particularly those of a technical nature, to which the labour market can assign a value. For blue-collar workers, Cole (1971, p. 77) noted that the foreman looked for the qualities of "diligence, seriousness, lack of absence and lateness, productive performance, and cooperation with fellow workers". For white-collar workers, the criteria are very similar, with cooperation being a particularly significant factor. Beck and Beck (1994), quoting the manager of an Osaka-based semiconductor firm who saw his human resource development function as "creating *kintarōame*",[1] observe:

the Japanese salaryman must do more than perform cooperative actions. His entire personality must seem to fit into the organisation if he is to be positively evaluated in promotion decisions ... The most difficult part

---

[1] A children's sweet which is long and cylindrical in shape (like "rock" in the UK), which is cut up to reveal the figure of a folk hero, Kintarō, wherever the sweet is cut.

about the promotion process from the perspective of the employee is that the criteria are fuzzy descriptions like cooperation, dedication, personality and achievement. Because there is no job description in the typical Japanese job, employees end up devoting their whole lives to the company, rather than simply sharpening their work skills, in order to prove their worthiness for a promotion. (p. 82)

Given the criticality of horizontal communication across the firm, or what Aoki (1994) calls the "non-hierarchical information system", the ability to coordinate internally over departmental and divisional boundaries is an important subset of the virtue of "being cooperative". Itoh (1994, p. 240), in addition to confirming the lack of objective individual performance measures and the importance of cooperation among workers, finds that the Japanese firm "counts more on effort and capability at lower levels in the hierarchy (via more extensive delegation) than in the Western firm".

Salary structure

Base pay

Typically the main element of remuneration is basic salary (*kihonkyū*). While this was based explicitly on age and seniority in the decades after the war (and some firms still maintain an element of salary which is explicitly linked to age (*nenreikyū*)) base salary is now usually linked to a finely graded internal ranking system (based on the acquisition of knowledge and experience), designed, according to Dore, to give all employees the sense that they are "getting on" (1973, p. 102), where each of the many ranks will correspond to a certain salary figure. As mentioned above, white-collar employees will rise more or less in unison through the grades, with possibly minute differences depending on their merit assessments,[2] until they have been with the firm seven to eight years, with the big differentials appearing after fifteen years. The effect is that salary goes up automatically every year as employees rise through the bands. This process is called *teiki shōkyū*, or "regular

---

[2] Although the differences between salary are very small, workers are nevertheless very sensitive to them. Differences of a few hundred yen between one worker and another can cause workers to resign (Cole, 1971).

salary increase". The salary bands themselves are subject to annual increases (called "base-up") that are the outcome of the labour negotiations that occur during the spring offensive. In recent years, "zero base-up" has been the norm, because of poor economic conditions.

Allowances

The other key elements of regular compensation are the plethora of allowances that employees receive and their bonus, which will be dealt with below. The most significant of these allowances has been the "family allowance", introduced in the economically straitened post-war period (Dore, 1973), which starts on marriage, and increases as the size of the employee's family grows. Some 90% of companies with more than 1,000 employees pay their employees a family allowance (Rebick, 2005). Apart from family allowance, the other key allowances are for holding a management post, entertainment, commuting, housing and regional. Union members receive overtime allowances. Altogether, allowances add up to between 10 and 20% of total regular wages.

Bonus

In addition to regular salary and allowances, Japanese employees receive a bonus, which consists of two semi-annual payments, usually made in June and December. Although the summer and winter bonuses are negotiated separately, they usually end up being the same. The bonus is expressed in terms of a multiple of monthly basic salary (i.e. allowances and overtime are not included) and usually amounts to a total of four to six months' worth of basic salary. The number of months' bonus that employees are paid is decided during the spring offensive and is paid to all executives, whether they are members of the union or not. Some labour economists and other observers (Abegglen and Stalk, 1985; Gordon, 1982) have attempted to explain the bonus as a source of flexibility in the Japanese employment system representing profit-sharing that stabilises employment, or a return on firm-specific human capital (Hashimoto, 1979). Hirakubo (1999) observed that the "system allows a company to pay a small bonus in a bad year or even defer the payment of the entire bonus to a later year. Thus, a firm can cut its payroll by as much as 30 percent." Many observers, however, dismiss the concept that the Japanese bonus is a source of flexibility. While it is the case that companies in severe financial difficulties will implement cuts in bonuses, Japanese companies appear to do everything possible to maintain stable bonus payment levels. Toyota maintained a payment of 6.1 times basic monthly salary every year between 1967 and 1986 despite widely fluctuating business conditions and results, including two oil shocks. Koshiro (1994) attributes the origin of the bonus to supplementary payments in the inflationary period in the late 1940s to enable workers to keep up with living costs.[3] "Because of this, current payments were strongly tied to previous payments and were very sticky downward. So they are today" (p. 252).

With bonus being paid in multiples of months of basic salary, the only volatility in bonus comes from the fact that one person's basic salary is higher or lower than another's. For the first fifteen years of an employee's career, therefore, there is almost no variation in the bonus he or she receives in relation to his or her cohort and there is therefore a strong "taken-for-granted" nature from the employees' perspective.

Recent developments in reward systems

In the last fifteen years, there has been enormous pressure on the system of seniority-based wages as Japanese corporate performance has fallen in the wake of persistent economic weakness. Criticism has been aimed at the white-collar segment of the economy (e.g. Hori, 1993) where productivity has declined significantly relative to the blue-collar sector. In particular, there has been pressure for the decoupling of the system of seniority from the practice of lifetime employment, which became institutionalised in the post-war employment system as part of a complete "package".

As pressure has mounted to move away from a purely seniority-based reward structure, Japanese companies have tried to develop a more "scientific" and quantitative approach to setting objectives against which performance can be measured and many firms have

---

[3] Koshiro points out, however, that a system of bonus payments was in existence for white-collar workers prior to the war. The practice spread to the blue-collar sector in the post-war years.

instituted "management by objectives" (MBO) systems. There is also more specification of desired "competencies" at various levels of employees' careers, and evaluation of the extent to which employees have these competencies. In 2000, 50% of companies surveyed claimed to have implemented an MBO evaluation system, and 52% mentioned that "competencies" were evaluated. In a comparison of US and Japanese appraisals systems Shibata (2002) found widespread implementation of the MBO and competency appraisal systems at large Japanese companies. Japanese companies have augmented the "performance" element of base salary, either by changing the way base salary is calculated or by developing new salary categories that are based purely on short-term achievement measures.

There is evidence that companies are putting less emphasis on allowances and there is a movement to transfer them, particularly those related to family circumstances, to regular salary (JIL, 2004). This has certainly been a visible trend for senior managers, although Rebick (2005, p. 44) notes that there has been no change in the percentage of companies paying family allowances to junior employees and that, if anything, it has risen during the past ten years, "suggesting that the idea of compensating employees according to their needs is still present in Japanese enterprise policy". He notes, however, that allowances for management-grade personnel are disappearing.

There are efforts to create a more specific link between the bonus and individual and company performance, especially in those firms that have introduced an "annual salary" system, where bonuses are generally explicitly linked to performance evaluations (JIL, 2004; Rebick, 2001).

In short, there may be a real sense that Japanese firms are beginning to take performance-related salaries much more seriously and actually using the ability-based system for the purpose for which it was conceived: to identify and reward high-performing employees. The "taken-for-granted" nature of the salary increase that came about with the *"teiki shōkyū"*, or "regular salary increase", system has been altered considerably, with 41% of companies in a recent survey indicating that they had either stopped it completely or had limited it only to young employees. A further 34.5% had reduced the amount of the "regular increase" (*Nihon Keizai Shimbun*, 2004).

There has been, more significantly, a rapid diffusion of the "annual salary" system (*nenpōsei*) whereby employees' salaries are fixed for a period of one year and vary annually on the basis of their performance appraisals. By 2001, 46% of companies of over 1,000 employees had introduced the "annual salary" system in one form or another, compared to 17.8% in 1998. In a survey of 423 companies carried out in 1999, 73.6% responded that it was their intention to either widen salary differences "significantly" (20.6%) or "quite significantly" (53.0%), compared with 20.3% who thought "current levels are fine" and 6.1% who intended to increase them "very slightly" (JIL, 2004). These findings are reinforced in a more recent study (JIL, 2007) which estimated that 30% of Japanese firms were still committed to both long-term employment and seniority-based pay, but that the largest group, at 40%, were part of a "new model" of Japanese firm, which was still committed to long-term employment, but with a strong emphasis on performance-based pay (p. 80).

Many believe, however, that, even though there have been changes in the *way* employees are rewarded, this has not been reflected in a material difference in actual rewards. Even with the introduction of new appraisal systems such as MBO and the use of competency evaluation, Shibata (2002) saw little change in the linkage between the evaluation process and resulting pay. For union members, union resistance ensured that the introduction of these appraisal methods was not accompanied by any change in salary structure, and there is still widespread use of the explicit age-linked component and the maintenance of narrow remuneration differentials.

Shibata, like other observers of the Japanese employment system (e.g. Dore, 1973; Koike, 1994), notes its highly integrated features and concludes that the high levels of interdependence between its various elements would make change difficult. This was recognised by management who had no interest in working within some brand new template:

despite various pressures and the need for change, this key characteristic of integration has not been fundamentally changed in wage and performance appraisal systems or in other human resource management systems in Japan. Recent changes amount to moderate modifications of the "integration" characteristic of Japanese firms. Japanese management basically would like to maintain the strength of its integration property. (p. 650)

In other words, according to Shibata, given the strong inter-linkages between the component parts of the Japanese employment system, it was very difficult to make radical adjustments in one area without drastically affecting others. All of this caused the JIL to conclude that the "ability-based system", when actually put into operation, was no more than "pseudo-*nenkō*" (*giji-nenkō*) as, instead of giving employees credit for performance, "employees were evaluated by the proxy variables of length of service and accumulated work experience" (2004, p. 27).

The fact of the matter is, however, that a number of Japanese companies have attempted over the last decade to force a pay structure with a greater emphasis on performance and results on their employees, but these have not been successful. The most notorious example is Fujitsu. A former employee wrote a book (Joe, 2004) in which the failings of Fujitsu management to prepare its supervisors to design MBOs which could be perceived as fair and reasonable by the employees are vividly portrayed. The result of the sudden move to quantitative-derived targets to determine rewards was the lowering of productivity because employees tried to minimise the possibility of wage reduction by setting as low a target as possible. A blog from another former employee[4] points the finger of blame squarely at the management, who, in trying to introduce a "western style of management", made two mistaken assumptions: first that Japanese employees were motivated solely, or mostly, by money, and second that employees only performed tasks that were prescribed by clearly defined job descriptions.

Fujitsu was not alone. During the early 2000s, many Japanese companies introduced a much more performance-oriented remuneration

[4] Koichi Masada: http://homepage1.nifty.com/masada/manage/MBO.htm. Masada also makes the interesting observation that relations between a Japanese client and its Japanese supplier of a product or service are governed by different factors from the contract and economically driven relations with a western supplier. He asserts that, once a Japanese firm tries to "westernize" its management and put its client relationships on a more rational footing, it endangers the foundations upon which that relationship is built. Although I do not intend to explore the impact on client relationships of Japanese firms taken over by foreign companies in this book, it was certainly my experience at LTCB Investment Management that the clients looked upon us in a very different way when the firm was taken over by UBS.

structure with greater emphasis on rewarding employees who met clearly defined quantitatively established targets. Several years on, however, the evaluation of the academic community, as well as the media, would appear to be that, in focusing exclusively, or substantially, on results, traditional values highly valued by corporate Japan such as fairness and equality have been undermined, leading directly to a deterioration in teamwork and the passing of vital tacit knowledge from one generation to another. Many see the introduction of performance-based pay as a cynical ploy by management to reduce costs (by creating a framework within which salaries could be reduced). Writing in the admittedly slightly left-of-centre *Aera* magazine, Ryutaro Ito notes that "the performance-based pay introduced by Japanese companies was a system completely unrelated to motivating employees. The damage resulting from it should have been obvious to anyone." He concludes: "many organisations have been cast under the spell of performance-related pay. Attempts to escape from it are only just beginning"[5] (2008, p. 19).

Stock options and other forms of remuneration

A distinctive feature of Japanese remuneration systems has been the relatively small gap between the lowest-paid workers in a company and the senior executives. Many studies of Japanese corporate life emphasise the equality of salary levels, particularly in contrast to the US. Dore (1973) finds that, while directors at Hitachi did own shares in the company and received bonuses that fluctuated with the company's business fortunes, the bonuses reflected those of "salaryman directors" and had become "a relatively standardised part of their income" (p. 165).

However, during the 1990s, as Japanese companies began to perform poorly, there was increasing pressure on senior Japanese executives to take more personal responsibility for companies' results. As the idea of collective responsibility began to recede, at least on the surface, the concept of reward commensurate with the increased risk executives faced started to take hold and, in particular, the thought that a clearer link should be established between executive pay and

---

[5] Author's translation.

share price movements. In 1997, legislation was passed to permit the setting up of stock options, significantly not a government measure, but a diet member's bill. Uptake was initially quite slow, with only 150 listed firms setting up schemes in the first year, but this accelerated in subsequent years.[6] By 2005, over a third of all listed companies (nearly 1,400) offered stock options to employees (Uchida, 2006).

Alongside the proliferation of stock option plans for senior Japanese executives has come a movement towards greater transparency in relation to directors' pay. Currently companies are only required to disclose aggregate directors' pay and there is pressure to make more individual disclosure.

It is difficult to know, however, the extent to which the new alignment of management with the interests of shareholders through stock option schemes has really taken root in the Anglo-Saxon sense. Dore (2000) notes the comments of a steel company chairman in the *Nihon Keizai Shimbun* in the wake of the liberalisation of stock options in 1997:

At the time of the yen appreciation it fell to me to be the main flag-waver for our efforts at restructuring the firm. We didn't do too badly and the firm got back into profit. But that was by group effort. Supposing that my role as flag-waver in the process had been seen as important and I'd been given stock options and exercised them and made a lot of money. I don't think I would have felt too happy about that. And I don't think my colleagues, in the bottom of their hearts, would have accepted the justice of it.

[6] One such company is Toyota. While the company is considered quite traditional in its approach to employment relations, it is speculated that the high visibility of the company, and the leading role its management plays in the Keidanren, obliged it to "show the way" with "progressive" compensation systems for senior executives (Dore, 2000). According to data from the company's 20-F filing with the SEC (26 June 2006), the maximum grant of options to directors for 2002–2005 was for 20,000 shares. This increased to 40,000 shares in 2006. According to the author's calculations, if the options had been exercised on the first day they were exercisable (two years after grant), the value to directors would have been in the range of approximately ¥23–30 million for each of the 2002–2005 grants. The amount may seem large by Japanese standards, but are very small by US standards, especially considering the strong performance of the company's stock price in this period. The 2005 and 2006 series, while not exercisable at the time of writing, would theoretically be worth over ¥60 million calculated on the share price of 20 March 2007.

In individualistic societies like America and Europe stock option systems may fit in very well, but I really wonder about their suitability for Japan. (p. 68)

The key reference made by the chairman is to the possible feelings of his colleagues. The concept of stock options and more pay for greater responsibility for senior executives cuts across the deeply institutionalised principle of equality, and it is not clear yet that a sufficient degree of legitimacy has been bestowed upon the new practices for them to take root. As far as transparency is concerned, only fifteen out of 1,310 firms in a survey by the Tokyo Stock Exchange in 2000 revealed individual directors' pay, while only a further seventeen responded that they planned to disclose it (Tokyo Stock Exchange, 2000).

To summarise, therefore, the reward system under the communitarian template consists of the following features:

- a strong emphasis on equality;
- slow promotion at the early stages (first fifteen years) of employees' careers;
- cohort members moving up together during this period;
- employees showing strong coordination skills and teamwork are more likely to be promoted;
- an emphasis on family-related allowances;
- bonus considered as an element of salary, with little variation;
- a lack of share price-based rewards, such as stock options.

Conclusions from the literature:

- there has been a shift away from "life stage" or explicitly age-based pay to "job-" and "ability-"based pay (JIL, 2004);
- new evaluation systems have been introduced which take into account ability and competencies as well as setting clearer employee objectives (Shibata, 2002);
- the grading system reflects an apparent determination to create wider gaps in rewards between high and poorly performing employees (JIL, 2004);
- many companies have abandoned the system of automatic annual pay increases (*Nihon Keizai Shimbun*, 2004);
- in practice, however, while the systems have changed, the net effect on rewards is not significant, with seniority still the dominant determinant (Shibata, 2002);

- bonus is still determined as a multiple of base pay, with no strong link between short-term company or personal performance (Koshiro, 1994);
- allowances still feature strongly in overall compensation (Rebick, 2001);
- stock options have been introduced, but stock price is not yet a significant factor in senior management compensation (Ahmadjian, 2001).

Findings at comparator and case companies

While there is, then, little evidence pointing to the end of the concept of lifetime employment among the comparator companies, there are some signs that the traditions of lifetime employment and seniority wages are no longer necessarily joined as a "set" and that the seniority system is breaking down in favour of a much greater merit-oriented approach: "a growing number of companies are abolishing seniority-based wages and shifting towards performance-based wages" (JIL, 2004, p. 39). Insofar as the old seniority system is based on rational calculation by management towards enhancing employee loyalty and motivation, the logic no longer holds up. The former head of *Rengō*, the Japanese Trades Union Federation, observed the following, using the example of a lathe operator:

In the old days this was an extremely skilled job and required years of training. So for the growth period that lasted for thirty years from the 1950s, the seniority system was perfectly rational. Training took place inside the firm, inside the factory, so lifetime employment also made sense. To support this, you had intra-company labour relations management, which supported and reinforced these two phenomenon: hence the "three treasures". What brought about the change in this situation is the development of computerisation in the 1980s and 1990s. When computer control drives the ability of machine to design and produce screws, the old way of accumulating knowledge and experience, and the way this process is rewarded, doesn't make sense any more.

According to this analysis, even allowing for the build-up of tacit knowledge that accumulates with experience, we should expect larger gaps to appear between those who produce and those who do not, with less emphasis on seniority. To what extent, then, has seniority-based pay actually disappeared? In particular, has the implementation of new evaluation and pay structures really made any difference to the speed at which employees are promoted relative to their peers, and the amount they are paid?

Evaluation and promotion process

Below are two tables which show the extent to which differentials have opened up between cohort members between 1998 and 2003 for both comparator and case companies. Table 5.1 shows the number of years that elapse after a cohort enters the firm before a significant gap in salary (more than 5%) opens up between cohort members. Table 5.2 shows the number of years that elapse until the first cohort member (or members) reach the key career milestones of manager or *kachō*.

Table 5.1 *Comparator and case salary differentials (1)*

Salary differentials (1)		
	Years elapsed until difference in pay (>5%) appears among cohorts	
	1998	*2003*
J-Mfg Co	9	9
Nissan	9	2
J-Phma Co	3	3
Chugai	3	3
J-Fin Co	6	6
Shinsei	7	2
J-Svcs Co	3	3
F-Svcs Co 1	5	3

It can be seen from Tables 5.1 and 5.2 that in nearly every respect the period between 1998 and 2003 saw little actual change at the comparator companies. The time elapsed until differentials in pay appear among cohorts varies considerably among the companies, with J-Pharma Co and J-Services Co much faster than the other two companies. However, the situation in 2003 was the same as 1998 at all four companies. As can be seen, there is some variability between

Table 5.2 *Comparator promotion speed*

	Promotion speed earliest to manager (years)	
	---	---
	1998	*2003*
J-Mfg Co	15	15
Nissan	14	8
J-Phma Co	11	11
Chugai	16	13
J-Fin Co	9	9
Shinsei	14	8
J-Svcs Co	12	12
F-Svcs Co 1	13	7

the companies, with the range of between nine and fifteen years before the first cohort member became a manager.

Generally speaking, the emphasis in the promotion process is to adopt a more scientific approach that takes into account the abilities and the contributions of the employee to a much greater extent and from an earlier stage in his or her career. Again, looking at the current state of J-Utility Co gives us some insight into the workings of the community firm. At J-Utility Co, there are nine grades to go through before an employee enters management grade. High school leavers come in at the bottom grade while university graduates enter at grade 3. Each grade is further subdivided into fifty units to which is attached a salary level. On promotion to a certain grade, an employee will start at the first unit, and will generally be expected to be promoted by four units per year. However, the most able employees are promoted by five units, while the worst performers are promoted by only three. While the "top performers" account for 20% of a cohort group, the "worst performers" account for only 0.5%. It is extraordinarily rare to be placed in this category. In any case the difference in salary between one unit and the next amounts to only around ¥1,000 per month, so financial incentives for promotion at this level are very low. Promotion between grades takes a fixed amount of time. It takes twelve years to reach management grade when one becomes an assistant manager, but after that promotion speed varies, with the most capable reaching the coveted rank of manager in a further four years while most have to wait five years. For the fastest, it therefore takes sixteen years to reach the grade of manager. Lifetime employment is strongly emphasised at the company and there are no plans to make any radical alterations to the promotion system.

Promotions at other companies are generally faster, and the hierarchies are less finely graded. All companies now use some variation of MBO, with evaluation taking the form of a matrix, which measures performance against set objectives and competencies.

At J-Services Co, there are eight non-management grades (university graduates skip a grade and go straight to grade two) and six management grades. It generally takes two years to go through each grade, meaning that it generally takes the better graduates twelve years to reach the rank of manager. To be promoted, employees have to accumulate points, which are awarded as a result of the annual appraisal process. Differences within the cohort start to appear after only three years, when about 10% of the group is left behind in the promotion process. The appraisal process takes place twice-yearly for bonus determination and once a year for salary and promotion decisions. There is a tendency not to award extreme marks, especially on the lower grades, but that is changing. A senior member of the HR department noted:

We are refining the grading system by adding more grades, and sending the message that employees need to be assigned poor grades if they do not perform. So in evaluating management-grade staff, for example, we only went down to –3 but now we have grades down to –5. It's true that people find it difficult to give the absolute top mark of 4 and especially 5. Five really seems "almighty" and it's difficult to understand what kind of person that is. Also for the lowest grades, unless people have been off sick for long periods, it's difficult to assign them.

Thus, while the company has created a wider range of grades that employees might be assigned, actually placing the employees into these grades has proved to be more of a challenge. The only way to be assigned the poorest grade is to be physically unfit to work.

J-Pharma Co's grading system is close to J-Utility Co's, with five non-management grades and three management grades. These are finely sub-graded into 67 "steps" (e.g. "S-1" grade, just below the manager grade). The standard speed for reaching the rank of manager is fourteen years, but the fastest can reach it in eleven years. The evaluation system uses a series of letters, with "S" being outstanding, and then from A to G, with D as the standard grade. The HR department determined beforehand roughly what percentages should be assigned to each grade and departments were instructed to fit their employees into the grid accordingly. Although virtually no one got "S", "F" or "G" grades, there were a small number in the "A" and "E" brackets.

J-Financial Co continues to emphasise seniority during the first ten years of the employee's career as they feel that excessive stress on performance conversely makes young employees more conservative, fearing that failure and mistakes would count against them in the promotion race. As a result, there is no change in the rate at which the post of manager is reached (ten years as standard for the first group, but nine years in exceptional cases). While the company is keen to promote the more capable employees more quickly through the ranks thereafter, it is constrained by a top-heavy hierarchy. For the post of branch manager, which has considerable symbolic value, the CEO of J-Financial Co has decreed that younger candidates be nominated. Since the merger, the age of the youngest branch manager had crept up slightly to forty-two, but after the president's intervention, the youngest became thirty-six in 2003.

The appraisal system has become more transparent and rigorous, with 360° evaluations for 6,000 employees, which the company believes is the largest such exercise in Japan. The final arbiter on appraisals is the HR department, and they actively adjust employees' appraisals to take into account the different appraisal habits of managers. They also plot the distribution of appraisals to ensure that there are more employees at the extremes of the distribution curve.

For the purposes of evaluating employees, the HR department at J-Manufacturing Co have developed a competency and performance grid, which sets out expectations of employees at various stages of their careers (starting with the "acquiring basic skills" period, then the "acquiring core specialist skills", followed by "establishing professionalism" and finally "being a professional"). For a manager in the "professional" category, this means fulfilling criteria such as "he is capable of exercising a high quality of leadership that would be recognised as such in another company or overseas" and "he would be able to command a salary of over ¥10 million at another company". In addition, there is a grid, which lays out weightings for various attributes (e.g. creativity, execution, managing your subordinates, personal reputation, etc.). There are ten grades in all: six up to management and four in management. For the first eight years, promotion is automatic, with employees going up a grade every two years. In the ninth year, only 30% make it to the fifth grade, with 30% following in year ten, and 30% following on in year eleven or later. The speed taken to reach the equivalent position of manager is fifteen years at the fastest, with nineteen years being the standard trajectory, unchanged from five years previously.

One of the most important developments at J-Manufacturing Co during the last fifteen years has actually been the removal of the "manager" or *kachō* rank in a bid to flatten the hierarchy and redress the balance between the "managers" and the "managed" as the number of the former was increasing exponentially with a system that virtually assures promotion to the manager grade for university graduates. This reorganisation had some negative unintended consequences, which will be explored later.

This thinning out of management positions in the company's hierarchy, with the implication that fewer people will make it to middle and top management, has enhanced the importance of the appraisal process, even though, as we have seen, the length of time it takes to move through the hierarchy does not appear to have changed. As we will see below, the impact on wages has also not been significant.

Salary structure

Table 5.3 displays salary differentials over the 1998–2003 period. It shows the salary multiple of the highest to the lowest earner in a cohort ten years after entering the firm. With the exception of J-Services Co, there has been no change. At J-Services Co, the gap was already quite wide in 1998 and has since widened out further. The 1998 figure for J-Financial Co represents the faster (in promotion terms) of the pre-merger banks. J-Pharma Co did not have individual data for 1998.

While differentials may not have widened, there is no doubt that the process of evaluating employees has become more "scientific" and quantitative at the comparator firms. There is now also a higher proportion of pay that is dependent on factors other than years of service. As can be seen in Figure 5.2, at J-Manufacturing Co the company moved in 1990 from a system where 100% of managerial salary was based on length of service, with differences appearing after about

Table 5.3 *Comparator and case salary differentials (2)*

Salary differentials (2)

	Cohort salary differentials (10 yrs) x	
	1998	*2003*
J-Mfg Co	1.1	1.1
Nissan	1.15	1.5
J-Phma Co	N/A	1.3
Chugai	1.3	1.5
J-Fin Co	1.33	1.33
Shinsei	1.05	1.5
J-Svcs Co	1.4	1.6
F-Svcs Co 1	1.25	1.6

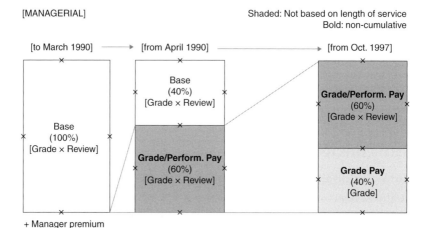

[MANAGERIAL]   Shaded: Not based on length of service
                                                     Bold: non-cumulative

+ Manager premium

Figure 5.2 **Changes in payment programme: J-Manufacturing Co**

fifteen years based on evaluations, but where salaries nevertheless increased annually, to a system where only 40% of base pay depends on seniority. In 1997 this was changed so that there is now no component of salary that automatically increases, with 100% reflecting an employee's grade, 60% of which would be subject to a performance and competency coefficient.

Despite these changes, and the fact that the hierarchy has been thinned out, the practical impact on salary differentials, at least in lower- to middle-management positions, has not been great. The underlying philosophy that determines salary at this level has remained consistent over time. A senior HR official explained the impact of the elimination of the rank of manager:

If you do that [i.e. abolish the manager rank] and you've taken away the prospect for whole layers of staff of becoming a manager, you get a real motivation problem. So what we did was to pay people of a similar age almost exactly the same whether they were managers or not. We were thus able to tell people that even though they couldn't make it to the senior ranks, if you work hard and do a good job, you'll be paid the same or pretty much the same. From the J-Manufacturing Co point of view, this kind of thinking is second nature. If you work as hard as someone of your age and he gets to be a general manager and you don't, you still have the same experience, expertise and so on of people of the same age and get pretty much exactly the same pay. Of course from the viewpoint of people from our overseas affiliates it doesn't make any sense. On the one hand there's the general manager with several hundred staff under him, a huge performance expectation and, on the other, someone with perhaps no responsibilities at all getting almost the same salary.

At J-Manufacturing Co, therefore, experience and expertise, from the standpoint of remuneration, were of critical importance as was the understanding by employees that hard work and loyalty should be rewarded in the long term. In addition to enabling the company to reap the benefits of experience and expertise, this served as a strong motivating factor for employees. Taking a radically different approach to reward might undermine the company's social fabric and, with it, the morale of the company's employees. But this was not just something specific to the company, or even the industry in which J-Manufacturing Co operated. There were wider historical and societal factors to consider:

You also need to take into account social norms and the expectations of the external labour market as a whole … The current seniority system has its roots in the post-war period where we would recruit young workers at very low cost. These wages were OK for a bachelor, but once they had families it wasn't sufficient, so we had a system of age- and family circumstance-related wages that forms the basis of our current system. This may change gradually but we can't change it all at once given the possible impact on morale.

At J-Services Co, there was a major revision in salary structure in 2001. For non-managerial staff, base salary prior to 2001 was divided 50/50 between age-related pay and grade-related pay (which was in any event highly correlated with years of service). Both categories went up every year: in the case of age-related pay, until the age of 55; and in grade-related pay, until retirement. After 2001, the age- and grade-related portions were retained (although annual increases for the age-related portion now stops at the age of 50) but a new element, based on performance/merit (*seika kasan* or merit supplement), was added. This addition, which accumulates annually, is calculated according to performance criteria with the top performers receiving double the supplement of the standard performer.

A further change is in the calculation of the allowances. While family allowances have been maintained, the "grade allowance" was changed into a performance/merit allowance. In contrast to the merit supplement, this does not accumulate and is reset at the beginning of every year. Again, grades are assigned from A to D.

For management staff, the salary structure also reflected a combination of age- and grade-related contributions until 2001. It was simplified and is now 100% related to grade, with there being a single wage for each of the six managerial grades. Salary increases are therefore now only available at the time of promotion. Family allowance has been eliminated for management grades and the overall ratio of salary to allowances changed from 65:35 to 70:30 as a result of the restructuring of salary in 2001.

The salary structure at J-Financial Co is quite similar to that at J-Services Co. The system at the pre-merger companies was explicitly based on seniority, but now salary is tied completely to grade, with the exception of a merit supplement (*seika kasan*). This supplement is based on evaluations and accumulates annually until promotion (subject to a ceiling), when it is reset to zero. The spread of salary (i.e. the gap between the top and the bottom between cohorts) is not greater than it was five years ago, but there has been a greater effort to reward the better performers in relation to the poorer ones – as a result, the distribution curve is not as bunched in the middle. The highest-earning employees in a cohort are earning the same amount in relation to the lowest paid; it is just that there are more people earning the higher and lower salaries. Prior to the merger, it was impossible for salaries to go down (except for economic reasons) but now 10% of salaries are actually reduced as a result of the annual appraisal process.

At J-Pharma Co, there were no fundamental changes in salary structure during the 1998–2003 period. For non-managers, there is still an age-dependent element of salary (called *honninkyū*, or "personal pay"), which accounts for 40% of basic pay. This goes up continuously with age until fifty after which it reduces annually by ¥1,500 per month. The two other elements of pay are related to job grade (*shokunōkyū*) and "job difficulty" (*yakuwarikyū*) and could stay the same or go up, but not down, and are therefore also quite highly correlated with age. For management-grade employees, salary consists of only two elements, "job difficulty" and job grade. Theoretically, seniority is not reflected, although in practice there remains a high correlation between age and pay.

Although Japanese companies appear to be reducing the weight of allowances as a percentage of overall salary, J-Utility Co's pay allowance structure demonstrates that, at some of the more traditional firms, the key elements of the community firm still survive. For all employees, both management and otherwise, in addition to base pay there are eleven separate allowances to which employees are entitled, including family allowance. In addition, there are a large number of benefits that are payable on the occasion of weddings, births and special birthdays of dependants (e.g. the twentieth birthday of a child, the eighty-eighth birthday of an employee's parent).

As noted above, we saw that little change has been reported in the structure of allowances paid by Japanese firms other than for management-grade employees (Rebick, 2005). My investigation shows that there has been more change at the comparator companies. Family allowances have indeed been more or less abolished for management-level employees at all of them. J-Pharma Co and J-Services Co still pay family allowance to non-management staff, and J-Pharma Co pay housing allowance to management staff. J-Financial Co stopped allowances of any kind at the time of the merger; family allowance is not paid to any employees. J-Manufacturing Co had never paid allowances to their managers, as their salaries and other benefits were already considered "high enough" according to the HR department.

Bonus

We have seen in previous chapters that a bonus is considered more or less a part of an employee's salary, expressed as multiples of monthly salary, with some variation year-by-year depending on

the performance of the company and how labour management discussions have progressed, but that there is little variation between
employees. There has been some change in recent years, particularly
with a greater emphasis on reflecting individual achievement and ability in the bonus amount.

At J-Utility Co, all employees receive the amount of bonus that has
been agreed between the union and the management as part of the
"spring offensive". It has remained very stable, and during the last
twelve years to 2005, the bonus has stayed in the range of 5.5–5.85
times monthly salary. However, there is variation of between –5%
to +10%, which depends on the employee's evaluation. In practice,
there are very few employees that receive less than the standard bonus
and those tend to be employees who had already received official
warnings about their work. The number who received more than the
standard bonus was quite high, amounting to almost 50%.

At J-Services Co, the bonus has both increased as a percentage of
total remuneration (from an average of about 80:20 in 1998 to 70:30
in 2003) and became more volatile between employees. Bonus determination is carried out twice a year and is determined according to
the same scale that is used for salary and promotion evaluation, with
grades from –1 to +5. At least 5% of employees are put into each of
these extreme groups, and within the same rank employees with the
best evaluation can receive up to five times the bonus of the lowest
evaluated employee, although in practice this situation is quite rare.

At J-Financial Co, the percentage of bonus that was tied to performance in the late 1990s was about 30% and that rose to 50% by
2003. As a percentage of total remuneration it rises gradually with
seniority, but for someone of 20 years' experience, the bonus accounts
for around 25%. The amount of bonus is calculated using a combination of company, divisional and personal performance. For employees
of management grade, the variation in bonus could be in the range
of –20% to +20% from the standard.

At J-Manufacturing Co, the way bonuses are calculated is similar for management and non-management. The only difference is
that a competency factor is added for management employees. For
management-level employees, the variation in bonus is –15% to
+15%, although the spokesman from HR said that the likelihood of
employees receiving above the standard amount is much greater than
receiving less than the standard.

Stock options and other forms of remuneration

At the time of my research, the only company among the four comparators to grant stock options to employees was, paradoxically, probably the most traditional: J-Manufacturing Co. In 2003–2004, the average director of J-Manufacturing Co was paid just under ¥74 million in salary and bonuses, a substantial increase from the previous year. While this amount is nowhere near the ¥146 million reportedly paid to Nissan directors, and although the majority of this increase is likely to have taken place on account of the sharp reduction in the size of J-Manufacturing Co's board, it is widely perceived that the remaining board members will have seen their remuneration increase in line with their responsibilities.[7] The fact that J-Manufacturing Co is increasing its disclosure of directors' pay would seem to indicate, first, that there will be increased transparency on the role and responsibilities of directors and, second, that the concept of responsibilities being rewarded with greater monetary compensation will be seen in a more legitimate light.

J-Pharma Co, after my research there, merged with another Japanese pharmaceutical company. It has introduced a system of stock options to directors and a limited number of employees. Neither J-Financial Co nor J-Services Co has introduced stock option plans.

Case companies

We have seen from the above that intense pressure for change on the institutionalised system of employee-reward determination has produced a more results-oriented philosophy towards pay. There is now a more systematic and scientific approach to employee evaluation, as

---

[7] Historically, Japanese firms have paid their directors generous lump-sum allowances on retirement. For example, in the four years between 2003–2004 and 2006–2007, directors' compensation at J-Manufacturing Co totalled ¥8.5 billion, while aggregate retirement allowances totalled ¥6.2 billion. Along with many other major Japanese firms, the company has abolished the retirement lump sum for directors and folded the retirement payment into directors' annual remuneration. This had the effect of adding an extra ¥70 million to each director's annual remuneration in 2007–2008 compared to the previous year, when the retirement lump sum was abolished.

well as the introduction of new reward mechanisms, such as the use of stock options. However, it has not yet led to a dramatic difference in salary or bonus dispersion at Japanese companies: a clearer distinction in the rewards of high- and poorly performing employees. This reflects the picture at the comparator companies, where new, more "scientific" systems had been introduced, but had not yet been implemented in a way that had produced large gaps between a cohort of employees, at least for the first part of their careers, which in some cases is fifteen years. Change has been gradual, and within the existing framework of the Japanese remuneration system.

We would expect a more radical approach from the new foreign shareholders who would adopt "global best practice" at the case companies. In particular we would expect:

- a marked move away from seniority as the principal determinant of reward;
- that the evaluation process produces bigger gaps between "winners" and "losers";
- better-performing employees to reach the key position of manager much earlier;
- an end of the "taken-for-granted" nature of annual salary increases;
- a different type of employee to succeed in the organisation;
- the issue of fairness to become more of an issue with employees as the objectivity of age-based reward is replaced with performance-based reward in which subjectivity can play an important part;
- salary to become more important to individual employees.

Findings: case companies

As can be seen in Tables 5.1 and 5.2 above, the difference between the case and comparator companies can most easily be seen in the change in promotion speeds. Generally there is a dramatic reduction in the time it takes to reach the key rank of manager after entering the firm from university. As indicated above, promotion to manager at large Japanese firms usually took between ten and fifteen years, even for the fastest employees, who would in any case reach that position six months or one year prior to others. At the case study firms, the length of time to reach manager fell by almost half for the best performers. A significant constraint for Chugai has been the large number of employees in managerial posts. This has kept promotion speeds down, but despite this constraint, it now takes about three years less.

The time that elapsed for an employee to open up a significant gap in salary (more than 5%) with members of his or her cohort also shortened, except in the case of Chugai (see Table 5.1 above). The most dramatic change was at Shinsei, where it used to take seven years for any gap to open up at all, but it now took only two years.

Employee perception

The change in importance of seniority is summarised in Table 5.4.

Table 5.4 *Change in importance of seniority*[8]

Seniority

Q: To what extent has seniority become less/more important in determining wages/promotion?
1 = as important as before
2 = somewhat less important
3 = much less important

Nissan	Chugai	Shinsei	F-Svcs Co 1	F-Svcs Co 2	Total	
2.18	2.31	2.80	2.50	2.55	2.48	
Male	Female	Career	MCH	20–35 yrs	35–45 yrs	45 yrs +
2.55	2.18	2.53	2.31	2.25	2.50	2.56

n = 60

It is apparent that the perceived importance of seniority as a deter-minant of reward had declined significantly at the case study compan-ies. The slight exception was Nissan: while there was still a feeling that seniority was less important, in line with employees' feelings on life-time employment, it appears that traditional elements are still present in the determination of reward at the company. At Chugai, hitherto the company with the lowest level of perceived change, there appeared to be a relatively strong consensus that the reward system was changing.

[8] No interviewees replied that seniority had become *more* important.

There were significant inter-employee group differences. Consistent with the finding that female employees did not see much change in the way they were treated, males were more likely to perceive changes in reward structures. Career employees and older employees were more likely to perceive change, which would be expected.

Evaluation and promotion process

There were many references made by the new management to the conflict between the traditional communitarian reward system and the new "performance culture", in particular to the weak link between responsibility, performance and reward under the old regime. For example, the (non-Japanese) head of HR at one case company commented on one senior manager:

When I start talking about high performers and poor performers he can't bear it; he'll say: "there are no low performers, they're all my workers and they all perform at the same level. There is no difference between them." [When it comes to] his performance reviews of his staff ... he'll say about someone: "No, that rating is too high. She's from a rich family so she doesn't need that much but he's just had another child so he needs more." We're trying to develop a performance culture and when you're confronted with that you realise there's a long way to go. I'd like to say that I only see it at that level but I see it much further down the organisation as well. They want to keep going the way they've always gone. It's very hard to change things in a traditional Japanese company.

It was noted that at all five companies the evaluation process has become more "scientific" and quantitative. However, it is also true to say that the process of change in all cases had started before the foreign shareholder took control. The systems had continued to evolve and it is therefore difficult to isolate exactly the nature of the change that is attributable to the existence of the new shareholders. There are a number of features that are common to all five companies. For example, they have all adopted an evaluation system based on "management by objectives" (MBO) where personal objectives are set for each employee by his/her supervisor, and the employee is rewarded partially to the extent those objectives are reached and partially on the basis of various competency ratings.

The main difference between the case and comparator companies was the way in which employees were graded. As has been discussed above, the comparator companies had developed much more quantitative ways in which to evaluate staff and to remunerate them accordingly. However, there was in general a much greater willingness on the part of the case companies to force employees into the extreme categories (Table 5.5 from a case company and its comparator company below illustrates this point). At the comparator company, the most employees (half) are graded as "C", with the other half spread fairly evenly above, as "A" or "B". At the case company, there was an even bigger "mode" group at "B". However, there is a clearer attempt to distinguish the "super" performers and, more significantly, to establish who the sub-standard employees were. At this particular case company, too many years spent in either of these bottom categories was seen as a signal that one should seek alternative employment.

Table 5.5 *Distribution of evaluation grades: comparator vs case companies*

Spread of evaluation grades (%)

Grade	Comparator co	Case co
S	N/A	5
A	20–30	20
B	20–30	60
C	50	10
D	1	5

Two companies, Chugai and F-Services Co 1, had introduced a points system for promotion, so that employees had to accumulate a certain number of points during the evaluation process to be promoted to the next stage. Written exams were compulsory at Chugai for significant milestone promotions, but not at the other firms. Important innovations at Shinsei were the introduction of a Group Evaluation Committee to determine compensation strategy and an Executive Evaluation Committee to coordinate and monitor the evaluation and compensation of executives at the company. This function had previously been carried out by the HR department, which had used its power extensively in the old days to preserve a proper "balance" between the departments. Competency ratings were generally done with grades, letters or numbers, such as "A" to "D". A common issue for firms was the tendency for evaluators not to assign extreme ratings for their subordinates. The head of HR at F-Services Co 1 summed up the problem:

We have to force people to put their subordinates into different groups. Everyone wants to give all their subordinates good marks, but I stress that that isn't necessarily in their best interests. They have to learn what their weaknesses are and correct them.

F-Services Co 1 and Shinsei also had mandatory 360° evaluation for managers and above. F-Services Co 2 had a 360° evaluation process, but it was voluntary and consequently did not appear to be taken seriously.

A senior manager at Nissan summarised the change between the old and the new Nissan in the following way:

At Nissan, even before Ghosn-san got here, we had introduced a 100% performance-driven system. But while the system was there, it didn't work properly. We didn't identify people of high potential and develop them, we didn't set clear objectives, for the company, for the division, nor for the individuals, so that they could be rewarded properly for achieving them. There have been no big changes in the system since Ghosn-san got here. But what we've done is to make clear to everyone what is expected of them. The system and its implementation are entirely different things. You go to any Japanese organisation and they'll tell you: "Oh yes, we have 100% performance-related pay now." But if you ask them whether their top performers are earning twice what the poorest performers are getting of course they'll say no. The problem is that, in order to implement this kind of pay structure properly, you've got to give to all employees a job description and clear guidelines as to what is expected of them, and by doing that, you can tell them what they can expect if they reach or exceed those objectives. It's no good just changing the system. If you check what systems Japanese companies are adopting, I'm sure you will find that there's not a lot of difference between Japanese and US or other foreign firms. But it's the implementation that's different. Japanese tend to think and do things in teams. As there's no particular sense of one's individual responsibilities and what commitment they are expected to make as individuals, it's not possible to have a properly functioning meritocracy.

His comments reinforce our findings: Japanese firms are certainly introducing the necessary systems to enable greater distinctions between various levels of performance. However, there is a great disparity in the way the systems are implemented between the case and comparator companies. He also makes the important point that merely introducing meritocratic pay systems into an organisation that has hitherto emphasised teamwork and had no job descriptions for individual employees will not have the desired effect.

Salary structure

Salary differentials between cohort groups ten years into the company (see Table 5.3 above) also show dramatic change at the case companies: it is noteworthy that in the cases of Shinsei and F-Services Co 1 they started off in a more conservative position than their comparators. In relative terms the biggest change has taken place at Shinsei – indeed the HR representative indicated that the differentials may in fact be wider than the figures indicate if one included the absolute top earners in the investment banking area.

All five case companies employed a variant of the *shokunōkyū* system, where salary is tied completely to a particular grade. Nissan and Chugai most resembled the traditional Japanese company, with a large number of "steps" (twenty-five for management grades in the case of Nissan,[9] twenty-one in Chugai's), each with a fixed, single-salary figure attached to it. Indeed, at Nissan, the explicit age-related element of salary existed for non-management employees until April 2004 when it was finally abolished. F-Services Co 1 had only six salary bands (down from fourteen) and, while one could not be paid outside of the band, there was 20% flexibility within the band. Shinsei was by far the most flexible, with nine salary bands, but with a great deal of overlapping and vague limits to permit maximum flexibility. Whereas at Chugai and to a certain extent Nissan there was a sense of staying at each "step" for a certain amount of time (usually one year), this was not necessarily so at Shinsei.

There had been great change in the structure of allowances. All five companies had scrapped the payment for management staff of what

---

[9] However, this has since been reduced to eight. See section on "Hierarchy" in Chapter 7.

was perhaps the most symbolic element of the communitarian array
of allowances paid by Japanese firms, the "family allowances". This
was a variable amount depending on the size of the family. However,
all companies except F-Services Co 1 still paid this allowance to the
non-titled (i.e. non-management employees). Shinsei still paid housing
allowance to management-grade staff, having sold off all company
housing facilities after the company's nationalisation in 1998. Nissan
and Chugai still had company housing facilities for younger staff.

Bonus

Bonus determination was the area that saw the widest array of outcomes. The traditional way bonuses are paid, as we have seen above,
was twice annually, an equivalent of a fixed number of months of
basic salary. To a great extent, this is still the system used at the comparator companies, as we saw in the last chapter.

The greatest changes in the bonus structure have come at Nissan
and Shinsei. At Nissan, the bonus component has been renamed "variable compensation". The basic salary, renamed "annual basic salary"
("ABS"), is equivalent to 16 months of the old salary, thus recognising
that the greater part of the old "bonus" was basically considered as
a salary entitlement. The variable compensation element comprises a
number of elements: the extent to which company, divisional and individual "commitments" (i.e. targets or objectives, including, of course,
financial targets based on sales and profitability) are met. There is a
pool of overall variable compensation available for the whole firm,
and each divisional head is expected to fight for their own allocation
of this pool, a process of negotiation which may be familiar to foreign
firms, but not to Japanese manufacturing firms. Variable compensation can account for up to 25% of ABS. For non-managerial staff and
blue-collar workers, bonus determination has not changed from the
old method, negotiated between labour and management during the
"spring offensive".

The bonus system at Shinsei bears no relationship to the old LTCB
system. It is determined very much along the lines of an Anglo-Saxon
financial institution (i.e. an overall bonus pool being determined for
the firm as a whole) followed by a negotiation by divisions as to how
much they are allocated, divisional performance being the key determinant. There is no upper or lower limit, but employees can earn

more than 100% of their annual salary. It is possible to receive no bonus at all, although in practice this is still quite rare.

The system at Chugai had not changed substantially insofar as bonus was still expressed in multiples of monthly salary. However, there had been an increase in bonus variability, with a greater emphasis on individual performance. At F-Services Co 1, the method of bonus payment had not altered greatly, with a fixed five months (two months in summer, three in winter), with the increased variability coming from the fact that there was now more salary variation than before. In F-Services Co 1, there was an extra element of bonus (discussed below) that was explicitly linked with company performance.

Stock options and other forms of remuneration

Although it is true that schemes such as stock option plans are still not commonly used in Japan, and that setting up such schemes is much more cumbersome than it is in countries such as the UK or the US, it is still a little surprising that only two of the case study companies have ventured beyond the traditional salary and bonus concept of remuneration. Nissan have introduced a stock option scheme for the top 500 executives of the firm, which they were considering expanding to a wider group of employees.

A major break with tradition, and the carefully preserved sense of equality that pervades Japanese organisations, was Nissan's remuneration policy towards directors. Total pay for directors at Nissan is now many times what it was at the old Nissan. According to the 2006–2007 annual report, total compensation for the nine directors of the company amounted to ¥2.518 billion (an average of ¥280 million per director, or approximately US$2.8 million each). While this may not be out of line with compensation levels at other global firms based in North America or Europe, it has drawn a considerable degree of press comment in Japan. By way of comparison, in 2006–2007 Toyota's thirty directors received an aggregate ¥2.492 billion (or an average of ¥83 million per director, or approximately $830,000) which itself represents a slight decrease from 2002–2003 (average of ¥91 million) despite a 76% growth in net income in the intervening five years.

In addition to the fixed bonus scheme, F-Services Co 1 introduced a scheme which exists for other members of the parent company's global employee base called the "short-term incentive plan" ("STIP") which was calculated using a number of profitability, cash flow and customer satisfaction measures. It also included an element to incentivise managers to meet particular corporate goals that the company might have had at any given time, such as increasing the share of data transmission as a share of total revenue.

Employee reaction

Given the extent of change in the remuneration system at Shinsei it is not surprising that the employees there felt the change most keenly. While there were some areas where seniority was still quite prevalent, particularly among the old LTCB client relationship managers, other areas had moved over more or less completely to a merit- and results-based environment. The reaction of the old LTCB employees could be summed up with the following comment from a deputy general manager:

In principle pay is based on performance and skills. People understand that the days when your salary would rise naturally by just keeping your nose clean are over. It will not go up unless you actually make a visible contribution and we do have people in their 20s who earn more than people in their 40s.

At Chugai, employees perceived seniority as being less important a determinant of reward, something attributed by many to the influence of the former Nippon Roche employees who had joined the firm. A manager in Chugai's HR department said:

I think this trend [i.e. seniority] has been changing. It used to be very uncommon for someone to be reporting to a boss younger than they were and now there's more of it. The phenomenon of getting paid more just because you're older is also disappearing. I think it's unstoppable. There's definitely been an influence from Roche in this respect.

It was perhaps somewhat surprising that Nissan employees appeared to perceive the least change to their system of remuneration. Many of the employees interviewed, while acknowledging that a remuneration system based on seniority was a thing of the past, nevertheless felt that this had not actually made any significant difference to their take-home pay. The following comment from a middle-ranking manager may reflect the more gradual approach that the company's management has in forcing the pace:

I don't think there's been much change. Of course there are exceptions, with young people receiving a high evaluation and getting well paid, but overall, it's much the same as before. The company has abolished seniority as an element of salary determination but this has not been reflected in the actual result. I don't think that's necessarily a bad thing. It's probably better to implement this type of thing gradually.

This more "balanced" approach (to use the words of Thierry Moulonguet, the Nissan CFO quoted above) manifested itself in a greater emphasis on benchmarking, more targeting of promising younger managers for promotion, which in turn led to more instances of employees reporting to executives younger than themselves, but not the more dramatic pay differentials that had developed at Shinsei.

In practice, according to many respondents, for people in the middle of the pack not a lot had changed in terms of reward. The impact was felt most keenly by those at either edge of the performance distribution curve. Thus, at F-Services Co 1, one manager noted:

There is a tendency to mark people in the middle during evaluations and maybe from that point of view things aren't so different and that's something HR is thinking about. But at the extremes, people who really didn't perform used to be promoted and they are now being marked down. Also, I think outstanding people are being pushed up quicker.

Not surprisingly, many employees had misgivings about the new, more meritocratic, system of rewards. Its fairness and objectivity were questioned. Even some who had benefited under the new system expressed reservations. A young executive at F-Services Co 1 who had been promoted rapidly since the takeover summed up the advantages of the old system:

I was promoted before a lot of people and I'm sure there are many who have doubts about that ... There are these new rules for promotion established by HR but it seems to me that many of those being promoted are not being promoted in accordance with those rules. Somehow, the old seniority system seemed fairer. Age is quite an objective thing.

This is one of several examples we have seen of employees displaying sensitivity to the opinion of others and a sense of unease, perhaps even guilt, that they have been singled out prematurely for favourable treatment over others.

At Shinsei, it was clear that, for some of the old LTCB employees, it would take some time to get used to the new remuneration philosophy. The feeling of change was accentuated by the new working environment in which responsibilities were clearly laid out in job descriptions and there was a perception that the new employees stuck to their jobs and did not "muck in" to fill gaps like the old LTCB employees would do unquestioningly in the old organisation. Second, in a homogeneous and closely knit hierarchical order of the kind that existed at the old LTCB, excessive rewards to any one individual were bound to invite criticism and make the employee's life uncomfortable in the same way that it did for the F-Services Co 1 employee above. Whereas raised eyebrows would be quite commonplace in the new environment, they would have been far less welcome at the old LTCB. The comment of an old LTCB employee illustrates the complex way group solidarity is affected by efforts to single out high-performing individuals more clearly:

[Money] does become important, but for the old LTCB people it's still not just about money. If for some reason I get a much bigger bonus than other people, I'm sure that would change the way people look at me. For people who come in from the outside, they don't have that feeling. They think that those were the terms on which they were hired so it's quite OK to receive a big bonus. Their relationship with their colleagues is quite different.

We can see that, in attempting to align HR policies to "global best practice" in institutionally distant mergers, the issue of remuneration represents a significant challenge. A stronger emphasis on individualism and financial reward in a system in which a homogeneous group of insiders with a strong sense of cohort identity have dominated does not necessarily have the desired results, at least initially. Understanding the starting point of employees is clearly an important step in designing a path to a new destination.

Rewards: what are the new success factors?

The change in career success factors is summarised Table 5.6.

Table 5.6 *Change in career success factors*

Career success factors
Q: To what extent have the factors that determine career success changed?
1 = not changed
2 = changed somewhat
3 = changed a great deal

Nissan	Chugai	Shinsei	F-Svcs Co 1	F-Svcs Co 2	Total	
3.00	1.69	2.79	2.80	2.36	2.51	
Male	Female	Career	MCH	20–35 yrs	35–45 yrs	45 yrs +
2.54	2.36	2.57	2.31	2.38	2.48	2.61

n = 60

The nature of the people perceived as likely to succeed in the new environment changed significantly. The apparently anomalous reading is again Nissan, where, despite only a moderate perception that seniority had given way to meritocracy, every single employee who was interviewed was under the strong impression that the organisation demanded new and different skills to succeed. In line with our previous findings, male, older and career employees were more likely to perceive change than female, young and mid-career hire employees.

In a Japanese organisation, it was clear that, while the concepts such as knowledge, ability, skills and leadership were important, they took on a slightly different meaning under foreign ownership and needed to be displayed in a different way, particularly at the junior and middle-management level. A large number of case company interviewees referred to "*chōsei nōryoku*", which literally means the "ability to coordinate", as being a key skill for getting on in the old organisation. This referred to one's ability to create consensus by communicating with people within one's own division or department and with people within other divisions and departments to iron out differences in opinion to get a proposal through.

Employees who were seen as high-fliers at large Japanese firms tended to be from the prestigious universities and, as the old organisations emphasised generalists over specialists, it was important not to have had a narrowly focused career. A former Nippon Roche employee at Chugai observed:

Chugai put more emphasis on balance. So they don't want people with extreme leadership qualities. I think it's the result of a system that brings up generalists. In a hierarchical organisation like Chugai's, it's people who understand the total organisation and how to get things done within it that do well. In Japanese society we don't like people who are extreme.

In a more hierarchical organisation, the attribute of a "balanced" style of leadership and the ability to coordinate smoothly between individuals and groups was seen as a positive. In a fluid, loose organisation, however, a more extreme and individualistic form of leadership was seen to be more likely to succeed.

On becoming a foreign firm, the pressure to produce results was much more keenly felt by individuals, and it was first and foremost individuals who could "perform" that were seen to be rewarded. However, it was clear that "performance" was not just about producing results. It also entailed letting those around you know that you were the one to have produced the results. Many emphasised that presentation skills, and particularly a facility with English, were critical in the new organisation. You were much more likely to be accepted than before if you were apt to speak out and get your opinion heard. Thus, a female manager in the sales department of F-Services Co 2 remarked:

It's important to be able to present yourself and your opinions. You have to be a good speaker, someone who can persuade other people. It was the same in the Japanese organisation but actually people who voiced their own opinions too strongly were rather disliked. They are the "sticking-out nail" that are supposed to be hammered in in Japanese society, but they are liked by foreigners because they speak their own opinions clearly.

Most of all, it was the definition of leadership that was changing at these organisations, from one which emphasised stability and internal coordination to something more extreme and outward looking. A senior manager of F-Services Co 1's customer services department summed up the change:

Before it was based on seniority. Now, the company is much younger, from the President downwards. People with leadership skills get promoted and this quality of leadership is different between a Japanese company and a foreign company. In a Japanese company, you've got to be good at negotiating with the people around you, whereas foreigners have a more direct style of leadership. They are clear in their pursuit of company objectives in terms of profit and, based on that, they inspire their subordinates to follow.

Summary

At Japanese firms, there have been changes to the system of rewards, with a more scientific and quantitative approach emphasising ability and contribution over seniority. The "taken-for-granted" nature of annual salary increases that used to occur under the *teiki shōkyū* system has disappeared and the widespread introduction of the annual contract system (*nenpōsei*) has meant that, theoretically at least, salary can go down as well as up. However, changes in the systems of evaluation and pay has not necessarily resulted in employees actually being paid any differently. The difficulties many Japanese firms have had in implementing performance-based pay systems demonstrates how difficult it is to shift deeply institutionalised practices, particularly those with normative foundations.

At most case companies, a key part of the enhanced "performance culture" demanded by the new management was a greatly enhanced market-oriented reward structure designed to separate more clearly employees who produced and who were either leaders or identified as leadership material. This manifested itself in a clear break from the "late promotion" system (Koike, 1994) with much faster promotion to the rank of manager and a widening out of cohort pay differentials. There was also a general feeling that a different type of person was destined to reach the top echelons of management.

References

Abegglen, J.C. (1958) *The Japanese Factory: Aspects of Its Social Organisation*. Boston, MA: Massachusetts Institute of Technology Press

and Stalk, G. (1985) *Kaisha, the Japanese Corporation*. New York, NY: Basic Books

Aera (2008) "Midoru No Fukken Koso Datsu Seikashugi No Kadai" ("The Restoration of Middle Management and 'De-Meritocratization'"). 7 April: 16–21

Aoki, M. (1990) "Towards an Economic Model of the Japanese Firm", *Journal of Economic Literature*, 28: 1–27
    (1994) "The Japanese Firm as a System of Attributes: A Survey and Research Agenda". In M. Aoki and R. Dore (eds.) *The Japanese Firm: Sources of Competitive Strength*. Oxford: Oxford University Press

Beck, J. C. and Beck, M. N. (1994) *The Change of a Lifetime: Employment Patterns among Japan's Managerial Elite*. Honolulu, HI: University of Hawaii Press

Cole, R. E. (1971) *Japanese Blue Collar: The Changing Tradition*. Berkeley, CA: University of California Press

Dore, R. (1973) *British Factory – Japanese Factory: The Origins of National Diversity in Industrial Relations*. Berkeley, CA: University of California Press
    (2000) *Stock Market Capitalism: Welfare Capitalism. Japan and Germany versus the Anglo-Saxons*. Oxford: Oxford University Press

Gordon, R. J. (1982) "Why U.S. Wage and Employment Behaviour Differs from That in Britain and Japan", *The Economic Journal*, March, 13: 44

Hashimoto, M. (1979) "Bonus Payments, On-the-Job Training, and Lifetime Employment in Japan", *Journal of Political Economy*, 87: 1086–1104

Hirakubo, N. (1999) "The End of Lifetime Employment in Japan", *Business Horizons*, November–December: 41–44

Hori, S. (1993) "Fixing Japan's White-Collar Economy: A Personal View", *Harvard Business Review*, November–December: 157–172

Itami, H. (1994) "The 'Human-Capital-Ism' of the Japanese Firm as an Integrated System". In K. Imai and R. Komiya (eds.) *Business Enterprise in Japan*. Cambridge MA: MIT Press

Itoh, H. (1994) "Japanese Human Resource Management from the Viewpoint of Incentive Theory". In M. Aoki and R. Dore (eds.) *The Japanese Firm: Sources of Competitive Strength*. Oxford: Oxford University Press

Joe, S. (2004) *Uchigawa Kara Mita Fujitsu: "Seika Shugi" No Houkai (The Inside of Fujitsu: The Collapse of Performance-Related Pay)*. Tokyo: Kobunsha

Koike, K. (1994) "Intellectual Skills and Long-Term Competition". In K. Imai and R. Komiya (eds.) *Business Enterprise in Japan*. Cambridge, MA: MIT Press

(1994) "Learning and Incentive Systems in Japanese Industry". In M. Aoki and R. Dore (eds.) *The Japanese Firm: Sources of Competitive Strength.* Oxford: Oxford University Press

Koshiro, K. (1994) "The Employment System and Human Resource Management". In K. Imai and R. Komiya (eds.) *Business Enterprise in Japan.* Cambridge MA: MIT Press

Lincoln, J.R. and Kalleberg, A.L. (1990) *Culture, Control, and Commitment: A Study of Work Organization and Work Attitudes in the United States and Japan.* Cambridge: Cambridge University Press

Mincer, J. and Higuchi, Y. (1987) "Wage Structures and Labor Turnover in the US and in Japan", *NBER Working Paper Series* (Cambridge, MA): 1–43

Nihon Keizai Shimbun (2004) "Teiki Shoukyuu Minaoshi Ichinen De 14.3%" ("14.3% Revise Regular Salary Increase System During the Past Year"), 23 June, 15

Rebick, M. (2001) "Japanese Labor Markets: Can We Expect Significant Change?" In M. Blomstrom, B. Gangnes and S. La Croix (eds.) *Japan's New Economy: Continuity and Change in the Twenty-First Century.* Oxford: Oxford University Press

(2005) *The Japanese Employment System.* Oxford: Oxford University Press

Sato, H. (1997) "Human Resource Management Systems in Large Firms". In M. Sako (ed.) *Japanese Labour and Management in Transition.* London: Routledge

Shibata, H. (2002) "Wage and Performance Appraisal Systems in Flux: A Japan–United States Comparison", *Industrial Relations*, 41: 629–652

Uchida, K. (2006) "Determinants of Stock Option Use by Japanese Companies", *Review of Financial Economics*, 15: 251–269

6 | Female employees

I T MIGHT be argued that the issue of gender does not fit easily into the "varieties of capitalism" debate, nor has much relevance to the theoretical coverage of the "organisation-oriented" vs "market-oriented" ideology. Indeed, the varieties of capitalism literature has little, if anything, to say on gender. However, it was my experience working for a foreign firm in Japan that many ambitious female university graduates would express a strong preference for working in a foreign firm, where they saw their prospects for advancement as being far greater than in a Japanese firm (e.g. Ono and Piper, 2001). This same phenomenon would not exist in western countries and gender is an important element in determining the allocation of resources in firms operating in a traditional communitarian framework. It is therefore worth exploring changes in HR policies, and the reaction of employees, particularly females, when a Japanese firm is taken over by a western one.

The rights of female employees, or rather the lack of them, within the Japanese employment system, has been a consistent theme within organisational literature on Japan. Abegglen (1958, p. 75) wrote: "there is no more striking instance of the kind of tension and other strains caused by the lag between changes in the broader society and the present factory system than the role of women in the Japanese company".

There is no doubt that the role of women in Japanese society has changed a great deal since the end of World War II. The mass transfer from the agricultural to the manufacturing sector before and after the war contributed greatly to the growth in output, particularly in the automotive and electronics sectors, and the labour participation rate of women has risen gradually to match the 60% OECD average in recent years. The increase in educational attainment of Japanese women has led to a gradual erosion in the earnings gap with men (Rebick, 2005). Legislation, as well as court decisions, during the last half century, has gone a long way to emancipate Japanese women as well as to reinforce the principle of gender equality. The Equal Employment Opportunites Law of 1985 was designed to provide a comprehensive platform for eliminating discrimination against female employees. Moreover, in a rapidly ageing society, where a decreasing working population gives the Japanese an in-built output-growth disadvantage, the issue of how to increase female participation has in recent years received wider media and academic attention. By increasing the female participation rate from the current 60% to US levels (just under 70%), an extra 4 million people would be added to the workforce (*Nihon Keizai Shimbun*, 2007).

However, it is also true to say that women still expect to fulfil the role of housewife and mother on a full-time basis and, to a great extent, this "idealised" figure of womanhood appears still to be firmly entrenched, particularly among university-educated women (Sasagawa, 2006). This has led to a persistence of the so-called "M-curve", showing the tendency of women to drop out of the labour market after childbirth, to re-enter it at a later stage in their lives, most commonly in their late 30s and in non-regular employment (Nakata and Takehiro, 2002). This reinforces the idea of a distinctive "female employment system". The very same laws that promote equality have also constrained opportunities for women by protecting them on physiognomic grounds (Macnaughtan, 2006). While the wage gap with men has narrowed, the disparity is still, after Korea, the largest among OECD countries. Gender is the most significant explanatory factor behind wage differentials (Tachibanaki, 1996; Tachibanaki and Taki, 2000). As we saw in Figure 5.1 age has a very different effect on the wages of Japanese men and women. The difference is particularly marked for high school graduates.

At the management level, women are very under-represented in Japanese firms. In 1999, Japanese women accounted for only 8.2% of corporate managers, compared to 43% in the US, 33% in the UK and 26% in Germany (Gross, 1999). Many Japanese firms still divide employees, particularly white-collar, into two categories, *sōgōshoku* and *ippanshoku*,[1] with the latter generally being understood to refer to female clerical staff (commonly known as "office ladies"). In a survey

---

[1] *Sōgōshoku* literally means "comprehensive employees" and refers to employees who are on the fast track to management positions recruited

of 215 companies of various sizes conducted in 2000–2001, it was found that 168 firms still made this distinction, and that of the total of 139,322 *sōgōshoku* employees at the 168 firms, only 3,042 (2.2%) were female (JIL, 2001).

The government has been attempting to effect change and there has been considerable legislative activity. An important milestone for the rights of female employees was the 1985 Equal Employment Opportunities Law, which entitled females to exactly the same rights of employment as males. With the passage of this act, companies that had not hitherto employed any females in their executive streams began to do so and, to this extent, there was some change, particularly in the white-collar sector. However, much of the onus on the part of companies to comply with its statutes were of a voluntary nature, and there were no penalties laid down for non-compliance. Ultimately there was little change in the more front-line workplaces (e.g. the factory floor) as the law restricting female working hours both institutionalised and legitimated separate career paths for male and female employees (Sutoh, 2002).

Recent developments

Social consensus appears to be changing slowly. For female employees at the bottom of the employment ladder (i.e. the vast majority) prospects, if anything, have worsened. Office ladies working in administrative functions who might have been hired previously as *ippanshoku* would at least have been treated as full-time employees (which they were) even if the expectation was that they would leave when they got married, or became pregnant. At many large Japanese firms, these administrative jobs have been "de-regularised" and transferred to external outsourcing companies. At a recent visit to the headquarters of a large Japanese manufacturing company, I was told that there were almost no regular female employees left in the entire building.

Expectations of female employees, both by the employers and by the female employees themselves, have been slow to change. In a recent survey, it was found that over two-thirds of women left their

directly from universities. *Ippanshoku* means "ordinary employees" and refers to clerical staff who are recruited from high school or junior college (i.e. two-year universities).

job on the birth of their first baby and did not return (JIL, 2003). Even among university graduates, nearly half of all females who have left employment to raise children would prefer to work part-time, effectively sealing off a managerial career for women (Rebick, 2001).

More recently, however, economic recovery and demographic reality have encouraged Japanese firms to re-examine the role of women in management. By 2009, Asahi Life Insurance aim to increase the ranks of female managers by 50%, Kirin Brewery to 100 from the current 31 by 2015 with Sharp doubling the number of female executives in one year to 60. An important part of this process will be making it easier for female employees to re-enter the firm after a period of three to five years of looking after ageing parents or giving birth. Mitsubishi Corporation, Mitsui & Co, Toppan Printing and Toshiba are among a number of firms that have announced these changes to employment practices recently (*Nihon Keizai Shimbun*, 2007).

One increasingly attractive alternative for female Japanese white-collar workers is to work for a foreign firm. Returns to seniority have been demonstrated to be less marked at foreign firms in Japan. Foreign firms also have a reputation for low employment security, which is partially compensated for by higher wages. Female employees, less likely to be able to make long-term career commitments, are more likely to be attracted to the higher-risk, higher-return proposition offered by foreign firms (Ono and Odaki, 2004). As a result, women made up a higher percentage of the management cadre at foreign firms in 2003 (12.3%) than at Japanese firms (5.5%). Three of the top ten firms in Japan with the highest percentage of females of management grade are foreign: L'Oréal Japan (ranked top with 51.6%), Manpower Japan (31.3%) and Unilever Japan (21.9%) (Sakaguchi and Miyake, 2008). Employees at foreign firms are also entitled to more annual leave and actually take more of their leave entitlement, and work fewer hours, than at domestic firms. They are better suited to female work patterns and family obligations (JILPT, 2005). Macnaughtan (2006), however, suggests that even in the case of foreign-affiliated firms in Japan, "where there is deemed to be a greater sense of awareness of gender equality in the workplace and a greater attempt made to tap into a pool of under-employed and well-educated women in the labour market, there is still a large gender divide because of the affiliate's very operation in the Japanese market" (p. 44).

Female employees

Communitarian template:

- low level of recruitment of females into the executive stream;
- few females in the management group;
- persistence of the *sōgōshoku* vs *ippanshoku* divide.

Conclusions from the literature:

- there are some signs of changing attitudes even in traditional industries (Sutoh, 2002);
- there is still strong normative pressure for women to conform to traditional roles (Rebick, 2001);
- women continue to be under-represented in management – large wage gaps still exist with male employees (Wakisaka, 1997).

While recognising that complete equality would be difficult to achieve, especially in the short term, we would nevertheless expect there to be:

- a more active effort to promote female managers, and
- more female managers as a result,

at a Japanese company taken over by foreigners.

Table 6.1 below would seem to indicate that there has been some change at the comparator companies, with two companies, J-Services Co and J-Pharma Co, showing a marked increase in the number of female executives as a percentage of the total. The number of female executives at J-Manufacturing Co doubled during the period 1998–2003, although from a low base. The company did not start recruiting females into the managerial stream until 1990. At J-Utility Co, only 3.5% of the total workforce is female. Of the 80 managerial stream employees hired every year, ten are female and none are of management grade (the highest-ranking female in 2004 was an assistant manager, who joined in 1990). Until recently, late shift working for female employees was legally a problem and the HR department pointed to the tendency for females to leave the company once they married or started a family. Average annual turnover for female staff was just under 8%, ten times that of male employees.

In terms of the percentage of management-grade staff who are females, the comparator companies lag considerably behind the

Table 6.1 *Female executives: comparator vs case companies*

	Females as % of executives	
	1998	*2003*
J-Mfg Co	0.1%	0.2%
Nissan	0.3%	1.5%
J-Phma Co	0.5%	1.1%
Chugai	1.7%	3.0%
J-Fin Co	1.2%	1.0%
Shinsei	1.0%	10.0%
J-Svcs Co	0.9%	2.5%
F-Svcs Co 1	0.2%	3.4%

national average, where 5.5% of managers (*kachō*), and 3.2% of general manager-grade employees, are female (JIL, 2001).

As mentioned above, an important feature of Japanese companies is the split between *ippanshoku* (clerical stream) and *sōgōshoku* (executive stream). We found at all the comparator companies that this distinction persists and there are no plans to end it. This again is in line with national practice.

Case companies

In the area of gender equality, we do see quite a dramatic difference between the case and comparator companies. Shinsei's move has been the most eye-catching, but the other three companies have also greatly increased the number of female executives.

The changes appeared to come as a result of three factors. The first was a more direct top-down intervention by the new management, which was exemplified by the case of Shinsei, where the president was clearly committed to increasing the number of women in the management ranks. He had asked each of the divisions to double the number of female managers within three years and this message was clearly understood by the employees. This has led to a remarkable ten-fold increase in the number of female managers as a percentage of total management-grade employees, as can be seen in Table 6.1 above. The company opened a childcare facility at its head office in September 2003, and in the last three years over 94% of female employees who took maternity leave returned to the bank. Since the opening of the child-care centre, applications from female university graduates have increased between 20 and 30%.

Second, even if it was not part of a conscious effort to increase the number of female managers, by increasing the number of mid-career hires the number of female managers increased naturally. This was partly because Japanese females apparently have a better command of English. A manager from F-Services Co noted:

Before we didn't recruit many management-grade (*sōgōshoku*) females so there weren't that many to promote. The female executives we have taken on recently are on the whole bi-lingual. If you want to recruit mid-career hires and you establish a condition that they be bilingual, you always end up with more female candidates.

In the case of Chugai, there was an influx of female managers from Nippon Roche, which was responsible for the creation of a new environment and the possibility of the faster advancement of female employees in the future. A manager from the HR department noted:

I think Chugai was more advanced in its thinking towards women than the average Japanese company but, despite that, we had no female general managers. Now that we have merged, we do now have a number of female general managers and the atmosphere has changed. Females make their opinions heard much more in the workplace and we need proper explanations for why people aren't promoted.

Employee perception

The change in opportunities for female employees is summarised in Table 6.2. Notwithstanding the jump in female executives, especially compared with the comparator companies, overall the scores for perceived change in the treatment of female employees were among the lowest of any of the domains. Only at two companies, Shinsei and F-Services Co 1, was the average perception greater than "changed somewhat". There was not significant inter-employee group variation, but females themselves, as well as younger employees, were less likely to perceive change.

This finding was slightly at odds with the fact that there had clearly been an effort at all the case study companies to promote

Table 6.2 *Change in opportunities for female employees*

Female employees
Q: To what extent are there greater/less opportunities for women to advance in this company? 1 = no change[2] 2 = somewhat greater 3 = much greater

Nissan	Chugai	Shinsei	F-Svcs Co 1	F-Svcs Co 2	Total	
1.82	1.62	2.33	2.20	1.64	1.92	
Male	Female	Career	MCH	20–35 yrs	35–45 yrs	45 yrs +
1.94	1.82	1.96	1.77	1.63	1.97	1.94

female executives, with the most dramatic increases between 1998 and 2003 taking place at Nissan, Chugai and F-Services Co. Fully 10% of employees in managerial posts (defined as manager, or *kachō*, and above) at Shinsei were females, compared to only 1% in 1998.

There was substantial evidence of conservative attitudes prior to acquisition and this can be seen from the extremely low numbers of female managers at Nissan and F-Services Co 1. A potent symbol separating male and female employees were the uniforms that female *ippanshoku* staff were expected to wear. An important change was therefore the abolition of the uniform, one of the first moves made by the new management. In the words of the head of retail sales at Shinsei:

We had uniforms to accentuate the difference between male and female employees. So from day one, the CEO said "no uniforms". There was consternation. People didn't understand what that had to do with performance and meritocracy. But looking back, I think it was important because it made people realise there was no difference between male and female when it came to performance.

---

[2] There were no responses that opportunities had decreased. I have therefore graded the responses differentiating between perceived increases in opportunities.

At Nissan, F-Services Co 1 and F-Services Co 2, there were attempts to change the cultures of the firms to create a more hospitable environment for female employees and there was a certain amount of success, although it was uneven across divisions. One female executive from Nissan's finance department said:

There are areas of course where Renault has made a difference. For example Moulonguet-san [CFO seconded from Renault] is very keen to see women advance and he has helped me with my career. The Finance Department was a difficult place for women to work and they didn't tend to last very long but it's better now. The situation will improve further over time and this will be a combination of overall social change, accelerated by the "Renault factor".

Generally, those in charge of HR would indicate that the company was fully committed to promoting equal opportunities regardless of gender, but the message was not getting through. A young female executive at F-Services Co 1 noted:

I don't think a lot has changed with the merger with [the parent company]. There aren't so many female managers. I don't think it's necessarily unequal, but I don't think the company has made a really big effort to create a workplace where women can build a career and cope with family pressures. There are companies in Japan that seem to make a special effort to help working mothers. I'm married but don't have children yet but I'm wondering what's going to happen if I start a family.

Even in the cases of executives who thought that the message was getting through, larger, societal, factors were cited as to the reasons more progress was not being made. Thus, a senior (male) executive at Nissan, who had spent many years in the company's US operations, observed:

This has still a long way to go. It was zero before so it's certainly better than that, but compared to the US, it's still pretty backward. This is not just a problem for Nissan but Japanese society at large. But the message to the staff is clear and the company appears to be determined to do something about it.

If one looks at the increase in the number of female executives at the case companies, there would appear to be quite strong erosion of institutionalised practices concerning the promotion of female executives. However, it is also clear that mere top-down desire for change was not going to be sufficient to achieve it. What was required was a combination of a long-term strategy to alter the attitudes of both male and female employees, plus the resources to create an infrastructure for women to participate more fully in the workforce. Even at the apparently most progressive of the case companies, Shinsei Bank, the management appreciated that numerical targets for female managers would not be enough. In a recent interview, Tom Pedersen, Deputy General Manager of the Investment Banking Division, said:

I think we hit our 20% target of [titled employees being women] last year. But there's a lot more that we can do. Even within gender diversity, it's a lot more complex than saying a certain amount of women ought to be in titled positions. Gender diversity, I believe, is about recognising that individual employees have different aspirations about how they engage work. What if someone wants to take a career break to have a child? How do they re-enter work? What about the women who aspire to those leadership roles versus the women that don't want to? How do we accommodate them, and what specific programmes do we put in place for them? How do we take something like this very innovative childcare centre concept that we have available to attract and retain a key demographic force? Those are the more difficult things. It's very easy to say "20%" but what happens when you over-promote people when you have this goal and you don't develop them or you don't look at their total career? Again, it has some unintended consequences and we are living with some of those. We need to have holistic, sustainable, well thought-through solutions to this. They're not slogans, they have to be backed up by substance.

The company has justifiably developed a reputation for innovative solutions for increasing female participation in management and, in many of the interviews, there was a sense from both the old LTCB employees as well as those who had come in from the outside that the management had a clear commitment to achieve its goals in this area. Even here, however, it is clear that establishing numerical goals and making crèche facilities available at the head office represent only small steps on the long road to the achievement of gender equality.

Equality of opportunity across gender is clearly not just a Japanese issue. Some Japanese case company employees who had travelled to their new overseas headquarters had noticed that the situation there was only slightly better. However, attitudes in Japan have been particularly conservative and this has led to difficulties for female advancement. One gets the feeling that, however hard the management of the case companies tried, embedded societal norms would ensure that progress towards gender equality would be slow: getting male employees to accept the prospect of a female boss continued to present difficulties. One case company manager summed up the problem:

I don't think we will revert to the old "we can't hire so many women as they will go off and get married and have babies" philosophy. We simply need good people and we can't be constrained like that. However, I think in many ways the old thinking remains, and that goes for the way males, including me, would think if they had a female boss. I think most people would think that it just wouldn't go as well compared with having a male boss. This is a problem for Japan as a whole ...

Summary

Across the board, there appeared to be greater opportunities for female employees at the case study firms compared to the comparator firms. Symbols such as uniforms were abolished, as well as the distinction between *ippanshoku* and *sōgōshoku*. One firm in particular, Shinsei, had increased the number of female employees in management positions. However, the perception of change among the employees, both male and female, at the case companies was not as great as one might have expected and was the lowest of the domains that we examined. Again, this suggests that changing ownership is not of itself a sufficient condition to change deeply entrenched attitudes to gender.

References

Abegglen, J.C. (1958) *The Japanese Factory: Aspects of Its Social Organisation.* Boston, MA: Massachusetts Institute of Technology Press

Aera (2008) "Hataraku Josei No 20 Nen" ("Working Women, 20 Years on") 12 May: 30–33

Gross, A. (1999) "New Trends in Japan's Recruiting Process", *SHRM International Update*

JIL (2001) "Few Female Workers on Management Track", *Japan Labour Bulletin*, 40: 311–325

(2003) "Two-Thirds of Working Women Leave Job upon Birth of First Baby", *Japan Labour Bulletin*, 42: 1–2

JILPT (2005) "Business Management, Personnel Management and Industrial Relations of Foreign-Affiliated Pharmaceutical-Related Firms", *JILPT Research Report*, 20: 10

Macnaughtan, H. (2006) "From 'Post-War' to 'Post-Bubble': Contemporary Issues for Japanese Working Women". In P. Matanle and W. Lunsing (eds.) *Perspectives on Work, Employment and Society in Japan*. Basingstoke: Palgrave

Nakata, Y. and Takehiro, R. (2002) "Employment and Wages of Female Japanese Workers: Past, Present and Future", *Industrial Relations*, 41: 521–547

Nihon Keizai Shimbun (2007) "Josei Wo Chouki Senryaku Ni" ("Making Females Part of Long-Term Strategy)". 1 April

Rebick, M. (2001) "Japanese Labor Markets: Can We Expect Significant Change?" In M. Blomstrom, B. Gangnes and S. La Croix (eds.) *Japan's New Economy: Continuity and Change in the Twenty-First Century*. Oxford: Oxford University Press

(2005) *The Japanese Employment System*. Oxford: Oxford University Press

Sasagawa, A. (2006) "Is It Worth Doing? Educated Housewives' Attitudes Towards Work". In P. Matanle and W. Lunsing (eds.) *Perspectives on Work, Employment and Society in Japan*. Basingstoke: Palgrave

Sutoh, W. (2002) "Joshi Hogo Kitei No Kaisei to Danjo Kongou Shokka" ("The Revision of Rule to Protect Rights of Female Employees and the Gender-Mixed Workplace"). In M. Nitta (ed.) *Roushi Kankei no Shin Seiki (Labour – Management Relations and the New Century)*. Tokyo: Japan Institute of Labour

Tachibanaki, T. (1996) *Wage Determination and Distribution in Japan*. Oxford: Oxford University Press

and Taki, A. (2000) *Capital and Labour in Japan: The Functions of Two Factor Markets*. London: Routledge

Wakisaka, A. (1997) "Women at Work". In M. Sako (ed.) *Japanese Labour and Management in Transition*. London: Routledge

7 | *Organisation and decision-making process*

Board of directors

Given the status of the Japanese company as an "organic community which admits selected recruits to life membership" as opposed to the paradigm of employment of the British company being based on the "contract, specific in its obligations and limited in time by a specified period of notice" (Dore, 1973, p. 222), it follows that the standing of the company's directors should be different. Dore likens the board of Hitachi to a "council of elders of the corporate community", in contrast to the board of English Electric, a "collection of men appointed for their capacity to contribute to the direction of the company in the best interests of the shareholders" (p. 223).

At the top of the organisation, the concept of "leadership" as embodied by the CEO also deviates from the Anglo-Saxon norm, being about "creating the atmosphere within the firm that ensures that all employees work as hard and as conscientiously and as cooperatively as possible so that all the decentralised decision-producing structures of the firm produce the best decisions" (Dore, 1994, p. 381). The recent trend in the US for company boards where the majority of directors are external, and the increasing trend in choosing CEOs from outside the firm (Khurana, 2002), has not remotely affected Japan. The Japanese CEO is almost always an insider. Unless the firm is controlled by a foreign company, he is invariably Japanese (and, of course, male). He is on average much older than his counterparts in other countries[1] and is less well paid.[2] He has achieved his position because of the

---

[1] According to a study of the world's top 2,500 publicly traded companies by Booz, Allen and Hamilton, the Japanese CEO started his tenure at an average age of 58.4 years, compared with 49.1 years for the US, 50 for Europe and 47.4 for non-Japan Asia. See *Nikkei Shimbun*, 9 July 2004.

[2] A survey by Towers Perrin, a human resource consultant, in 2003 revealed that average CEO compensation in Japan was $456,937, compared with

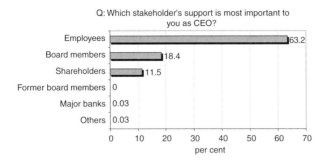

Figure 7.1 Importance of stakeholder support for Japanese CEOs
Source: Yoshimori (1995)

support he has received from the organisation, and it is to the organ-isation that he owes his loyalty. A comprehensive quantitative analysis (Ahn *et al.*, 2004) has shown that Japanese CEO changes, even of the non-routine kind, have little impact on firm performance, firm investment policies, and financial policies. In the survey by Yoshimori (1995) referred to earlier, 113 CEOs of major Japanese corporations were asked whose support was the most important to them. The overwhelming majority indicated that the employees were the most important (see Figure 7.1 above). Radical change or reform, which is likely to harm the interests of the organisation and its employees, would therefore not come easily to him.

Japanese boards are characterised by a number of features. First, they have traditionally been relatively large. In a study of 1,029 Japanese firms listed on the First Section of the TSE by Miwa and Ramseyer (2002), the mean number of directors was 19.5, compared to twelve for US companies. Second, like the CEO, the majority of Japanese board members are insiders, meaning that they have had their careers inside the firm and that there are few non-executive directors. Only 1% of Japanese board members were non-executive directors towards the end of the 1990s (*Global Proxy Watch*, 1997). Of the remain-ing 99%, the great majority will be men who had spent their entire careers with the company. Indeed, the method for selecting those who

$545,024 for CEOs in Brazil, $830,223 in the UK, $954,726 in Germany and $2.2 million in the US. See *The Wall Street Journal Online* (2004) 'American CEOs Meet Resistance when Taking the Helm Overseas', 26 May 1994.

make it to the board is described as "an extension of the *nenko* system for employees" and in these circumstances it is not surprising that directors should "take on the appearance of representatives of their employees" (Imai and Komiya, 1994, p. 22). In Miwa and Ramseyer's study, fourteen of the mean 19.5 directors were career employees. By contrast, of the mean twelve US directors, nine were outside directors and three inside directors (Ahmadjian, 2001).

Decision-making process

Abegglen (1958), not surprisingly, gives a cultural explanation of the Japanese decision-making system, saying that it is rooted in "the tradition of family counsels, in which the entire family joins in reaching a decision about family problems" (p. 62). Insofar as the family and the company are similarly all enveloping, interpersonal relations become the more critical: "it is impossible to expose an individual to the hazard of direct individual responsibility for a decision ... When a man must spend his entire career in one factory or company, it is important that his prestige and reputation and his relations with others retain their integrity. The decision-making system is admirably adapted to this end." Despite the fact the system is slow and cumbersome, "the Japanese choice is in the direction of the support and maintenance of interpersonal relations within the company at the expense of maximum efficiency" (p. 63).

Aoki (1994) sees Japanese organisational design as one consciously fashioned to optimise decisions. In Japanese organisations, while the management may appear very hierarchical from the viewpoint of administrative structure, the distinction between decision making and operational implementation is blurred: "the former function is never limited to management, as operational workers also participate in considerable collective decision-making" (p. 13). Even strategic decisions "are not made unilaterally by top-management on the basis of centralising relevant information, but rather are formed inductively through intensive vertical exchanges of information and opinions across various levels of administrative hierarchy" (p. 13). This non-hierarchical information system, combined with extensive job rotation, maximises organisational information sharing and is, in turn, combined with an incentive system that minimises threats to senior and middle management who therefore are willing to delegate responsibility to a far greater degree than in western organisations.

Oliver and Wilkinson (1992), in developing a dependency relations model for the Japanese organisational form, identified a high level of inter-dependency in Japanese organisations. Strategies of direct control require a strict division of labour and tight control, while those of responsible autonomy, found in Japanese organisations, entail "delegation of authority down the organisation ... [and] is closely related to an organisational design based on self-contained tasks (work teams, cells and so on) and also on lateral communication and a customer-oriented ethos" (p. 81). While considerable power is distributed to lower parts of the organisation in the form of heightened responsibilities, this also comes with tight controls and high levels of surveillance and monitoring. The control mechanisms are reinforced by measures to reduce "goal heterogeneity", particularly those that give employees long time horizons.

The decision-making process of Japanese companies, with its strongly participative and "bottom-up" flavour, means that little, in the formal sense, has traditionally been decided at the board level. The board certainly has not in the past played a major supervisory role: the board consists of heads of divisions who are not in a position to monitor management – they themselves are the management (Ahmadjian, 2001). By the time any matter has reached the board, it is only for formal rubber-stamping. Prior to that, there will have been a process of formal coordination and informal discussion, both horizontally across the hierarchy and vertically through it, in which the manager, or section chief, plays a key role (Dore, 1973, p. 227). This system is known as the *ringi* system, after the *ringi-sho*, the document that is circulated to which key senior, middle-level and junior employees put their personal seals to indicate that they have participated in the consensus-building process on any given issue. An important part of the process at the board level is the discussion that takes place in the inner circle of the board (*jōmu-kai*), usually consisting of managing directors (*jōmu*) and above, where differences are thrashed out. Even before that takes place, however, there is likely to have been informal negotiation among the key senior directors during the *ringi* consensus-gathering process.

Hierarchy

The finely graded nature of the Japanese organisational hierarchy was observed by Abegglen (1958, p. 58): "there are three main features of main office organisation. First, the organisation is elaborately and minutely divided into separate, formally distinct groupings. Second, a very high proportion of persons hold formal positions and titles. Third, the complexity of the organisation is heightened by the presence of large numbers of deputies and assistants to department and section chiefs." Dore (1973) asserts that the purpose of the more finely graded hierarchy of functional authority positions is to reduce the appearance of "sharp discontinuity breaks". He also comments on the fact that the number of posts is far in excess of what is needed to take and implement decisions and attributes the "latent" function of Japanese hierarchy to the distribution of prestige, a function which "can have just as much ultimate importance for the organisation's effectiveness as the manifest function of distributing authority" (p. 259).

The tight and finely graded hierarchical design also fits well into the dependency relations model where high levels of responsibility are delegated far down the organisation, but are accompanied by high levels of monitoring from above (Oliver and Wilkinson, 1992). This is reinforced by the findings of Lincoln and Kalleberg (1990) who noted that tall, finely graded status hierarchies raised labour commitment and dependency:

by increasing the proportion of employees with management responsibilities as well as the density of relationships formed around a status difference. Moreover, tall hierarchies ... imply job ladders and promotion opportunities which hold out the promise of career advancement to employees who invest heavily in the fortunes of the firm. (p. 183)

It is necessary to distinguish here between "external" and "internal" grades. By "external" I mean the rank that appears on the employee's name card by which he/she is identified to the outside world and which indicates his/her importance within the corporate hierarchy to outsiders. Particularly at the lower levels, there is a wide variety in the nomenclature, with, for example, titles appearing in Japanese banks that do not appear in other industries. Titles on the factory floor are generally quite different from those in administrative functions. Management grades generally begin at *kachō* (manager), then *jichō* (deputy general manager) and then *buchō* (general manager), although there are many variations. *Buchō* was generally the final rank before joining the board, which at Japanese firms was much larger than those at their Anglo-Saxon counterparts, and where the lower-ranked directors would have executive divisional responsibility. As we will see below, companies have in the last ten years been drastically reducing the size of their boards and introducing the "corporate executive officer" system; general managers who were promoted to heads of divisions at firms with this system are now not directors, but *shikkō yakuin* (corporate executive officers).

By "internal", I mean grades which are uniquely tied to each company, which are generally (but not always) tied to the external rank and to which salaries are tied. In Japanese firms, there would traditionally be a large number of these grades to help give employees, particularly those in the first ten years of their career, the sense that they are "moving on", as Dore suggests.

The human resources department

As might be expected in an organisation in which the employee enjoys special status in the governance hierarchy, the department that controls human resources plays a significant role. While we have seen that *de facto* delegation is a key feature of Japanese organisations, the exception is the HR function, which is highly concentrated. Itami (1994) observes:

One rarely finds an American equivalent of a Japanese firm's headquarters Personnel Office. In the United States, personnel decisions depend on department heads; your boss is your personnel officer. In Japan, although department heads contribute personnel evaluations, theirs is not the only input the personnel office receives, and generally departmental heads have no power over job reshuffles. (p. 78)

In a comparative study of US and Japanese HR departments, Jacoby (2005) found that the average tenure of a senior HR executive at Japanese firms was twenty-six years, three times the US figure. Consistent with the concept of job rotation, Japanese HR executives were less likely to be HR specialists, and more likely to have experience in fields other than HR, while 77% of US HR executives had spent their careers in the HR field. A key indicator of the influence of HR was the experience of board members. Some 85% of Japanese board members had at least one member with HR and/or union experience compared with 34% in the US.

The values of Japanese and US HR executives were also contrasted: "maximising the share price" was seventh in the ten priorities for Japanese HR managers; for US managers, it was second. For Japanese HR managers, job security was their second most important concern; for US managers it ranked ninth: "that difference is big, and emblematic of the distinction between the stakeholder (organization-oriented) and the shareholder (market-oriented) visions" (p. 154).

There are signs of change, however, in the standing of the HR department of Japanese companies. The HR department has come in for considerable criticism as representing the forces of reaction. The overwhelming influence of the HR department in controlling the allocation of resources effectively means it has control over a company's strategy, according to its critics (e.g. Yashiro, 1998, p. 47). Jacoby and Saguchi (2002) highlight possible differences in the interpretation of the concept of "strategy": in Japan, strategic decisions are related to identifying and building the company's core competence, with the pool of human resources at the company's disposal, whereas in the US, "growth is more likely to occur through acquisition and divestments, that is, through financially determined criteria for restructuring" (p. 20). In other words, Japan, which lacks a market-related view of human resources, is limited strategically by its current human resources, while for the US firm no such limitation exists.

Recent developments in organisation and the decision-making process

Just as the employment system has proved remarkably impervious to change, the same can be said for the way in which Japanese companies are organised and how decisions are made. On the surface, there appears to have been change. For example, Japanese companies have been urged to speed up their decision-making process by shrinking the size of the board of directors and reducing hierarchy. Calls have been made to improve the monitoring function of boards by increasing the appointment of external directors. To a great extent this has already happened. In 1997, Sony dramatically cut its board from thirty-eight to ten, intending to separate strategic decision making, which would be the board's responsibility, with implementation and operational management the responsibility of "corporate executive officers" (*shikkō yakuin*) who had previously held board positions as the junior directors. Since Sony's move, a large number of other firms have moved to reduce the size of their boards and install the "corporate executive officer" system (see Takahashi, 1999; Tokyo Stock Exchange, 2000).

However, there is a considerable degree of doubt that the system has had any real impact, especially in establishing any form of monitoring role on behalf of shareholders. As Ahmadjian (2001) points out, the end result is that one set of insiders supervises another set – not so different from the previous situation. As far as the speed of decision making was concerned, the purpose of the board in most Japanese companies was to rubber-stamp decisions made by a subset of directors; it is difficult to see how the reduction in board size would make much difference. A report by the Policy Research Institute of the Ministry of Finance concluded that there was no change in the nature or speed of decision making at Japanese companies, and that the introduction of the corporate executive officer system was "nothing more than a cosmetic device to reduce the number of directors" (*Nihon Keizai Shimbun*, 2003, p. 1). There does not appear to be any strong evidence that other features of the decision-making process, and in particular the use of the *ringi*, are undergoing significant change.[3]

To summarise, therefore, the JWCO template for organisation and decision making has the following features:

- large boards, playing a symbolic, rather than an executive or overseeing, role;
- a consensual, bottom-up decision-making process;
- accountability dispersed through the organisation, rather than concentrated on individuals;
- widespread use of the *ringi* system;
- tall, narrow hierarchies;
- a powerful and centralised HR department.

Conclusions from the literature:

- Japanese boards are indeed large and composed largely of insiders, but recent moves to cut board size and introduce the "corporate

---

[3] Although most Japanese companies now have an electronic form of *ringi*, which does hasten the process of minor decision making, such as procurements, expense claims, and so on.

executive officer" system suggest a determination to introduce more clarity and speed into the decision-making process (Takahashi, 1999);

- most firms now have computer-based *ringi* systems, again emphasising speed;
- many commentators, however, suggest that such changes are cosmetic (Ahmadjian, 2001; *Nihon Keizai Shimbun*, 2003);
- the perceived power and influence of the HR department is high but there are some signs of companies trying to cut back the size of HR and decentralise some of its functions (Jacoby, 2005; Yashiro, 1998).

At the case companies, in line with the new management's desire to enhance the "performance culture" of these organisations, it was expected that they would:

- attempt to increase speed of decisions as well as improve quality of decisions;
- attempt to slim down the hierarchy by shrinking the board, removing layers of management;
- increase individual accountability for decisions;
- move away from the consensual, bottom-up style of decision-making to a more top-down approach.

As a result:

- the influence of the HR department would reduce;
- key decisions on human resource matters (recruitment, training, promotion, salary, etc.) would be made by the operating divisions; and
- as a reflection of this, the standing of the head of HR would decline within the firm.

Findings at comparator and case companies: board of directors

There was certainly evidence at the comparator companies of a perception that the decision-making process needed to be overhauled. The starting point was the board; by 2003 there had been substantial reductions in the number of comparator company directors. Whether this was the result of a genuine feeling that faster, better-informed decisions would result is not clear. A senior figure at one comparator company alluded to the strong role that shareholders were exerting to cause the company to reconsider the way its board was structured:

When we are told we have too many directors by institutional investors, we think we should put that in our thinking ... We are responding to external pressure.

In a press release in March 2004, J-Manufacturing Co said that the board would be restructured, a move "aimed at accelerating managerial processes by streamlining the number of board members and at speeding up operations by making the decision-making structure less vertical".[4] As part of this reorganisation, J-Manufacturing Co cut its board by half in 2003. At the same time, they introduced the "corporate officer" system (it will be recalled that the "corporate officer", or *shikkō yakuin*, is more or less equivalent to the old junior board members, who were generally divisional heads). At other firms, too, there have been efforts to slim down the board. Both J-Financial Co and J-Pharma Co have radically cut the number of directors and introduced the corporate officer system.

J-Services Co had slightly increased the number of its board members (by two) in 2003, but in 2005 it introduced the corporate officer system and drastically reduced the size of its board. By the end of the 2006–2007 fiscal year, there were only twelve board members. This brings it more or less in line with the other comparator companies.

Board size

As can be seen in Table 7.1, the comparator firms are making considerable changes to the size of their boards and are introducing the corporate executive officer system. J-Pharma Co has made the most drastic cuts and, with J-Services Co's post-2003 cuts, all the comparator firms have moved decisively to reduce board size.

Case companies

It is clear from Table 7.1 below that the reduction in the number of directors at most of the case firms has been even more dramatic, especially when one strips out the non-executive directors. If one looks at just the executive directors, the contrast is particularly striking. At the

---

[4] Taken from the annual company report.

Table 7.1 *Change in board size: comparator vs case*

	Reduction in board size (2003 as % of 1998)	2003 non-executive directors (% of total directors)	Use corporate officer system (2003)
J-Mfg Co	49	0	Yes[5]
Nissan	20	20	Yes
J-Pharma Co	31	43	Yes
Chugai	85	46	Yes
J-Finance Co	N/A	10	Yes
Shinsei	54	87	Yes
J-Services Co	108	4	No
F-Services Co 1	30	67	Yes

case companies, there are on average 4.5 executive directors at the case companies compared to nineteen at the comparator firms.

The composition of the board is also of interest. At Nissan, Chugai and F-Services Co 2, the heads of the major operating divisions, such as manufacturing, sales, purchasing and R&D, were board members, as were the respective CFOs. Shinsei and F-Services Co 1 had extremely small boards. Shinsei reduced the number of executive directors to two and introduced the "company with committees" board system, in line with Anglo-Saxon governance structures. F-Services Co 1 had only three executive board members, with only the finance function represented at board level.

Hierarchy

J-Manufacturing Co's move in 1990 to reduce layers of management has already been referred to. At that time, the management ranks were, in ascending order of seniority, supervisor (*kakarichō*), deputy manager (*fuku kachō*), manager (*kachō*), chief (*shusa*), deputy general manager (*jichō*) and general manager (*buchō*). As we have seen, after the change, there were only two ranks in the new management

---

[5] J-Manufacturing Co introduced the corporate officer system, coinciding with a considerable reduction in the size of its board in June 2003.

organisation, general manager, and a newly created post, "office head" (*shitsuchō*). While the objective of this change was to reduce the number of "checkers" and increase the number of "doers",[6] the drastic reduction in the number of supervisory staff had some unintended negative consequences, particularly on the passing on of tacit company-specific knowledge from one generation to the next. While the "checkers" continued to have broad training and development responsibilities for their subordinates, the "doers" were evaluated solely on the basis of their output. Thus, when the first line of management suddenly went from "supervisor", who had a responsibility for four to five employees, to "office head", with responsibility for fifty employees, an intolerable strain was put on the system. In the short term, according to one executive, the response was to install two to three "staff leaders" under the office head:

But they didn't officially have a supervisory role; they were still staff. Officially the first line manager was still the *shitsuchō*. But the mentality of the staff leaders was that they were staff, not managers. They would be evaluated on the quality of their output, not on their ability to train staff, as that was not officially part of their responsibility, so there was no incentive to train their juniors. That would just take time and they wouldn't be able to get their own work done.

The overall effect of these changes was to weaken one of the very features that had been seen as a key ingredient to J-Manufacturing Co's success: training and development. The executive continued:

When I joined J-Manufacturing Co, what really impressed me was, when I was having problems at work, the guys who were one or two years above me would call me into their rooms at the bachelors' dorm and tell me what I was doing wrong and how to put it right. They wouldn't say anything at work as they had other responsibilities and there were also other people around. But they would still take the time in the evenings to do this for me. This was very much the culture at J-Manufacturing Co. This was the way they were raised so they did the same for me. This changed a little bit with the organisational change that took place in the late 1980s and that

[6] If the company had not implemented this change, the company would evidently have ended up with 15,000 out of 19,000 head office staff as managers of one sort or another by the end of the 1990s.

weakened the organisation. This stopped the development of young people
that took place so naturally at J-Manufacturing Co before.

A senior member of the HR department takes up the narrative:

After ten years of operating the flat organisation we found that the staff
development had suffered decisive damage. We decided to introduce a new
layer called "*groupchō*" ["group leader"] and in addition to the 200 GMs
and 600 *shitsuchō*s we now have 2,000 of these *groupchō*s. A *groupchō*
usually has about ten employees under him and is somewhere between the
old *kachō* and *kakarichō*. A *kachō* used to have about 20 subordinates
whereas the *kakarichō* had 5 or 6. You would get to *groupchō* in about
eight years at the earliest although some might be in their 40s by the time
they got there. A *groupchō* would often have older people reporting to him,
and this kind of more flexible, merit-based organisation was one of the
merits of the flatter organisation ... So the reason we put in this new layer
of *groupchō*s was that we had confidence that we had a better balance of
managers and staff but also that we needed to restore education as a top
priority as it is a core strength of our group.

In the case of J-Manufacturing Co, therefore, it would appear that,
in attempting to speed up decision making by eliminating layers of
hierarchy, some of the key competitive strengths of the company had
been imperilled and this has resulted in a partial reversal of the policy. Put another way, a key benefit of a finely graded hierarchy is the
clearer responsibility to bring on subordinates, and more scope to be
able to do so. At other firms, as can be seen in Table 7.2 below, there
has not been a great deal of change in the hierarchy.

In a reorganisation in 2004, J-Services Co flattened the internal hierarchy in order to reduce the number of grades and improve communication, and there has been a reduction in the number of internal grades.

At the case companies with the exception of Chugai, where the
number of internal grades has remained the same (six grades, compris-
ing twenty-one different "steps"), they have reduced. Nissan is a typical example. With further changes announced in 2004 (see footnote
8), the number of internal ranks has decreased from twelve grades and
sixty sub-grades in 1998 to six grades and twenty sub-grades in 2004.
At Shinsei, whereas there were six grades with twenty-four sub-grades,
there were now nine grades, with no sub-grades. At F-Services Co 1, the
number was reduced from fourteen to six. There was little change in

Table 7.2 *Comparator and case hierarchy*

	\multicolumn{4}{c}{Hierarchical structure}			
	\multicolumn{2}{c}{External grades}	\multicolumn{2}{c}{Internal grades}
	1998	*2003*	*1998*	*2003*
J-Mfg Co	4	5	11	11
Nissan	5	5	12 (60 sub-grades)[7]	10 (43 sub-grades)[8]
J-Phma Co	5	5	8 (finely graded)	8
Chugai	7	6	6 (21 steps)	6
J-Fin Co	6	6	15	15
Shinsei	3	3	6 (many sub-grades)	9
J-Svcs Co	5	5	19	14
F-Svcs Co 1	9	6	20	6

the external grades, or ranks, of the employees as these were important signals to outsiders (i.e. clients, suppliers, regulators, etc.) as to the significance of the employee within the organisation. To the outside world, therefore, the case company hierarchy looks much the same as before.

There were substantial changes in office layout at Shinsei, F-Services Co 1 and F-Services Co 2 so that it was not easy to understand the departmental hierarchy just by looking at where people were sitting, as one can in a normal Japanese company.

Decision-making process

There has been an emphasis at all comparator firms on speeding up the process of decision making, with the introduction of the corporate officer system being the most obvious manifestation of the change. While all firms use the *ringi* system (and none report fundamental changes to the structure of senior management meetings), the nature of the role of the board, which had not historically been a forum

---

[7] There were thirty-five sub-grades for junior posts, and twenty-five for senior posts.
[8] As of the end of March 2003, there were still thirty-five sub-grades for junior posts, but senior sub-grades had been cut from twenty-five to eight. In 2004, Nissan further cut internal grades to six (from ten) and total sub-grades now number twenty (twelve junior and eight senior).

for serious strategic discussion as there were so many directors, had altered. With slimmed-down boards (only four executive directors at J-Pharma Co and an average of nine at the major operating subsidiaries of the J-Financial Co) there is more strategic content in the discussion and board meetings are less of a formal "rubber stamping" of decisions. At J-Manufacturing Co, there is some feeling that the consensual process through which decisions were arrived at is changing. The former HR executive observed:

> It's become more top-down. We still have the *ringi* system and it's still critical to coordinate between departments but the old system of having people of each rank going around the various departments doing the *nemawashi* has changed. Now it's more a matter of the senior people getting together and deciding something and getting their juniors to sort it out. It's getting much speedier. You need that kind of speed to be promoted now, and there is less emphasis on the ability to create consensus. But the J-Manufacturing Co style of top-down doesn't mean that you ignore the opinions of other departments. It means that the general managers carry out the discussions with the other general managers themselves. That's the way it seems to me. It wasn't so clear before, where the decision was made.

It appears, then, that, at least in the area of decision making, the subtle bottom-up, consensus-driven style is shifting slightly in favour of a more top-down approach.[9] It may also be the case that the kind of people who thrive in the new environment, tomorrow's leaders, are not quite in the same mould as the leaders of today.

Case companies

There was quite sharp inter-company variation in perception of how the decision-making process had changed (see Table 7.3). Great change was noted at Nissan and Shinsei and, to a certain extent, at F-Services Co 1.

---

[9] Dore points out (private correspondence) that there has also been a change in the lateral spread of consultation and this has also had an impact on the speed of decision making. Formerly, any department which would be affected had, at the very least, to be formally consulted before a decision would be declared as having been reached. The narrowing in the range of the consultation process is a significant part, perhaps almost as significant in the reduction of lower-level consultation, of the shift in the decision-making process.

Table 7.3 *Change in the decision-making process*

			Decision-making process			

Q: Has the decision-making process changed since the merger?
1 = no change
2 = changed somewhat
3 = changed a great deal

Nissan	Chugai	Shinsei	F-Svcs Co 1	F-Svcs Co 2	Total	
2.91	1.62	2.80	2.30	1.91	2.32	
Male	Female	Career	MCH	20–35 yrs	35–45 yrs	45 yrs +
2.31	2.36	2.38	2.08	2.25	2.24	2.50

n = 60

Change appeared to be more modest at F-Services Co 2, while the finding at Chugai was very much in line with our other findings at that company. Inter-employee group variation was quite modest although older employees were more prone to perceive change than their younger colleagues.

Generally it was observed that the consensual, bottom-up decision-making process had given way to a more top-down approach. This was strongest at Shinsei and F-Services Co 1, while at Chugai it was felt that the consensual style was still present. At Nissan, it was perceived that the nature of leadership itself had changed and that the nature of the "top-down" process was not simply a matter of the management giving orders for subordinates to follow. What was expected of management was the creation of a vision, with the implementation of the vision being a process in which all employees participated.

The way decisions were arrived at changed in a number of ways. First, there was a much greater emphasis on clarity and transparency. There had not been a tradition of minute-taking at the case companies and it was seldom clear who had made the final decision or why it had been made. A senior executive at Nissan said of the decision-making process there:

Before, it wasn't even clear whether a decision had been made. Japanese companies are quite haphazard about [record keeping]. Memos and minutes are rarely produced. Minutes mean that what has been decided, by whom and why, and what has not been decided, is very clear.

The decision-making process became much more formal, with individual responsibilities being assigned more clearly through job descriptions, and committees with specific decision-making tasks.

Second, the criteria for decision making changed, with a much greater emphasis on the shareholders' perspective. At Shinsei, for example, the way lending decisions were made changed considerably. A middle-ranking relationship manager lamented:

In the old days, the relationship with the client was the most important thing. Even if it meant losing some money, or if there wasn't anything in it for you, if the client wanted you to lend them money, you had to do it. Now, the person who is in charge of risk control is a foreigner. The risk control meetings are held in a public way; they are minuted very carefully, so who made what decision is clearly there for all to see. In the old days it was not really clear who was responsible. The reaction of the committee management now is always first to consider what the risks are to the company and not the relationship with the client, so for us old LTCB people it was really stressful at first but we've come to understand the way they do things so I suppose now we've become used to it.

For many employees the more "rational" approach to decision making represented an important break with the emotional approach of the past, which interviewees often characterised with the word "*shigarami*", which translates as "emotional bonds" or "ties", and refers to the adhesive quality that strengthens, for example, the relationship between a manufacturer and its suppliers. Thus, *shigarami* tend to strengthen links between insiders, whether they be employees of the same department, cohort or firm, or the links between companies inside a *keiretsu* network, and sharpen the differences between those inside and those outside. A relationship manager at Shinsei commented:

The biggest change in the inside [of the organisation] is the decision-making process which is completely free of the old "bonds" [*shigarami*] and which has therefore become extremely rational. For us externally, this is both good and bad. The good part is that the range of products has greatly increased. The bad point is that as the process is now so rational our clients, who sometimes expect a more Japanese approach, feel alienated.

The suggestion here appears to be that the "system" in which a Japanese company operates constrains its business behaviour and that there is a "legacy" which affects a Japanese firm even after it is taken over by a foreign firm. For the acquiring firm, the extent to which the "emotional" approach is forcibly abandoned for a more rational approach is an important judgement call. The benefit of relationships based on *shigarami* is that, being based on more than rational calculation and mere contractual obligations, their foundations are made more robust by higher degrees of trust, and are therefore more durable. This in turn enables both parties to make long-term plans based on higher degrees of confidence concerning the counterpart's behaviour. The difficulty is that, in attempting any form of change, the existence of *shigarami* makes it very difficult for insiders to unravel the web of relationships to set the organisation on a new course. A middle manager at Nissan summed up the changes that had resulted from the weakening of *shigarami* as follows:

The difference I've noticed is that formerly the problems that had to be solved to get from the "as it is" to the "as it should be" state were too big and, although the management understood where the company should be going, they did not have the courage to try and fill that gap. These problems were the *keiretsu* supplier chain, the lifetime and seniority employment systems. They were basically the system of relationships [*shigarami*] that had built up around and within the firm that the old management, who grew up inside the system, could not break down. The new management has tackled these issues one by one and found solutions.

One important aspect of the more "rational" approach was that the finance function became much more involved in the decision-making process. While this led to a more disciplined approach to important matters such as budgeting, there was a perception at some of the case companies that decisions were based on much more short-term considerations than before. This was particularly true at F-Services Co 1 and F-Services Co 2, where the heads of finance were both sent out from the home office. The increased influence of finance, and a greater focus on the bottom line, was associated by some with a more short-term orientation. An executive in F-Services Co 1's sales division commented:

We are intensively profit-driven. Having merged with a foreign firm I feel we have become extremely short term in our focus. Japanese firms are said to be more long term and I always felt some question mark as to whether this was the right approach but this is too far the other way. We put the requirements of the shareholder at the top. I can understand that but I think our company is failing because of it. We are so intent on increasing short-term profits that we are squeezing sales incentives to the bone. It's been reduced by half and that's resulted in sales declining dramatically.

While the decision-making process was generally considered to be more top-down, it did not necessarily mean that it was faster. In particular, it appeared that the more control that was exercised from the overseas shareholder, the longer decisions appeared to take, especially important investment decisions. At F-Services Co 1 and F-Services Co 2, which, according to interview feedback, were subject to the greatest degree of control from head office, there were many who thought that the decision-making process had slowed down. A typical comment was the following from an F-Services Co 2 manager:

For investment decisions it's become slower. For investments of over a certain size, you need permission from head office and that takes two or so weeks. Before, I could disturb the president while he was having his lunch and explain I was in a rush and he would put his stamp on it there and then. Now we have to wait for head office to approve these things. The president used to be all-powerful but now he's a bit like a branch manager and his power is more limited.

At Nissan, by contrast, authority had shifted back to Tokyo after Renault took over. An executive in the finance department noted:

Now it is much more global in scale. It was a very decentralised organisation before, with each operating company looking after its own finances. We now have a much tighter grip from Tokyo.

As we have seen, the management of Roche have given the management of Chugai considerable autonomy to run the company. At Chugai, employees from the old Chugai and Nippon Roche had very different viewpoints about the speed and nature of decision making. While Chugai employees thought generally that the process was moving away from the traditional Japanese model, former employees of Nippon Roche noticed a big difference in decision-making styles. A former Nippon Roche manager commented:

I suppose in the Roche decision-making process it is the top-level meeting that makes the decision so in that sense it is "top-down". Chugai's way is for everyone at the bottom level to do the "*nemawashi*" [i.e. "preparing the ground"] and for the decision to be made there to be ratified at some ceremonial meeting of top executives. That's the traditional Japanese "bottom-up" method.

It is significant that all five companies maintained the *ringi* system in one way or another. At Nissan and Shinsei, it appeared to be as a supplement or alternative to minute taking and has lost its original significance. However, at the other firms, the *ringi* retained a degree of importance that is difficult to explain in rational terms. An expatriate senior executive at one of the case companies viewed the reluctance of Japanese employees there to give up the *ringi* in the following way:

Having arrived from head office the thing that struck me about the decision-making process was the *ringi* system. We introduced the [parent company] approval process for things like capital expenditures and they start running but the *ringi*s are still going around because it seems to me that across the organisation people will only make decisions on a collective basis. I sign off on them as well if it comes around to me because I'm not going to be awkward about it and if it's a way to make everyone happy with the decision and come in line, that's fine, but that doesn't make the decision as far as I'm concerned. So that's an example of how we have introduced our own approvals and governance system but the old system has carried on in an overt way from the old days.

The result was a hybrid of the Japanese and home office system, where the *ringi* was used to enable local staff to "feel" or "see" the decision being made, but had no practical meaning in the global context of the firm.

The HR department

The picture as to whether the influence of the HR department is declining is mixed at the comparator firms, with J-Manufacturing Co having reduced HR headcount, but J-Pharma Co having increased the size of the department slightly. J-Services Co's HR headcount has remained steady over the period. However, if one takes the position

of the head of HR in the organisation as a proxy for the HR department's power, then the picture is much clearer. At the comparator
firms, at all firms the head of HR is still a board member. The only
exception is J-Pharma Co, where the head of HR was not a board
member even in 1998. (See Table 7.4.)

Table 7.4 *Comparator HR department*

| | Significance of the HR department | | | |
| | HR dept employees as % of total employees | | Head of HR on board? | |
	1998	*2003*	*1998*	*2003*
J-Mfg Co	0.8%	0.6%	Yes	Yes
Nissan	0.2%	0.2%	Yes	No
J-Phma Co	0.6%	0.8%	No	No
Chugai	0.6%	0.6%	Yes	No
J-Fin Co	N/A	0.7%	Yes	Yes
Shinsei	2.0%	1.5%	Yes	No
J-Svcs Co	1.2%	1.2%	Yes	Yes
F-Svcs Co 1	2.0%	3.8%	Yes	No

The case of J-Financial Co illustrates the subtle nature of the change
that is taking place in Japanese organisations. Executives felt that
increasing complexity and specialisation in the financial field had clear
implications for the role of the HR department. This meant that there
would be an inevitable dispersion of power and influence away from HR
and there were concrete examples of the increase in role of the business
divisions in recruitment, training and career development. However, it
was felt that unfettered competition between the business groups was
not a desirable outcome, and one way to limit this was by maintaining
a balance between the power of the HR department and the divisions,
and the continued exercise of central control on allocation of human
resources, particularly in intra-group resource allocation.

The picture at the case companies is also somewhat mixed. A common theme among the case companies was that, in the immediate
post-merger period, the HR department was extremely stretched in re-
designing the companies' HR practices and cutting HR headcount had
not been an immediate priority. Notwithstanding this, there had been

some dramatic decreases in HR headcount, particularly at Shinsei, where it declined by more than half. A valid comparison is not possible with J-Financial Co who did not have meaningful figures for their pre-merger organisations. Nissan also declined, but this was in line with decline in overall headcount. Headcount at J-Manufacturing Co also declined, but the size of the department is considerably larger than Nissan's. HR headcount at Chugai remained stable relative to the overall size of the enlarged firm while it increased substantially at F-Services Co 1. However, a senior official at F-Services Co 1's HR department explained that the 2003 headcount number includes various functions that were not included in 1998 (such as regional HR employees and General Affairs department employees). He indicated that pure HR numbers were roughly the same in 2003 as they were in 1998.

The second proxy for HR influence, representation of HR on the board, is perhaps more significant. At all four case companies, the head of HR, who was a main board director in 1998, was no longer on the board in 2003.

Employee perception

There was plenty of evidence of the power of HR in the traditional Japanese firm. The expatriate head of HR at Nissan noted that a large number of the most senior executives on the board had, at one time or another, been members of the HR department.

This function was at the same time very powerful and at the same time very bureaucratic and administrative. In fact it was not a development function. It was a function with the power of the policeman who catches you when you go through the red light. It applied to the mobility system, promotion and so on.

Given that the role of HR is particularly important in the immediate aftermath of mergers, it is perhaps not surprising that there had not been a strong sense of the decline in their role. The exception was Shinsei and this was partly a function of the especially powerful position HR occupies at Japanese financial institutions and the rapid transfer of this power at Shinsei to the divisions. Moderate change was also experienced at Nissan, F-Services Co 1 and F-Services Co 2, with Chugai employees perceiving least change. Inter-employee group

Table 7.5 *Change in role of HR department*

Role of HR department

Q: Do you feel the HR department's role has become more/less central since the merger?
1 = no change[10]
2 = somewhat less central
3 = much less central

Nissan	Chugai	Shinsei	F-Svcs Co 1	F-Svcs Co 2	Total	
2.09	1.54	2.93	2.21	2.36	2.22	
Male	Female	Career	MCH	20–35 yrs	35–45 yrs	45 yrs +
2.29	1.91	2.24	2.15	1.75	2.15	2.56

n = 60

patterns of perception were exactly in line with perception of change in other domains, with male, career and older employees much more likely to feel change. The gap between older and younger employees is particularly striking. (See Table 7.5.)

What has occurred at Shinsei, and to a certain extent at F-Services Co 1 and F-Services Co 2, is a dismemberment of not just the HR function, but also corporate planning, traditionally another key department, with power to design corporate and human resource strategy being passed on to the divisions. At Nissan, there is now a smaller planning department focusing on a much narrower range of highly strategic issues, closely related to the finance function.

An executive at Shinsei, a senior manager from the old LTCB, observed:

HR was very powerful under the old system and completely controlled staff moves. Under Shinsei, this has passed on to each of the divisions so the role of HR has changed to becoming a coordinator among the divisions and also to develop expertise in staff welfare matters. The planning function also is transferred to the divisions so the old planning department disappears. Even today, with banks' planning departments designing

---

[10] There were no responses at the case companies to indicate that the HR department had become more central.

strategy, all financial institutions look the same as the others. So the two most powerful divisions at the old LTCB (which are still very powerful at other Japanese financial institutions), HR and planning, disappear, and the divisions become much more dynamic.

By contrast, the finance function grew considerably in influence and at all companies, except Chugai, the finance function was headed by an expatriate by 2003. As mentioned above, all finance heads are board members, with the exception of Shinsei, where there are only two executive directors.

Summary

The case company organisations have been remodelled to increase transparency, accountability and speed. Boards have been reduced in size, and hierarchy trimmed. Finance drove the decision-making process, and the concept of the budget as a yardstick against which performance should be measured appeared to become more deeply ingrained in employees. Hurdles have been set and benchmarks more clearly identified. Time horizons have become shorter (although the influence of finance in the decision-making process in some cases meant that power flowed away from the Japanese entity to the head office of the new shareholder, causing decision making to slow down). Employees generally felt the decision-making process was more top-down and less consensual. The HR department has generally lost influence compared to the finance function.

References

Abegglen, J.C. (1958) *The Japanese Factory: Aspects of Its Social Organisation.* Boston, MA: Massachusetts Institute of Technology Press

Aoki, M. (1994) "The Japanese Firm as a System of Attributes: A Survey and Research Agenda". In M. Aoki and R. Dore (eds.) *The Japanese Firm: Sources of Competitive Strength.* Oxford: Oxford University Press

Dore, R. (1973) *British Factory – Japanese Factory: The Origins of National Diversity in Industrial Relations.* Berkeley, CA: University of California Press

(1994) "Equality–Efficiency Trade-Offs: Japanese Perceptions and Choices". In M. Aoki and R. Dore (eds.) *The Japanese Firm: Sources of Competitive Strength.* Oxford: Oxford University Press

Global Proxy Watch (1997) "Japan's First Code", 1: 40.

Imai, K. and Komiya, R. (1994) "Characteristics of Japanese Firms". In K. Imai and R. Komiya (eds.) *Business Enterprise in Japan*. Cambridge, MA: MIT Press

Itami, H. (1994) "The 'Human-Capital-Ism' of the Japanese Firm as an Integrated System". In K. Imai and R. Komiya (eds.) *Business Enterprise in Japan*. Cambridge, MA: MIT Press

Jacoby, S. (2005) *The Embedded Corporation: Corporate Governance and Employment Relations in Japan and the United States*. Princeton, NJ: Princeton University Press

Jacoby, S. M. and Saguchi, K. (2002) *The Role of the Senior HR Executive in Japan and the United States: Companies, Countries, and Convergence*. 13th World Congress of the International Industries Relations Association, Berlin

Khurana, R. (2002) *Searching for a Corporate Saviour*. Princeton, NJ: Princeton University Press

Lincoln, J.R. and Kalleberg, A.L. (1990) *Culture, Control, and Commitment: A Study of Work Organization and Work Attitudes in the United States and Japan*. Cambridge: Cambridge University Press

Nihon Keizai Shimbun (2003) "Shikko Yakuin Seido Koka Wa Genteiteki" ("The Limited Impact of the Corporate Officer System"). 7 February, p. 1

Oliver, N. and Wilkinson, B. (1992) *The Japanization of British Industry: New Developments in the 1990s*. Oxford: Blackwell

The Wall Street Journal Online (2004) "American CEOs Meet Resistance when Taking the Helm Overseas". 26 May 1994

Yashiro, N. (1998) *Jinjibu Wa Mou Iranai* (*Who Needs an HR Department Any More?*). Tokyo: Kodansha

Yoshimori, M. (1995) "Whose Company Is It? The Concept of the Corporation in Japan and the West", *Long Range Planning*, 28: 6, 126–126(1)

8 | *Discussion and conclusion*

W E HAVE NOW examined the literature pertaining to Japanese organisations and the employment system, and looked closely at a number of Japanese companies, five that have been taken over by foreign companies and four that have not. Let us now try to pull together what we have learned from the data we have gathered from the case and comparator companies and try to draw some conclusions. We have already established that the organisational practices and structures of Japanese firms taken over by foreign firms look quite different from the Japanese comparator firms. We will now re-examine the evidence gathered in the empirical chapters and, through an institutional lens, try to gain some understanding of the factors that underlie persistence and change at the case and comparator companies, as well as gaining an insight into the factors that might account for differences in the trajectory of change at the case companies.

Japanese firms: few signs of deinstitutionalisation of organisational practices

It is clear from even a cursory glance at the business media that the organisational landscape has undergone considerable change in the last two decades. The certainties that existed in the 1980s as to the long-term competitiveness of Japanese organisational practices have given way to a great deal of debate about the role of the market mechanism in determining employment practices. The strong emphasis on reform of the Koizumi administration contributed greatly to the way in which this debate has been conducted, even if the reformist zeal appears to have abated somewhat in the post-Koizumi administrations.

A central element in this debate has been the role of the market for corporate control. How far do companies exist for the benefit of their employees and, insofar as they do, should trading in them be restricted? Alternatively, should shareholders exercise their rights as owners more vigorously and punish managers' non-share price-maximising behaviour by making the potential threat of takeover a real one? The rapid rise in the volume of mergers and acquisitions in Japan (*Financial Times*, 2005) shows the extent of this change. There have been a number of high-profile contested bids in Japan during the past five years, of which Sumitomo Mitsui FG's challenge to an already-agreed acquisition by Mitsubishi Tokyo FG of a third major bank, UFJ, the battle over Fuji TV instigated by Livedoor in 2005, as well as the hostile bid by Oji Paper for Hokuetsu Paper in 2006 stand out. These episodes gave rise to questions about the nature of Japanese capitalism, and the role of the company in society, that had not been seriously asked during the fifty years of virtually continuous economic growth during the post-war period.

There is clear evidence that the division of company profits has shifted significantly away from employees in favour of shareholders, with a substantial increase in the level of dividend payouts and share buybacks (Dore, 2006). At board level, there have also been noticeable changes. Japanese boards are now slimmer; stock options have been introduced at a number of Japanese companies; and there seems to be a slightly greater emphasis on speed and individual accountability in decision making and more top-down leadership. All this has led to a widening of the gap between the rewards of directors and ordinary employees. The increased emphasis on responsibility and accountability is mirrored in changing HR practices with evidence that many "taken-for-granted organisational actions" are being questioned by both employers and employees. We have seen in preceding chapters some evidence in the literature of companies making adjustments to time-honoured practices in response to new economic conditions and pressure from shareholders.

To what extent, however, do these changes amount to a "deinstitutionalisation" of Japanese organisational practices or, to put it another way, has the legitimacy of such practices been undermined to the extent that they are no longer accepted as mainstream? The rhetoric emerging from large Japanese companies during the past decade would indicate a far greater attention to the concept of shareholder value, and to some extent, as we have seen, with the rise in dividends and share buybacks, an argument could be made that Japanese managers are embracing an alternative version of capitalism. However, it would appear to me that such moves do not necessarily represent a closer alignment of management and shareholder interests, but are merely an exercise to "reduce social uncertainty ... through the introduction of symbolic rather than substantive control mechanisms" (Westphal and Zajak, 1998, p. 129).

In some ways, the "institutionalised definition of success" (Oliver, 1992) has altered slightly, with a greater emphasis on returns, rather than market share or sales. This has come about because the audience that measures success has changed, with the advent of a more militant shareholder base. Crucially, however, there has not been a marked shift in the insiderist nature of Japanese firms. We have seen that the vast majority of directors and CEOs of large Japanese companies are still insiders (Ahmadjian, 2001) and that the CEOs feel that the support of employees is significantly more important than that of shareholders (Yoshimori, 1995). Incidents such as Oji's hostile bid for Hokuetsu, while highly newsworthy, are still freak occurrences and do not in any way mark a permanent departure from institutionalised norms. Management has responded to increased pressure from shareholders by adjusting the balance of rewards among stakeholders: increasing levels of dividend and share buybacks and a decreased share of value-added to employees rather than through a fundamental change from viewing employee welfare as a positive concern to viewing employees instrumentally and labour as a commodity, a shift which would have been revealed in a major realignment of work practices.

I would therefore argue strongly that deinstitutionalisation is not occurring at large Japanese companies and that the "employee-favouring" company has not yet transformed itself into the "shareholder-favouring" company. We can see in the field of recruitment, for example, that, while the recruitment of mid-career hires at the comparator companies has increased, they still form a small percentage of total employees. While there has been some progress in the advancement of female employees, they still form a tiny part of the management cadre. The distinction between *sōgōshoku* and *ippanshoku* still persists at Japanese companies. "Office ladies" still wear uniforms. Employment stability is still a key (perhaps *the* key) driver of employment policy from the sides of labour, employers and the government. Tenure at large companies is increasing, rather than decreasing (Rebick, 2001). While large Japanese companies have been downsizing, there is strong evidence that they will go to considerable lengths to avoid laying off the core workforce (Kato, 2001). As we have seen in the study of the comparator companies, they recognise that there is a crucial link between mobility and a fluid external labour market and flexible corporate strategy formation. This has led to some adjustments in employment practices, notably a sharp increase in irregular workers. However, for employees in the (admittedly reduced) group of core workers, the implicit promise that the employee will be gainfully employed until retirement is still being kept, even if it comes with "guaranteed outplacement", meaning that he will probably not remain at the same company for his entire career. The reward system does take ability and contribution more into account and we saw evidence of this, particularly at J-Financial Co's securities area, which was the most exposed to foreign competition. The level of differentiation between cohort employees is also increasing somewhat, as we saw at J-Services Co. But change has been gradual and there was no change in the speed at which employees are promoted at the comparator companies (see Shibata, 2002). As we saw in Chapter 5, the Japan Institute of Labour describes the current "ability-based" reward system as something akin to "psuedo-*nenko*" (JIL, 2004). Beyond the reduction in board size at Japanese companies, there is little change in the decision-making process and the use of the *ringi* is still widespread (see Ahmadjian, 2001). J-Manufacturing Co made the organisation flatter in the early 1990s, but have quietly restored a key layer when it appeared that too flat a hierarchy caused an erosion of some of the key competitive advantages that are seen to accrue from their distinctive employment practices.

   The examination of the comparator companies illustrates vividly the factors that underpin the durability of the communitarian model and why, once practices and organisational structures become institutionalised, they are hard to dislodge. The "taken-for-granted" nature of Japanese HR practices, with their strong emphasis on predictability in promotion, wage increases and employment stability, may have altered slightly in the wake of enthusiasm for reform in the Koizumi era, but their institutional foundations are still intact. There has been no fundamental shift to an alternative mode of organising based on another template of capitalism.

At the level of the individual, it is apparent from the statements of a number of managers at the comparator companies that the twin principles of employee sovereignty and equality still provide a robust foundation for the employment system at large Japanese companies. At J-Manufacturing Co, long-term employment stability and seniority-based pay, the kind of thinking that permitted someone with few responsibilities to receive almost the same salary as a general manager with hundreds of employees reporting to him, just because they are of similar seniority, was "second nature".

From the "shareholder value" perspective, maintaining such practices may be "rational" insofar as the embeddedness of these practices in "widespread understandings of social reality" makes changing them extremely costly and therefore damaging to the interests of shareholders. Large Japanese companies such as J-Manufacturing Co would also argue that such practices are rational, in that they are a key element in a wider social structure which contributes significantly to the company's manufacturing excellence. However, they are also not challenged because they are seen as legitimate by key societal institutions and this is just as important a factor in explaining their resilience.

In our study of the comparator and case companies, the link between these ideas may provide a framework for understanding the reasons for change or the lack of it and the trajectory of change, once the process has started. If we consider first Oliver's "empirical predictors", it is quite clear that, in the case of the comparator companies, the three types of pressure that she mentions, political, functional and social, are not present at the intra-organisational level in sufficient strength to cause deinstitutionalisation to occur. "Increased workforce diversity", for example (under "political distributions"), would have occurred if Japanese firms were prepared to disturb cultural homogeneity by hiring significantly larger numbers of mid-career hires than they appear to have done. Under "social

consensus", we do not have evidence of "increasing turnover or succession", nor "weakening socialisation mechanisms". As corporate
restructuring has accelerated over the past ten years, mergers and
alliances are taking place at an even faster pace. However, as we
saw in Chapter 1, the tradition of Japanese mergers being those of
"equals" has not substantially diminished and, notwithstanding the
hostile nature of the battle over UFJ or Hokuetsu Paper, the way
integration has taken place in the wake of Japanese mergers would
suggest that the interests of employees are taken into account ahead
of those of shareholders.

Second, we found that the pattern of "value commitments"
(Greenwood and Hinings, 1996) of the key interest groups may have
altered slightly and given rise to a level of discourse that envisages
alternative ways of organising, but there was certainly no consensus
that it was seen as legitimate to head forcefully in that new direction.
We found this in the words of the HR director of one of the comparator firms, who indicated that the company had come to understand through its problematic international expansion that a flexible
corporate strategy required a flexible human resources strategy, but
stopped short of taking positive action ("it's only something we are
thinking about ... we've got to be careful").

Third, the system itself appears not to admit readily the influence of outsiders. We have seen from the literature that Japanese
organisations strongly emphasise homogeneity (Dore, 1973; Nitta,
1997; Rohlen, 1974). The way employees are recruited, trained and
rewarded all conspire to keep the internal labour market strong, and
the external market weak. The development of a stronger and more
fluid external labour market has not been actively encouraged by
government policy (Hanami, 2004; Weinstein, 2001). At the level
of the individual and the firm, we have seen in the literature, and
at both the comparator and case companies, many references to the
"bonds" (*shigarami*) that bind employees, clients, suppliers and other
related parties together. The nature of *shigarami* is far more than a
mutual or legal/contractual obligation: there is a strong emotional
element implicit in the notion. Employees at a number of the case
companies referred to the fact that major decisions on strategy and
resource allocation under the previous regime could not be made
without taking these bonds into account. As a result, expectations

were that all related parties would each behave towards the other in accordance with certain implicit, but strict, rules, which, while being seen as one of the Japan's key strengths, also tended to constrain management behaviour and company strategy. It was the presence of *shigarami* that prevented Nissan from taking action on its *keiretsu* network and the old LTCB from establishing more rigorous credit policies, as employee testimony showed in Chapter 7. The mode of organising that these bonds create can only be sustained if outside influences and the possibility of illegitimate and deviant behaviour can be kept at bay.

The employment system itself is an "institutional project" – an outcome of political interactions between labour, capital and the state, which crystallises into an institutional blueprint in which "institutionalized differences may become the very source of economic advantage, as various resources allow countries and firms to follow various pursuits in the global economy" (Biggart and Guillen, 1999). The stability of employment systems rests on the fact that they are "templates for action ... [which] organise existing interests and reward certain groups who then have a great deal at stake in defending them" (Fligstein, 2001, p. 121). Employment systems are "crystallised" and "frozen" at critical moments in history with the prevailing "power constellations" providing the blueprint for the templates. In the case of the Japanese employment system, the mutual interests of labour, capital and the state have not been served by altering the status quo. It is certainly true that the balance of power between the three has ebbed and flowed in the fifty years or so that the current employment system has been in existence. In particular we have witnessed a decline in the power of the labour movement (Hanami, 2004; JIL, 2003), with no sign of reversal. This has led to a weakening of the bargaining position of labour who have surrendered the right to virtually automatic wage increases ("base-up") in return for the maintenance of job security and a rethinking of the role of the ritualistic annual wage bargaining system known as the "spring offensive" (JIL, 2004), which was effectively killed off by the long period of deflation. Some of the taken-for-granted routines, or "automatism" (i.e. associated with Japanese organisational behaviour), may have dissipated over time. However, the conclusion from the literature, which has certainly

been backed up by the empirical data from the comparator companies, is that the sense of legitimacy bestowed upon communitarian
practices and its philosophical foundations have not been seriously
undermined within the groups that make up the critical "power
constellations" in Japan. The conclusion in the case of Japan is that,
once institutionalised, employment systems are hard to dislodge, at
least from the inside, by insiders.

Case study companies

Analysis

What were the factors that shaped the outcomes at the case companies? What were the underlying forces that caused change? Why did
some of the case companies change more than others?

The role of the management, as agents of the new shareholders,
was of great importance in determining how the new shareholder
orientation manifested itself. All the senior management interviewed
talked of "cultural transformation" and in particular about the need
for a focus on the "performance culture". Although there has been a
strong sense of continuity at Chugai, Osamu Nagayama, the CEO,
linked his aspiration to "transform Chugai, our staff and our culture"
through the merger with Roche to expectations of enhanced performance to deal with the harsh realities of an increasingly competitive
landscape.

For the new management of the case companies, the institutionalised definition of success is different and "performance" is a much
more market-driven concept. To a greater or lesser degree, they have
confronted the challenge of institutional distance by trying to impose
"global best practice" on the acquired Japanese company. New
employment practices have been introduced that make individuals
and divisions compete for resources, whether human or capital, in a
way that did not previously happen.

The result of this was that most elements of what might be considered "global best practice" have been introduced at the case companies. We have seen in the preceding chapters that, in the domains
of recruitment, training, employee evaluation and remuneration, gender, organisation and decision making, there have been significant
changes at the case companies, albeit not on a uniform basis across
the companies.

Institutional change at the case companies

Were there any institutional factors that might have given us some clues as to what trajectory the process of change, or "deinstitutionalisation", would take at the case companies? Let us now use Oliver's "empirical predictors" of deinstitutionalisation to analyse change at the case companies.

In trying to gain some insight into the relationship between the "empirical predictors" and the trajectory of change, I have tried to quantify the presence of the predictors in each case and illustrate this graphically in Table 8.1. In determining the different levels, I have drawn on a combination of the numerical HR data that I collected, as well as the "quantised" interview data. It should be stressed therefore that the table has not been scientifically derived. However, I believe it is useful for illustrative purposes. For the sake of clarity, I have defined below what each of the factors means in the context of this research and described what factors I took into account in the quantification process. It should also be noted that some of the "predictors" were either not clearly defined by Oliver, or had a very broad definition which was difficult to quantify (e.g. "increasing goal clarity"). In such cases, I have chosen a narrower definition so that it could be measured with data that I had collected.

Changes in political distributions:

- *Increasing workforce diversity*: a perception in the quantised interview data that the recruitment process had changed,[1] along with the HR data revealing a greater tendency to hire mid-career employees.
- *Declining performance or crises*: refers to the financial state of the company prior to the takeover by the foreign firm. Thus, the fact that Shinsei had been made bankrupt and Chugai had been consistently profitable, prior to their respective takeovers, put them at opposite ends of the scale.
- *Power reallocations*: I took the perceived shift in influence away from the HR department (therefore representing a shift *to* the

---

[1] I took a score of over 2.5 to show a "very strong" presence of a predictor, between 2.0 and 2.5 to show a "strong" presence, between 1.5 and 2.0 to be "moderate" and under 1.5 to show a "weak" presence.

Table 8.1 *Empirical predictors of deinstitutionalisation at case companies*

Intra-organisational factors constituting empirical predictors of deinstitutionalisation (Oliver, 1992)

Factors	Nissan	Chugai	Shinsei	F-Services Co 1	F-Services Co 2
Changes in political distributions					
Increasing workforce diversity	Strong	Strong	Very strong	Strong	Moderate
Declining performance or crises	Strong	Weak	Very strong	Moderate	Moderate
Power reallocations	Strong	Moderate	Very strong	Strong	Strong
Threat of obsolescence	Weak	Weak	Strong[2]	Weak	Weak
Changes in functional necessity					
Increasing technical specification	Very strong	Moderate	Very strong	Very strong	Very strong
Increasing goal clarity	Very strong	Moderate	Very strong	Strong	Strong
Changes in social consensus					
Increasing turnover or succession	Strong	Weak	Very strong	Very strong	Very strong
Weakening socialisation mechanisms	Strong	Moderate	Strong	Strong	Strong
Increasing diversification, dispersion or differentiation	Strong	Moderate	Strong	Moderate	Strong

[2] LTCB's business model had been under threat for some time by deregulation and, of the three companies that had long-term credit banking licences, none remain in that business.

operating divisions) to be a proxy for a shift in power allocations within the firm.

- *Threat of obsolescence*: refers to the extent to which the business model of the company was threatened at the time of the takeover.

Changes in functional necessity:

- *Increasing technical specification*: refers to the extent to which employees now perceived a greater emphasis on specialisation in the organisation.
- *Increasing goal clarity*: refers to the extent to which the decision-making process was perceived to have altered and had become more top-down.

Changes in social consensus:

- *Increasing turnover or succession*: refers to the extent to which the composition of the board has changed, and whether the CEO is an outsider.
- *Weakening socialisation mechanisms*: refers to the extent to which employees perceive the recruitment and training process to have altered.
- *Increasing diversification, dispersion or differentiation*: refers to the extent to which the business model of the company has altered under foreign ownership, and the extent to which it resembles its competitors less than it did before.

It is apparent from this table that a great deal of the changes that have occurred at the case study companies can be explained by the varying degrees to which the "empirical predictors" are present in each case. Thus, the strong presence of predictors at Shinsei is indicative of a large degree of change at that company. The opposite holds true at Chugai: a weak presence of predictors suggesting a greater degree of continuity. However, it is also apparent that the antecedents are just that – "a thing or circumstance which goes before in time or order; often implying causal relation with its consequent" (OED) – and that, whilst causality is indeed implied, it is not established.

The "insiderism" that still pervades major Japanese firms, and the fact that the main stakeholder groups (i.e. management, employees, unions and much of the domestic institutional shareholder base) share a common understanding of, and attachment to, the status of the employee-favouring firm, has ensured its survival through the years of economic difficulty.

However, with the appearance of new actors (in the shape of foreign shareholders) embedded in a different institutional framework and who have no emotional or philosophical attachment to a particular organisational form (or if they do, it is not to the Japanese version), the change in the balance of power is much more likely to lead to radical change. They are likely to look for weaknesses in the existing organisational template, seeking out practices that are inconsistent with shareholders' interests. They are less likely to be sympathetic to the idea of the holistic nature of the Japanese employment system, that it comes as an integrated "package" and that component parts cannot be tampered with without affecting the whole. The new management bring with them their own organisational templates, which they will not hesitate to impose.

Implicit in this analysis is the potentially critical role that exogenous forces will play in the process of radical change. The CEOs from all the case companies except Chugai were outsiders. Three of the four were non-Japanese. At all case companies except Chugai, the CFO was non-Japanese. In two cases, even the head of HR was non-Japanese. These are outsiders, people whose careers and attitudes have not developed in Japan, and, while they will be to a greater or lesser degree sensitive to local customs, their institutional frames of reference and ideas of legitimate behaviour will be different from that of the previous management, all insiders, whom they have replaced or supplemented. They are managers sent by the shareholders and, to that extent, employees at the case companies will expect them to bring the values of the new shareholders. They are people who will try to persuade Japanese employees, in the words of one case company CEO, that they should "feel good" about making a positive return to shareholders and that having these feelings was not "playing to [their] basest elements". Symbols and traditions, such as uniforms worn by female employees, office layout, or the fact that all new employees joined the company on 1 April, would mean little to these new managers. Similarly, it might be easier for outsiders to see the nature of *shigarami* in a more dispassionate light, both in the way it binds employees together internally as well as the way in which large Japanese companies are typically locked in a web of interdependent relationships with suppliers, customers, banks and so on. Nissan is prepared to sell off holdings in almost all the companies that form its *keiretsu* relationships as it considers the funds tied up in those companies to be a waste of much-needed capital; Shinsei changed its lending policies so that the credit standing of even long-standing clients became the sole criterion for lending decisions. A client-relationship manager from the old LTCB said:

The reaction of the [credit] committee management is always to consider what the risks are to the company and not the relationship with the client, as it was in the old days ... it's a lot more transaction-oriented and there's little emphasis on the relationship ... I'm not sure that all Japanese financial institutions can behave like Shinsei. The Ministry of Finance puts a lot of pressure on companies like us to behave in a certain way and support government policy.

In the Japanese institutional context, these actions may be seen as illegitimate (see Iwaisako, 2004), and would be difficult for lifelong insiders to implement. The workings of the credit committee are clearly rational and are doubtless in line with best practice at other global banking institutions. To many former LTCB employees, however, the new emphasis on risk would inevitably be questioned by the wider business community. The apparently reduced status of the client in lending decisions represented a significant departure from the traditional decision-making methodology. Foreigners, however, are just the kind of non-establishment fringe players (Kang, 1991) to whom Hirsch (1986) refers, who can afford to engage in this kind of "deviant innovation" (i.e. deviant to what is acceptable, or traditional local practice)

This point was made forcefully by a case company CEO, who was considering whether it would be feasible to appoint a Japanese national as his successor:

The leadership culture of an organisation is led by the CEO and I guess simplistically in my mind there is this idea that Japanese accept expatriates as agents of change. So for me to put more radical ideas on the table and push for change is the Japanese expectation of what I'll do anyway. I'm an expatriate so there's a *de facto* mandate to push for change. In a traditional Japanese sense, it seems to me that, if the CEO is Japanese, then delivering more radical change is more difficult because of cultural bonds ... A typical Japanese CEO is typically ... not personally a decision maker or an agent of change but more a senior figurehead that promotes consensus and promotes bottom-up rather than top-down decision making. A typical Japanese CEO would look for change from the bottom while a western CEO would promote change from the top. That engenders completely different dynamics in the way companies evolve.

Although his characterisation of a Japanese CEO as "not personally a decision maker" may be exaggerated, the important point is that he feels that as an outsider, he is in a position to introduce radical change in a way that Japanese leaders are not. This feeling was clearly shared by Japanese employees given the frequent references to the paralysing effect of *shigarami*.

We are reminded at the case companies of Walter's (1985) analysis of conflicting values that emerge during institutionally distant mergers. As we discussed above, the introduction of the concept of market forces into organisational practices is the key method for the introduction of a shareholder-oriented performance culture – it is this more than anything else that conflicts with the underlying emphasis on equality that characterised the communitarian ethic. This has a profound impact upon the employment system of the case companies, as we have seen. The increasing number of outsiders in the organisation as a result of increased hiring of mid-career employees has served to undermine the homogeneous social fabric of the company and, combined with, in some cases, frequent "voluntary" early retirement programmes, has altered the taken-for-granted attitudes that existing employees had about their own careers. Increased competition among employees has had some impact on cohesiveness: the meaning of pay has increased markedly and this has changed the way employees view each other compared to the days when, at least for the first fifteen years, there was virtually no difference in pay and promotion speeds. A market-based approach to resource allocation has inevitably intensified inter-divisional conflict as they compete for the best employees, increased bonus pools and capital. In the analysis of Walter, we have an example of the central conflict in merger and acquisition events: that between property rights, as espoused by a shareholder-driven approach, and human rights, as emphasised by an employee-favouring approach. All in all, the environment was less comfortable and the potential for conflict had increased, even if many employees acknowledged that the market-based approach enhanced organisational survival prospects. A young manager at a case company summed up this feeling:

The culture has changed. Before it was like "tepid water". Everyone got along together and we tried not to offend each other or get in each other's way. To put it positively, it was quite family like. Now it's much more competitive. That makes it uncomfortable and people try to drag others down. There wasn't much of this before. I think overall, it's moving in the right direction. We were too relaxed before.

Company analysis

While we have been able to observe some important common trends at the case companies, as we have seen there have been equally important differences. What, then, are the factors that lie behind the different trajectories of change at the case companies? Let us now try to integrate the three concepts in trying to answer this question. We will examine the particular contextual factors at each of the case companies, focusing on the two extremes, Shinsei and Chugai, but also on Nissan, which appears to display elements of both stability and change.

Shinsei

Of all the five case companies, the changes that had been intended, and implemented, at Shinsei were by far the most radical. The new CEO, Yashiro, had in mind the creation of something entirely new. This was not something for which a template existed, something he could just bring in wholesale from the US and implement in Japan. Tett (2004, pp. 194–195) describes the challenge facing Yashiro:

What Yashiro wanted to do … was build a new vision of banking that was different from the old convoy system, but also *Japanese*. "I never felt this was an American bank or that I wanted to make this an American bank," Yashiro later explained. "When I arrived I knew that we could not follow an American model, but we could not follow the old Japanese way either. So we had to create something new – a new way of being a Japanese bank."

If we examine Table 8.1 above, it is clear that the antecedents were present most clearly at Shinsei. The financial state of the company prior to the acquisition was the worst among the five case companies, having been in a state of receivership ("declining performance or crises"). In an effort to build an investment banking business of a kind that had not previously existed at LTCB, large numbers of outsiders were hired, with almost entire teams arriving from firms such as Lehman Brothers and Bear Stearns (Tett, 2004). The homogeneous fabric of the organisation had been greatly impacted by the large influx of mid-career hires, including a number of foreigners and Japanese who had worked at foreign firms ("increasing workforce diversity"). There had been considerable "power reallocations" – the authority of the once powerful HR department was almost entirely reallocated to the operating divisions. It had radically altered its business model ("increasing diversification, dispersion or differentiation"). Almost in every domain, employees, especially those of the former Shinsei, perceived a great deal of change from the previous organisation, or from the way a typical Japanese financial institution should look.

The extra insights afforded to us by the analysis of the precipitators and enablers of radical change, and the role that outsiders play in the process, is evident at Shinsei. A reformative commitment had been imposed and had been supported by changes in the business model, a sweeping away of the old HR practices and a dismantling of the power of the HR department, which was reallocated to the operating divisions. These changes, along with the influx of outsiders, had created a capacity for action, an ability to move the organisation from one template to another, with relative ease. Yashiro emphasised the critical role of the top management in the process of change, implying that it was difficult for insiders who were constrained by the bonds that develop within a traditional Japanese company to promote change and that his status as an outsider was critical:

You need to start at the top. If you want to change, if you don't start there, nothing will happen. It's very difficult to change [Japanese organisations] and so people shy away and they don't stay long as chief executive. If they want to be treated like their predecessors they won't change.

It is possible that, in its efforts to create something different, the bank had allowed the cultural roots which bound it to the local business community to weaken somewhat and that this had had some negative consequences. It is interesting to note that, in the last few years, there has been a subtle, but nevertheless perceptible, change at the bank, with a stronger emphasis on the LTCB "heritage", rather than the "legacy", a useful differentiator for the bank to its foreign competitors. Thus, in the 2006 annual report, the CEO (Yashiro's successor, Thierry Porté) and the Vice Chairman state that, while the bank "strives to be more global than local by developing innovative products and services based on world-class best practice …", they "also take advantage of our proud and valuable heritage in terms of our long-standing customer relationships in Japan that make us more local than global competition". Tom Pedersen, who has been brought into the organisation as Chief Learning Officer, commented that the LTCB heritage was:

A big part of our culture here and not necessarily part of the culture that we necessarily want to throw out with the bathwater. It has real strengths to it, the strength of relationships, the strengths of expertise, things that are encoded in the DNA of the organisation …

This reappraisal involved a concerted effort to communicate the key elements of the heritage internally, to ensure that employees had a common understanding of its impact on the current organisation and how it fitted in with the overall corporate vision and strategy. This was especially important in an organisation that had absorbed a large number of new external hires and was eager to forge a unique position for itself as a bank with some foreign features (technological know-how) but with important local attributes (respect for long-term relationships).

This involved the re-assessment of some major HR issues. For example, there was an acknowledgement that simply paying market rates for outsiders coming into the organisation, on the grounds that they were specialists, while leaving the original members of the organisation on internal pay-scales, was problematic and that a fairer, more transparent process of deciding on pay was required. This was particularly important in insider-oriented and seniority-based organisations and illustrates the difficulties in effecting a smooth transfer to a market-based system: the two systems would not sit comfortably alongside each other in the same organisation. The second, related issue concerned the role of HR itself. As Pedersen put it:

The other thing that is fundamental is that, when Shinsei was born, they decentralised all the HR functions and that has some unintended consequences. You don't have consistent ways to hire, develop, to retain and to pay people. It looks really good but the reality is that it's perceived as unequal: we need to be explicit about the differences and have consistent ways of looking at talent and benchmarking it externally and internally ...

This has had two implications for the HR function. One was its re-creation as a stronger unit across the bank, as "centres of excellence", or "communities of practice", within each of the operating divisions that delivered best practice and process in recruiting, training and pay in a consistent way across the firm. HR now reports direct to the CEO, rather than the Corporate Affairs Group, which was the previous arrangement. This was a crucial shift in the effort to redirect the firm from a "transactional" focus to a more "relationship"-oriented one. According to Pedersen, "We have to be more respectful of our DNA and that's not possible if HR doesn't have a strong relationship with the business leaders and the President."

F-Services Co 1 and F-Services Co 2

The presence of antecedents at F-Services Co 1 and F-Services Co 2 was also strong, although not as strong as at Shinsei. Neither company had been in the same painful financial circumstances prior to acquisition as Shinsei, nor had the business models of the two firms altered in the same way. Nevertheless, it was clear that power dependencies had been realigned, with new management clearly empowered by the new shareholders to enhance financial returns and who were prepared to take radical measures to ensure that those returns were achieved. The new management clearly understood the "new conceptual destination", although at F-Services Co 2 reference was made to certain elements of the old guard that were resisting the journey to that destination.

Chugai

Chugai is almost the inverse image of Shinsei. Of all the five case companies, the antecedents of deinstitutionalisation were least in evidence at Chugai. Given that the new shareholder Roche had majority control over Chugai, there was the potential for as much change as had appeared at Shinsei. Indeed, we do see that, in important areas,

Roche was making its presence felt. Ambitious financial targets had been imposed at Chugai, of which the employees were universally aware. It is also clear that Nagayama himself desired change, with his reference to the need to "transform our staff and our culture". While felt more subtly, the changes were nevertheless evident to employees. The use of English was now much more widespread and ability with languages a more important factor for "getting on". Organisational structure had also been modified to fit in with Roche's global structure: the number of divisions had been reduced from seven to three. Most importantly, Chugai employees were affected by the influx of employees of the old Nippon Roche. Thus, a middle-ranking manager from the HR department noted:

Maybe the biggest thing is that people with different values have come into the company and work together with us. I used to take a lot of things for granted and this has been a good opportunity for me to reconsider things and look at things in a different light.

Overall, however, the company had shown the greatest degree of continuity, by a considerable margin, of all five case companies. While they had taken on more female executives and salary differentials had widened slightly, all other HR data had shown that the status quo was being maintained. Interview responses confirmed that employee perception of continuity was the highest among the case firms in almost all domains. Of all the case companies, communitarian features were by far the most prominent.

Whilst it would have been possible for Roche to rearrange the power dynamics given its position as majority owner of the firm, it has so far chosen not to do so. An institutional analysis using the power dependencies framework might go along the following lines. First, Chugai was the first major company in its sector where majority control was purchased outright by a foreign firm. The Japanese pharmaceutical market is the second largest in the world and is very attractive to foreign firms. Roche had been present in the Japanese market for over a century and had not built up an organisation with sufficient business momentum. Chugai was consistently profitable, well managed and was therefore potentially a very attractive partner for Roche, putting the management of Chugai in a relatively strong bargaining position. "Declining performance or crises" and "threat of obsolescence" were certainly not present in the case of Chugai. Simply put, there was no immediate need for Chugai to sell.

We see that the management of the company is almost exactly the same as it was prior to the acquisition. There are no representatives of Nippon Roche on the Chugai board and the only Roche representatives were two non-executive directors. In the immediate aftermath of the acquisition, Roche did not send a single expatriate to work in the company. The Chugai management were still all insiders (although, unusually, only one of the board members was a lifelong Chugai employee). While Nagayama is very "westernised" he has always worked at Japanese firms, organisations that are embedded in the Japanese institutional context. A senior general manager from Chugai commented on the feeling of continuity and the importance of the leadership:

The people who are running the company are the same as before so I don't detect much change ... but if Nagayama-san were to leave, things might change drastically. The atmosphere would alter a lot, I think. So far, we don't think of ourselves as a foreign firm, rather I think it's a matter of the Roche people thinking they've joined a Japanese firm.

And this, after all, is what both Nagayama and the CEO of the new shareholders thought were crucial elements for success in Japan: a key element, perhaps *the* key element, of overcoming the liability of foreignness was to be *seen* as a local player. Franz Humer, Chairman of Roche, touched on the "liability of foreignness" in Japan:

I am absolutely sure that, in Japan, if you are regarded as a Japanese company and not as a foreign one, you have a different status, a different relationship with government, different access to government, universities, opinion leaders. This was one of the strong underlying reasons for doing it [i.e. acquiring Chugai]: to tap into the different potential of knowledge science and know-how.

As with Nissan, there was with the Roche–Chugai relationship a strong emphasis on partnership, with the word "alliance" being used rather than "acquisition". Chugai was to be for Roche a key global "centre of excellence" in research and development and decidedly not a mere marketing arm in Japan for Roche products developed in Switzerland

and other centres. While there would be sharing of research resources between the two firms, insofar as the firms had developed similar products, they would be free to compete with each other in the market. The integrity of an independent Chugai was seen as vital to maintain the spirit of entrepreneurship and R&D excellence that would enable Chugai to contribute meaningfully to Roche's global product pipeline. Humer was optimistic about the medium-term future:

We'll be launching in a year's time [in 2008] the first original product coming from Chugai research, Actemra, which worldwide could be a major success story, and their research pipeline looks extraordinarily interesting. So if they focus on these things the next five years should be golden years for Chugai. So I think in that sense a model like ours you can sustain so much more easily if the partner is successful.

Humer believed that maintaining the local management and local roots was critical in its ability to take successful rationalisation measures in the wake of the acquisition:

Nagayama-san closed down factories, research sites, sold businesses, streamlined his entire operation, without a noise in the market, without damage to their reputation … any foreign company trying to do that would have been killed in Japan. I have enormous respect for how that was handled.

At the very least, outsiders would not have shown the proper sensitivity in navigating the organisation through a period of difficult restructuring. It is possible that, even if an outsider had made these difficult changes in exactly the same way as an insider, he would have been under a much greater degree of scrutiny simply because he was an outsider.

Thus, while it may appear that there is less of a reformative commitment at Chugai relative to Shinsei, this is the outcome of a conscious strategy by the parent. Nagayama's feelings on lifetime employment and the critical importance of the stable workplace set him apart from the leaders of the other case companies. Significantly, he mentions the importance of maintaining the company's "profile" by continuing to offer stability of employment. This would seem to indicate that both he and the company's management are not

prepared to ignore societal norms to indulge in deviant and illegitimate practices.

The trajectory of change at Chugai has therefore been quite different from the other case firms, and will continue to be so. Chugai
employees felt the increased influence of shareholders just as strongly
as employees at other case firms. The impact of the influx of Nippon
Roche employees means that, at the level of the individual employee,
there is potential for a re-evaluation of long-held beliefs and taken-
for-granted assumptions about the meaning and value of certain
employment practices and the future direction of his or her career.
However, there appears to be no indication that either the parent or
the management of Chugai wish to change dramatically the current
course of the organisation.

Nissan

The situation at Nissan is considerably more complicated, with seem-
ingly contradictory responses from employees which make a simple
institutional analysis difficult. The antecedents are clearly present at
the company and the reformative commitment appeared to be strongly
felt by management and employees alike. Employees at Nissan felt
the second-highest degree of change *overall* after Shinsei. But, while
they felt the greatest degree of change among all employees of the
companies to the decision-making process, they did not perceive it
as having become a significantly more top-down process. They were
only slightly more inclined than the employees of Chugai to feel that
the commitment to lifetime employment had reduced, but felt very
strongly that career patterns within the company had changed, with a
much greater emphasis on specialisation. They were the least inclined
of all employee groups to view seniority-based pay as having given
way to meritocracy, but were unanimous in saying that, to get on in
the company under the new ownership, employees required different
qualities from those needed before.

What are the reasons for this apparent inconsistency? In my con-
versations with senior executives at Nissan, it appeared to me that
there was less emphasis there in singling out specific domains of the
Japanese employment system or organisational form that needed changing. That is not to say that there was a conscious desire on the part of
management that institutions such as lifetime employment should be

maintained, as was the case at Chugai. Rather, that in focusing on the role of senior management and the decision-making process, changes would naturally follow. A considerable degree of autonomy had been delegated to the cross-functional teams and, whilst it was clear to them what conclusions the management wanted them to come to, it was nonetheless felt that the decision-making process was still consensual. Many employees noted, however, the increased level of clarity and accountability demanded of them in the new decision-making process. This, combined with a setting out of clear strategic goals by the management, would lead to the most appropriate employment system and organisational form for the company. Management had re-defined what "performance" meant and had set clear long-term performance targets. It was expected that the employees would intuitively understand what the implications were for HR practices and organisational structure.

Thus, Thierry Moulonguet, EVP and CFO of the company,[3] noted that the biggest change was the "combination of a clear and transparent decision-making process with a rigorous execution and monitoring process", but with a "strong bottom-up flavour" for which cross-functional teams would act as a vital platform. As for lifetime employment and seniority-based pay, he commented:

> I couldn't say there is a guarantee of lifetime employment here, especially for the top people ... the spirit of performance-linked pay and meritocracy is spreading throughout the company but we are taking one step at a time and I don't think there will be any drastic adjustment in the short term to the career trajectory of younger staff.

On the new shareholder orientation, he said: "I would say that it was a rebalancing of the governance structure rather than a fundamental shift towards shareholders." In this more gradualist approach, the management might be emphasising, for example, that a new type of person would be promoted in the organisation, rather than emphasising the end of the seniority system, even if it amounted to the same thing. The stress of the governance structure would emphasise

---

[3] Moulonguet returned to Renault in 2004 to become Chief Financial Officer.

shareholders more, rather than employees less, again, even if the end result were the same.

The question of balance is clearly of great importance to Renault in the handling of its relationship with Nissan. Although Renault does not hold a majority of Nissan's shares (they own 44.3% of Nissan, while Nissan holds 15% of Renault) they are nevertheless in a position to exercise *de facto* control. However, management language strongly emphasises balance and "partnership". At the outset, Renault sent a limited team to Nissan (around thirty executives) while Nissan also sent the same number of executives to Renault. While Renault executives occupied key positions on the Nissan board (CEO, CFO and director of strategic planning), the majority of the board consists of Nissan employees. All major decisions regarding the Renault/Nissan alliance are made by a management company, Renault–Nissan BV. The company is owned 50:50 with an executive committee consisting of the CEO (Carlos Ghosn) and three executives from Nissan and from Renault. In order to reap the significant scale advantages that accrue to the alliance, the two companies have set up a joint purchasing organisation (RNPO) which now accounts for over 70% of the purchasing turnover of the two companies. Many new ventures in new markets are done on a 50:50 basis, such as the alliance's recent foray into India with Mahindra & Mahindra. The symbolism of 50:50 is critical to the way in which the alliance is managed. Moulonguet noted:

We were not forced to do it but it is part of the spirit of the alliance and it is rather unique where we share everything on a parity basis ... it [i.e. putting important initiatives like RNPO on a 50:50 footing] was an important move to show that we were "walking the talk" when we were telling Nissan that we are an alliance of equals.

In common with Roche (and with Shinsei, especially in light of the management's recent comments) Nissan was concerned to be seen as a locally embedded organisation. This was not easy and it appears that liability of foreignness was particularly acute in Japan, where the way outsiders operated was under particular scrutiny. Moulonguet expressed some of the frustration that came with this:

Carlos Ghosn was saying that "To be recognised as achieving one, I must achieve 3 in Japan!" I still sense that we are not exactly viewed as a normal Japanese company even though we have respected everything: Nissan's corporate entity, corporate identity, brand identity, a majority of the management committee and the board are Japanese. Even with the success of the initial years, which was good news for Japan to have this big company reviving, they still question our credibility. The Japanese media and financial analysts are much more demanding of Nissan than other companies like Toyota, Honda, etc.

The difficulties that Nissan is having convincing the Japanese media and public at large of its local credentials is doubtless a function of the high profile of the Renault management that came at the outset, particularly that of Carlos Ghosn himself. However, the expectations that foreigners will behave in a different way, that they will import different values that have emerged from a different brand of capitalism and will impose those values on the organisation they now control, is also an important factor. The management of Nissan has to work three times as hard as firms which are still Japanese-owned to be viewed as a firm that respects local institutions.

The strong presence of "empirical predictors" at Nissan would point to a considerable degree of deinstitutionalisation of established practices at Nissan. Indeed, the employee response to the first question – How much change do you detect *overall* at the company? – being the highest among the case companies, would indicate there had been a considerable change in practices at the company, as much as at Shinsei and F-Services Co 1 and F-Services Co 2.

The role of agency?

Giddens (1984, p. 14) states that: "action depends upon the capability of the individual to 'make a difference' to a pre-existing state of affairs or course of events. An agent ceases to be such, if he or she loses the capability to 'make a difference', that is, to exercise some sort of power." To be sure, there is considerable discussion of the idea of power in the writings of Oliver and Greenwood and Hinings. In introducing the concepts of value commitments, power dependencies and an organisation's capacity for action, Greenwood and Hinings have clarified considerably the institutional perspective of change. However, the arrangement of value commitments, power dependencies and capacity for action did not appear to differ significantly at Nissan compared to other organisations whose employees appear to have noticed far greater organisational change (Shinsei, F-Services Co 1 and F-Services Co 2).

In examining the interview data at Nissan, one phenomenon that stood out clearly was the prevalence of the CEO's name. Table 8.2 illustrates the difference between the number of times his name was mentioned by Japanese employees compared with the CEO of the other case companies.

Table 8.2 *Frequency of CEO mentions*

Number of times name of CEO of case companies was mentioned by Japanese employees in semi-structured interviews

Company	Times mentioned
Nissan	64
Chugai	20
Shinsei	16
F-Services Co 1	4
F-Services Co 2	7

More than at any of the other case companies, interviewees did not just talk in terms of change being wrought by the new shareholders, but also referred frequently to the ways in which the actions of specific individuals, particularly, but not exclusively, the CEO, impacted the process of change. A senior executive in the sales hierarchy of Nissan noted:

That sense of individual responsibility is perhaps the biggest change since Ghosn-san and Moulonguet-san arrived. That represented a big shock for the normal staff of Nissan. That sense of vagueness about where responsibility lies in the organisation that pervaded Nissan, which may be a common feature of Japanese organisations, has gone. However, while the concept of assigning individual responsibility may be a western concept, I don't really know whether implementation of this would have been possible by any western leader or whether it was *because* of Ghosn-san. After all, it's the CEO's responsibility to implement change and it's his determination to get it done which is the key to success and I really respect him for that. It's not just a matter of adopting western management practices.

It is noteworthy that the name of the CFO, Moulonguet, was frequently mentioned, either independently, or alongside Ghosn's. This was often in the context of the great change that employees had noticed in the decision-making process on important finance-related matters. One employee noted:

It's certainly got quicker. But the process has also changed. For example, in the old days, if we were making a proposal to the CFO, and the choice was between proposals A and B, and we felt A was the right one, we were trained to push hard for A and lay out the reasons in our explanation to the CFO as to why A was better. We would then hopefully get the CFO's agreement to go with proposal A. Now, we put all the facts in front of Moulonguet-san and he makes the decision. It's a management decision and it's our job to give the boss all the facts that are relevant to the decision.

This observation stood in particular contrast to F-Services Co 1 and 2, where many employees noted that decisions had become much slower, as everything had to be referred back to the parent company.

At Nissan more than any other case company, the style of leadership, rather than the ideology or strategic intent of the shareholder, appeared to be the most important determinant of the trajectory of change. That is not to say that the ultimate "conceptual destination" of the management at Nissan was any different from that of any of the other case companies. The words Thierry Moulonguet used to describe the shortcomings of the budgeting and planning process and the need to enhance the "performance culture" was a clear indication of this. However, there was also a strong perception among employees that they were not going to be frog-marched to this new destination. A young and promising executive from the sales function said of the new decision-making process:

As to whether it's more top-down now or not, Ghosn-san has managed this process skilfully. From the start he had his own top-down vision. But he didn't force it down people's throats. He challenged the employees to take up this vision for themselves. To realise the new goals of the company, the employees need to have these goals for themselves. Thus, while it was a top-down process, people didn't really think of it like that or even realise that it was being imposed upon them. The voluntary nature of the employees taking up this challenge makes a great difference in the way they take it up and the energy they put into their efforts.

It could of course be legitimately asked what the difference is between forcing employees to embrace change and trying to persuade them to embrace it by themselves. If the end destination is the same, some would argue that the latter course was little more than cynical manipulation.

I would argue, however, that there is a material difference. The organisational literature on M&A has shown us that the changes wrought by mergers often involve a high degree of employee conflict, tension and alienation (Marks and Mirvis, 1985, 2001) and it was clear from the testimony of employees at some of the case companies that a strong feeling of dislocation had accompanied the takeover.

At first glance, it would appear from Nissan's HR data that the company has moved away from the practices of its comparator company J-Manufacturing Co as much as Shinsei and F-Services Co 1 have moved away from their comparator companies. However, the employees of Nissan clearly believed, first, that there was still a strong element of continuity along with change and, second, that they had voluntarily participated in, or even played a key role in, shaping the process of organisational change. Although there is no suggestion that the process has not caused a great deal of stress in the organisation and its employees, employee testimony would suggest that the way the process of change had been handled had led more quickly than expected to a relatively stable organisational platform.

It is perhaps almost as significant that the second most frequently mentioned CEO was that of the company that showed the least change, Osamu Nagayama of Chugai. To employees at Chugai, his presence would appear to represent just as important a symbol of continuity as Ghosn representing the new order at Nissan.

In reality, and as we have seen, the process of delegitimation is quite uneven and often painful. It is not self-evident that an employee who has believed for his entire career that the life-cycle system of rewards is the most legitimate way for employees to be rewarded will be easily convinced that it is no longer so, even more so if he has been waiting for twenty years to reap the benefits of the system.

Although I found very little evidence of active resistance to the new management at the case companies, there were suggestions that, beneath the surface, institutionalised practices did not change overnight. An expatriate manager at Nissan said of the decision-making process:

It is changing and becoming more transparent but the trouble is that it often appears like the decision-making process is following the "western" way and all the proper steps are being followed, but if you look carefully, it's quite different.

Thus, while it might appear that employees were showing a positive attitude towards new values, appearances could be deceiving. The same manager pointed out that there was no use in introducing the concept of individual accountability to Japanese employees, especially as a western manager, if you did not understand the cultural context within which accountability was set in a Japanese organisation:

Before we teach them how to be accountable, we need to teach them how to say "no". People in my department have so many things to do and there is no use in having them accountable for things if they don't have this ability. They always say "yes" and you never get the results.

According to his analysis, while Japanese employees would not actively resist the notion of increased personal accountability, merely introducing it into organisational practices would have no effect unless this cultural context was understood and adjusted for. Japanese employees had a tendency to "muck in" and get the job done, even if it was not clearly within their prescribed duties. It would take time to adjust to the idea of accountability related to a set of responsibilities narrowly defined in a job description.

Attitudes to authority, and when and how to resist it, are culturally and institutionally bounded. Dore's comparisons (see also Abegglen, 1958; Benedict, 1967) of a large Japanese and UK firm shows us that substantial differences exist:

Very minor changes in work allocations can, if not preceded by consultation, cause a walk-out in a British factory; in Hitachi … managers' authority in work matters is rarely challenged. (Dore, 1973, p. 247)

While institutional change over time may lead to attitudinal and behavioural change (and the decline of union influence in the UK might have led to less walk-outs of the type described by Dore) institutional differences across national borders will give rise to differences in what employees perceive it is legitimate to resist and how that resistance should be carried out. In undertaking any form of cross-border M&A and the type of "culture change" programmes that inevitably follow, the possibility of resistance, what form it takes and how to manage it would appear to be crucial issues for the new management. Institutional theory focuses in an abstract way on legitimacy-loss as if it occurs in a uniform way across the organisation, so that we have either institutionalisation or deinstitutionalisation – persistence or change. The case of Nissan points to a more complex picture of both persistence *and* change and shows that there is also scope for human agency. The skills of leadership in interpreting the organisation's cultural context in trying to effect change can have a decisive impact upon the outcome.

Is there a nationality effect?

As I mentioned at the outset, it was not my aim to measure the impact of the acquirer's nationality on the acquired company. This was because the sample size was too small to measure and my own personal concerns about the difficulties of unravelling the effects of nationality in today's complex multinationals, themselves often built up over the years from successive cross-border mergers. Indeed, the management of the case companies were at pains to downplay the impact of nationality. Having myself observed at close quarters the success Swiss Bank Corporation had had in integrating many of its acquisitions, including the extremely complex merger with the much larger UBS, I asked Franz Humer of Roche whether this was a trait particular to the Swiss. He replied:

One is tempted to say, "This has something to do with the nation, something Swiss." This is not the case, because many Swiss companies are not able to do it, although some perhaps are.

Thierry Moulonguet of Renault also downplayed the impact of Renault's "Frenchness", emphasising that it was a global firm and that most of its organisational practices would be in line with "global best practice". Indeed, there was little difference in the performance-related pay *practices* that Nissan had introduced, compared with, say, F-Services Co 1, even though there may have been some differences in the way in which they were *implemented*. Both Carlos Ghosn and Franz Humer have extensive experience of the US, either working there (as Ghosn did for Michelin) or working for a US firm (as Humer did for Schering-Plough). Although Ghosn is a French national, he was born in Brazil to Lebanese parents. Humer is not Swiss, but Austrian.

In their study Child *et al.* (2001) do draw some definitive conclusions as to the effect of nationality in cross-border M&A and demonstrate that patterns based on the nationality of the acquirer do emerge in the way subsidiaries are integrated and in the way that the parent firm approaches HR policies. However, in analysing the way, for example, the French integrate their acquisitions, they conclude: "the overall picture that emerged of French companies' approach to integrating their acquisitions is somewhat variable, and depends strongly on individual company culture and specific circumstances" (p. 152). It was certainly difficult in the case of Nissan to draw out any particularly French characteristics in the new organisation. There was certainly no evidence of a "colonial" attitude to the relationship with Nissan, which Child *et al.* cite as a feature of French attitude to integration and control.

From the perspective of the employees, there was little evidence that they attributed any aspect of post-acquisition change to the nationality of the new parent, although this may well have more to do with the fact that these were all employees who had been working for a Japanese company for all their careers and were not in a position to understand clearly what the difference was between working for a foreign company of one nationality or another. There were only two explicit comments that speculated on the nationality effect. One was from a Chugai executive:

Many senior people are being forced to confront issues by their Swiss counterparts and give clear answers to their questions, a clear "yes" or "no", and that's something they're not used to. But I think the Swiss are still a lot softer than the Americans.

The other was from a Nissan manager who was inclined to down-play the effect of nationality:

For a Japanese company, I think we've come a long way. I don't think it's a matter of differences between Japanese and French management (actually Ghosn-san was in the US for quite a long time, so we might even say "US management" instead of "French").

Far from a colonialist attitude, the new shareholders of Chugai and Renault believed that having and displaying an understanding of other cultures was fundamental to the success of the acquisition. Moulonguet noted:

You need to have for running this kind of alliance people who are really open to other cultures, very globally minded, with a lot of understanding of different points of view. This is a very important point. In the team you had some people succeeding very well and clearly being big contributors to the alliance. You had some others who were not so open- or global-minded and not so keen to respect diversity and not so curious about Japanese culture, Japanese history, Japanese design. You need to show your interest and to share it. This is very important.

Respect, however, was not limited to the cultural domain. In fact, in the sense that respect for a partner company's (or even a nation's) core competences gave rise to learning opportunities, there were con-crete business benefits to be derived. At Renault, Moulonguet claimed that mutual learning:

… is a very important aspect of our relationship because there is an appe-tite from each side to learn from the other and this appetite is still there. In manufacturing, engineering, in quality management, we continue to learn from Nissan and Nissan is still learning from Renault in different issues such as financial management, cost management, relations with suppliers, marketing and sales.

This view was reflected by Louis Schweitzer, CEO (now Chairman) of Renault, and architect of the alliance. He said in an interview with *Business Week*:[4]

[4] See www.businessweek.com/bwdaily/dnflash/oct2004/nf20040101_ 1918_ db053.htm.

… we learned a lot. Some things that started in Japan have been copied from Nissan. One very simple and striking thing: we teach people [on the production line] to do like piano players – to do separate things with each hand for efficiency. It's using hands in a most efficient way. Today, Nissan Sunderland is still Europe's most productive plant. We try to be as competitive as Nissan. For the start-up of the Megane 2 [model], we used 100 Nissan employees – that was very significant.

In all of this, we see the senior Renault management strongly emphasising partnership and equality and downplaying the fact that the power relationship is decisively in their favour.

There was one important aspect which enabled acquiring firms to take a longer-term view of their investments: the parent company's shareholding structure. The shareholding structure of Roche, where a majority of voting shares are still controlled by the Hoffman family, afforded the management more leeway to take a longer-term perspective. Humer noted:

In any decision, including that one [i.e. regarding the investment in Chugai], I don't have to cater to what the flavour of the month might be. I think that is very important, because having to do that in general terms destroys many corporations. I have seen it myself.

For his part, Moulonguet acknowledged that the 30% shareholding in Renault by a combination of the French government and Nissan, the 4% employee shareholding, "plus some very long-term US investors", gave the company a stable platform to take a long-term view.

There may be to some extent a nationality effect here. There are significant differences in the nature of the US and UK capital markets compared to those of France, Germany and Japan. Historically, the importance of concentrated blockholders in Germany and France, and cross-shareholdings in Japan, as well as the lower levels of receptivity to hostile bids (Jackson and Miyajima, 2007), have served to insulate the management of the coordinated market economy firms from the demands of short-term profit maximisation. The cases of Nissan and Chugai stood in particularly striking contrast to that of F-Services Co 1. In case of the latter, there was considerable scrutiny of the Japanese investment in the home media of the parent company, with business setbacks at the Japanese subsidiary receiving a great deal of press attention. While the role of F-Services Co 1's parent company's institutional shareholders in using the media to highlight these setbacks is unclear, the net effect was to put enormous pressure on the management of the parent to act, leading to the eventual disposal of F-Services Co 1.

A word about performance

As in the analysis of nationality effect, it is difficult to find a pattern among the case companies that amounts to a "recipe" for success and, as I have indicated, it has not been my objective to do so. There are too few cases in the sample and the total number of major acquisitions by foreign firms is not large enough. There are also a large number of factors that have not been examined here, particularly related to the companies' strategies, issues related to broader economic or sectoral factors, that will have contributed to success or failure. Some firms changed a great deal, but others less so. The extent of change did not correlate with survival. In the case of both F-Services Co 1 and 2, both subsidiaries have been sold in recent years by their parent companies to a Japanese buyer. The poor performance of F-Services Co 1 was the direct reason for its disposal by the parent, but in the case of F-Services Co 2, the financial position of the parent company was weak, and the disposal of the Japanese subsidiary was part of a wider restructuring of the group to refocus the business.

As for the "survivors", all three firms have gone through periods of difficulty under their new ownership, particularly recently. In the case of Nissan, the sometimes wild hype that greeted the arrival of the new leadership from Renault and the remarkable turnaround in the company's fortunes led to a build-up of excessive expectation and, where these have not been fully met, have led to equally excessive, gloomy prognostications about the future of the alliance. Moulonguet emphasises that there are a large number of achievements on the part of both Nissan and Renault, particularly in the entry of new markets such as India and China, as well as expanding business in existing markets in developing economies, which simply would not have been possible for either firm without the alliance. He gave the example of their alliance in Latin America:

We have just announced [in 2007] that we are producing in Brazil the Logan for Renault in Mercosur but for Nissan to export to Mexico, so we are producing the Logan for both Renault and Nissan at that plant in Curitiba in Brazil. It will be sold under the Renault badge in Mercosur and under the Nissan badge in Mexico. Why? Because in Mexico Nissan is much more powerful than Renault and in terms of volume it's much better for the Logan to be sold by Nissan than by Renault. This is another very good example of what we can do together and when you see the amount of competition in these areas in this sector every competitive edge can make a big difference and with the alliance we can make key differences.

Getting the media, particularly the Japanese media, to understand this, he claims, has not been easy. After profitability hit a plateau in 2004 (although revenue still continues to grow) there have been a number of media articles commenting on the demise of the "Ghosn effect". Typical headlines have read "Driver of growth hits bumpy road"[5] and "Ghosn's Nissan: Hitting the emergency brake".[6]

In an extensive article in *Bungei Shunju* (2007), Hisao Inoue offers a detailed critique of Nissan's strategy. His main thrust is that, in its quest to deliver enhanced shareholder value, Nissan has become extremely short term in its outlook, with a narrowly based core strategy focusing on cost-cutting and financial sleight of hand to boost returns. The result is that suppliers have been squeezed to the bone and have had to lay off workers and R&D expenditures have been suppressed. All the while, dividends have been increasing relentlessly, from ¥24 per share in 2005 to ¥34 per share in 2007. Dividend payments to Renault during 2007 amounted to ¥66 billion, cumulatively ¥270 billion since the start of the alliance. Inoue concludes (p. 106):

Reflecting on Ghosn's career, he came in with rich experience as a turn-around artist in times of trouble, first at the tyre maker Michelin, and then Renault, but has never had the experience of putting a giant global firm like Nissan on a stable growth footing. The Ghosn management style is to increase shareholder value by quickly reducing headcount, cutting expenses and increasing profitability at a stroke: if anything it resembles the short-term approach of the foreign "vulture funds". Such an approach naturally has its limits.[7]

---

[5] *Financial Times*, 30 July 2007.
[6] *Asahi Shimbun*, 6 June 2007.
[7] Author translation.

This analysis seems as flawed as the original evaluation of Ghosn as a miracle-working messiah. While it is true that Nissan has sharply increased its dividend and has the highest payout ratio of the three large Japanese auto makers (just over 30% in 2007) the rise in dividend at two other major auto firms has been in some ways even more dramatic. During the 2005–2007 period, Honda increased its dividend from ¥25 per share to ¥67, more than doubling its payout ratio from 9.6% to 20.7%, and Toyota almost doubled its dividend (¥65 per share to ¥120) and raised its payout ratio by almost 30% (18.3% to 23.5%). Nissan has also budgeted to increase its investment in R&D by 5% in 2007, although this figure is well below Toyota's. It also seems unfair to blame Nissan for doing exactly what all Japanese manufacturing firms do in times of economic difficulty: squeeze the supply chain. What the article does is to offer a vivid illustration of the difficulties foreign firms have in treading the delicate path between delivering shareholder value and wanting to be seen as deeply embedded in local institutions. Guardians of institutional norms, including those in the media, will be quick to point out behaviour on the part of outsiders that deviates from those norms, even if in many respects insiders may be surreptitiously behaving in a similar way. We have shown that the case companies, for the most part, have become much more likely to display behaviour that is deviant to localised norms. Much closer scrutiny is the inevitable result.

We have seen that Roche's method of dealing with institutional distance and the liability of foreignness has been to define financial expectations of its subsidiaries, but to leave strategic and operational matters to the local management. Chugai's performance post-acquisition has, in general, more than met Roche's expectations, with a continuous rise in profitability which was reflected in a sharp rise in the stock price. However, in the last two years the company has suffered from considerable pressure on margins and in the past year the share price has fallen back substantially relative to its competitors.

Shinsei re-listed its shares on the Tokyo Stock Exchange in February 2004 and, despite a steady increase in net profit until 2006–2007, the share price has significantly underperformed that of other financial firms. The company made a net loss in 2006–2007, with a considerable deterioration in the consumer finance business, and decided to sell its head office building in 2008 to cover losses incurred in subprime loans. In the retail banking sector, competitors have copied Shinsei, and launched similar products, eroding margins. In May 2008, Yashiro returned to the bank as chairman,[8] and in July 2009 Shinsei announced its intention to merge with Aozora Bank.

Do these companies have anything in common? The empirical predictors would certainly have indicated that they have little in common and the degrees of overall change felt since acquisition by the employees were at opposite ends of the scale. In many important areas, such as what factors now determined career success and how people were recruited, there were enormous differences between employee perceptions at the three companies.

There are, however, some interesting similarities. In all three cases the new owners had delegated major decision-making authority to local management, sent from head office (in the case of Nissan), recruited locally (in the case of Shinsei) or that were already in place (in the case of Chugai). In the cases of both Chugai and Nissan, there was a sense of balance between the shareholders and the Japanese subsidiary or affiliate, characterised by a strong sense of trust between the two parties. Humer took great pride in the relationship that developed between himself and Nagayama:

We trust each other enormously and when things come to the crunch he and I sit down together and sort it out and then it flows again in the whole organisation and that is very important. Otherwise things would not work as well as it is working.

Louis Schweitzer, former CEO (now Chairman) of Renault, also emphasised the role of trust: trust between the two parties, and between himself and Ghosn:

We [Renault and Nissan] had great clarity in our relationship. In the fall of 1998, I presented Mr Hanawa, then Nissan's CEO, a draft press release of the alliance, including what we wanted to establish – with all the legal documents. Carlos and I presented Nissan's management [with] a turn-around plan. So, four months before we went public with the announcement of the alliance, it was clear to Nissan what we would do. After 1999, we did exactly what we said we would do. The most important point was trust. The next point was Carlos himself. I knew how good he was. He was

---

[8] *Nihon Keizai Shimbun*, 15 May 2008, p. 7.

the linchpin. Carlos went with a very small team. He had the ability, the charisma to succeed. That was essential.[9]

To a greater or lesser extent, the new shareholders of Shinsei, Nissan and Chugai have left Japanese strategy formation to local management and have preserved a distinct Japanese identity in the firms they have purchased. That is most in evidence at Chugai, but even if "local management" in the case of Nissan has meant, in part, a senior team sent from Renault, and the "new" Nissan feels to employees very different from the "old" one, there is nevertheless a strong feeling that the integrity of the Japanese unit has been preserved. As for Shinsei, the realisation of Yashiro's vision of a "different kind of Japanese bank" has caused inevitable cultural difficulties as the bank has absorbed large numbers of executives from foreign firms. Management has begun to appreciate, however, that an important element of building local corporate relationships will mean readjusting the balance between Japanese and non-Japanese bankers and between a relationship and transaction orientation. Although the long-term sustainability of the Shinsei business model is far from proven, the company's initial success in signing up customers would indicate that there is a strong appetite among the Japanese public for innovation in retail banking. If innovation and a strong relationship orientation can be successfully combined to build its corporate and investment banking businesses, Shinsei may be in a position to realise Yashiro's original vision.

Inevitably, when the relationship between the new shareholder and subsidiary is highly dependent on trust between key managers at the companies, the question of succession is highlighted. At Shinsei, the fact that Yashiro's successor, Thierry Porté, was identified well in advance (the appointment was announced in October 2003, almost two years before he became CEO, in June 2005) clearly smoothed the transition. At Nissan, many employees expressed concern about the succession during the interview process. For example, one employee noted:

However, when he [Ghosn] and Moulonguet-san go back, I fear the process of reform may slow down. In particular, the barriers between divisions,

---

[9] See www.businessweek.com/bwdaily/dnflash/oct2004/nf20040101_1918db053.htm.

which have been such a problem in the past, may be erected again. That would be a great pity.

It is significant, again, that Moulonguet's name is mentioned alongside Ghosn's. Renault's answer to the succession problem is, for the moment, to ignore it by having Ghosn run both firms as CEO. Whether this is a sustainable structure in the long run remains to be seen.

At Roche, while Humer considers the relationship he has been able to build up with Nagayama as a source of great pride, it is also a cause for concern. While he was very optimistic about Chugai's long-term prospects, succession was an issue of great consequence:

My big worry is that Osamu and I, we are both in our early 60s. How are we going to instil, inspire, the next generation to build the same thing, who are the players on both sides? I think it's something that requires a very special talent, to understand the other side, to understand oneself, to understand that he would do it differently but still let the other side do it their way. It takes chemistry and time and an enormous amount of [pause] … is tolerance the right word … empathy. Because it's so easy to have these generalised statements "all these Japanese … all these Europeans … all these Americans".

Roche, which started its long relationship with the US biotech firm Genentech in 1980 (acquiring majority control in 1990), has a long history of success in running arm's-length relationships with significant subsidiaries. Humer strongly believes that, while this capability was embedded in the culture of the firm, it was also strongly influenced by individual leadership style.[10]

In all three cases, but particularly in the cases of Nissan and Shinsei, strong doubts were expressed at the time of the acquisition as to the long-term sustainability of these firms under foreign ownership. To the extent that all three have survived and, in the cases of Nissan and Chugai, have become significantly more profitable and, in the case of Shinsei, developed a brand new concept of a bank from a virtual standing start, they should be regarded as a success. These successes

[10] In July 2008, Roche made an unsolicited offer for the 44% of Genentech shares it did not already own, suggesting a more hands-on approach in the future. The acquisition was completed in March 2009. See www.ft.com/cms/s/0/e33b48cc-574f-11dd-916c-000077b07658.html.

should all provide encouragement to non-Japanese firms considering acquisitions in Japan. While the number of cases is too small and the nature of the relationships between the acquiring and acquired companies in the cases is too diverse to draw any definitive conclusions, there are a number of features that exist in at least one of the cases which I believe has contributed to their survival and which may provide some food for thought for managers contemplating mergers with institutionally distant firms:

- respect for, and interest in, local culture by new shareholders and/ or new management;
- an ability to listen to local staff and to change one's mind;
- sending or recruiting a leadership team with an excellent track record, but not necessarily knowledge of Japan;
- giving a Japanese subsidiary complete, or at least considerable, autonomy, based on high levels of personal trust between head office decision makers and local management;
- understanding and patient shareholders at the parent level;
- understanding that the cultural and institutional context of organisational practices is very different from head office, and that change should be managed accordingly; and
- an understanding that learning is a two-way process, that the local operation almost certainly will have something to teach the rest of the global organisation.

This may all seem self-evident. However, it is my experience that the process of transforming a Japanese organisation is not necessarily a reflective one. It is the natural instinct of those who have crossed large institutional distances to reach for the familiar in implementing change: in my case, it seemed that the important thing was to turn the organisation as rapidly as possible into something that looked and felt like the foreign firms for which I had worked. This is perhaps what the employees had been expecting and many of the changes may well have been for the better. But organisational routines do not necessarily travel well across institutional distances. While putting an end to seniority-based pay and rewarding employees based on merit may seem like an obvious move, substantially increased monetary reward presents unexpected problems for some, as we have seen. Across the case companies, a common complaint was of the unevenness of the application of merit-based pay, and the different criteria used in evaluation – this was causing resentment and friction between employees.

In a tightly knit, homogeneously conceived organisation, great care is required to evaluate the impact of the importation of new and alien practices. Intensive efforts to educate and train managers and employees are needed if the legitimacy of these practices is to be accepted. It is not good enough simply to outline a new destination for the employees and expect them to move towards it smoothly and unquestioningly. What is required by the acquiring firm is to understand the present location of employees and to examine the institutional and cultural underpinnings of their current behaviour. Only when one has done this can one begin to design a sensible pathway towards the new destination. This is particularly important for major changes in direction in such important matters as how employees are rewarded.

Despite my many years in Japan, I found myself making the mistake at LTCB Investment Management of only thinking about the destination to which we should be headed. Take, for example, the simple matter of office layout. It seemed to me that the Japanese office layout was all wrong and that more space and enhanced privacy would increase productivity. The new company ought to look like a foreign firm and office space seemed the right place to start. We abandoned the Japanese-style group-based seating and put everyone in cubicles instead. But this had some unintended consequences. Employees were happy with the increased level of privacy, but a number commented that the ability of employees to communicate with each other had deteriorated substantially. I was reminded of this when an employee of F-Services Co 1 told me:

The working space per person has become much greater and the working environment has improved a lot … [but] competition [between employees] has increased also, and I think that has contributed to the decline in "coordination" skills. There's so much competition that there is no effort to create a meeting of minds. There's no effort to communicate. There's more space between our desks, but that means that communication is harder.

Instead of assuming that the western office layout was innately superior, I might have asked myself why Japanese firms had adopted this particular arrangement. What were the advantages and disadvantages? And if I were to make changes, what mechanisms could be put into place to minimise the negative consequences? These are some of the questions that, with the benefit of hindsight, I would ask myself were I to go through the process again. It means understanding the starting point before designing the route to the ultimate destination.

Limitations of research and scope for future work

This study has many shortcomings and is far from a comprehensive analysis of the entire Japanese employment system. I have only examined the impact of foreign ownership and control at large Japanese corporations. However, while the market for corporate control of large Japanese companies is still not a large one, and the entry of foreign firms into that market is still quite recent, Japanese SMEs have been bought and sold much more freely and foreign firms have participated in this process over a longer period. Given, on the one hand, the closely integrated nature of much of corporate Japan, especially in the manufacturing sector, and, on the other, the apparent separateness of the employment systems that apply to large and small firms, a study of the impact of foreign ownership and control of Japanese SMEs would be of great interest.

I have also focused solely on the white-collar sector. A similar study of the impact on blue-collar work routines and organisation would be a worthwhile exercise. The representative of J-Manufacturing Co's suggestion that employment stability and seniority-based pay were vital ingredients for the successful operation of the *kaizen* philosophy and the transfer of tacit knowledge both vertically and across the organisation imply that, for manufacturing firms at least, radical organisational change and the deinstitutionalisation of established practices would most likely have negative consequences. It would therefore be interesting to test this framework on the blue-collar sector insofar as the philosophies of *kaizen* and the importance of tacit knowledge underpin the work routines at these companies. Nissan, for example, has a large blue-collar workforce, as does Renault. Renault claims that they have as much to learn from Nissan as Nissan has to learn from Renault, particularly in manufacturing. The extent to which blue-collar working practices at the two companies have changed would be worthy of investigation.

There were a large number of avenues, both theoretical and practical, that opened up and invited exploration, but which were neglected.

There has, for example, been a renewed focus in the recent organisational literature on Japan on convergence and it struck me that there may be links between the ideas of delegitimation and deinstitutionalisation that underlie institutional theory and the concept of convergence (e.g. Kerr *et al.*, 1964). Convergence theory was popularised during the 1960s, but, criticised for its overly deterministic orientation, it fell into obscurity with the increasing popularity of culture during the latter half of the 1970s and 1980s. However, Japan, which has long been held up as the exception that disproved the convergence theorists, is now under strong pressure to adopt Anglo-Saxon governance structures and make its employment system more responsive to the market mechanism. There appears to be an element of "coercive isomorphism" in convergence theory, with its implicit conclusion that, ultimately, all organisational forms would converge on the most rational and efficient form, the Anglo-Saxon model.[11] As in the case of institutional theory, it seems to me that the uneven outcomes at the case companies highlight some of the shortcomings of convergence theory. It can only give us limited insights into the role of cross-border M&A in bringing institutionally distant organisational models closer together.

Conclusions

Our research question concerned the changes that took place when a Japanese company was taken over by a non-Japanese firm. We looked for contextual factors that might account for differences in the process of change at the various companies we examined. We also looked at Japanese comparators so that we could attribute more confidently the changes at the case companies to the fact of foreign control.

What, then, have we really learned from this exercise? Why is this research relevant, and why might it be useful, either to an academic or a practitioner? And in particular, has the examination of the process of change through the lens of institutional theory enabled us to see anything that we might otherwise not have been able to see? Did the research throw up any surprises?

---

[11] Kerr and associates, rather than specify the Anglo-Saxon model, distinguish between "middle-class" and other types of industrial forms: thus "successful commercial society is predisposed toward middle-class leadership of industrialisation" (1964, p. 53).

To this last question, on the surface, the answer is "no". The literature (Chapter 1) had informed us that Japanese organisations, despite fifteen years of economic stagnation, had not changed fundamentally. It was no surprise, then, to find that, on examining the organisational practices at the comparator companies, the basic tenets of the communitarian firm, the principles of equality and employee-favouring orientation, were very much in evidence.

When the "jolt" of foreign ownership hits a Japanese company grounded in the communitarian tradition, it is not surprising there is substantially greater attention paid to the needs of shareholders. Given this new shareholder orientation, the subsequent changes to HR practices and organisational structure followed quite naturally.

And yet, I was surprised. It was astonishing that, after a few short years, it would be inconceivable that a manager at case company Nissan would express the sentiments of the head of HR at comparator company J-Manufacturing Co, who told us that it is "second nature" to keep the wages of two people with vastly differing responsibilities the same because they are the same age and have the same experience. I was also surprised by the speed with which the functions of the HR department had been devolved to the operating divisions at Shinsei, while at J-Financial Co the HR department appeared to maintain strong control of intra-group resource allocation. It seemed perfectly natural for the head of one of the comparator firm's HR department to say they had only just started to think about the issue of increased labour mobility in relation to the company's ability to adopt a more flexible corporate strategy, but it would have sounded ludicrous coming from his counterpart at the case company. In each case, the sentiments expressed at the comparator companies would have been echoed at the case companies prior to their acquisition just a few years before. I could not help being surprised at the rate at which attitudes that had been held to be perfectly legitimate at an organisation could be deemed so illegitimate in such a short space of time and, while this is not a question for this book, I wondered whether an organisational study of, say, UK firms taken over by non-UK companies would have produced the same results.

The institutional literature has provided a good framework for understanding these changes. Institutional writers have been criticised for their lack of insight into the process of change and their analysis has provided valuable insight as to the circumstances under which there is a "discontinuity in the willingness or ability of organisations to take for granted and continually re-create an institutionalised organisational activity" (Oliver, 1992, p. 564). In particular, the link highlighted by Oliver between the interaction of the "predictive factors" and the course of deinstitutionalisation provided clarification of the different trajectories of change at the case companies. The idea of "institutional distance" has given us some insight into the difficult job that managers involved in cross-border mergers have confronting "institutional duality": balancing the pressures to make the local subsidiary conform to global best practice and the constraints imposed by local institutions to behave in a way that is seen as legitimate.

At the comparator companies, institutionalised Japanese organisational routines, even if there were variations among them, showed the extent to which they continue to accommodate institutional expectations. At the level of the employment system, Fligstein's analysis (2001) of the institutional arrangements that underpin a country's employment practices has gone some way to explaining the longevity and robustness of the Japanese system of human resource management.

The Japanese employment system remains just that, a system, held together by institutional complementarities that have endured an enormous amount of pressure during the last fifteen years. This has important implications for foreign firms taking over, or considering the acquisition of, Japanese firms. We have seen that the surviving case firms have in different ways and to varying degrees felt the liability of foreignness as they have steered, or have been perceived to have steered, their firms away from institutionalised practices that constitute the communitarian firm. However, even in the case of Shinsei which has moved the furthest away from the system, we have seen a shift from the practices that one might expect to see in other foreign financial institutions operating in Japan as it seeks to position itself as an organisation more embedded in the local institutional framework. Its practices are still a long way from those of J-Financial Co, but, rather than diverge further, may have inched a little closer recently. Renault, and especially Roche, have resisted the forceful imposition of "global best practice" and have made significant accommodation to local practices. The path of globalisation has not, by and large, followed the prescriptions of convergence theory. The greater the institutionalised distance that multinationals travel, the more carefully they need to consider the ways in which they adapt to local conditions.

This book has also made a number of practical contributions. For practitioners who are contemplating cross-border acquisitions, particularly of Japanese companies, this study, which examines the process of integration at five companies and the link between the process of change and the companies' institutional contexts, should be of great value. In attempting to change, or indeed in deciding whether to change, organisational practices in the post-acquisition process, the experience of the case study firms will provide useful pointers as to what to expect from an organisation and its employees. In trying to effect organisational change in cross-border M&A and to understand its likely trajectory, it is critical to understand the institutional context of the firm. This requires an understanding at two levels: the first at the intra-organisational level and the second at the level of the employment system into which the firm is embedded. A combination of Oliver's analysis of the empirical predictors of deinstitutionalisation and Greenwood and Hinings' concepts of precipitating and enabling dynamics is valuable as it provides a concrete framework for understanding the various ways in which "normative fragmentation" and eventual deinstitutionalisation occur. However, we have also seen that the role of external forces in effecting change is of great importance, particularly in a system that emphasises so greatly the distinction between insiders and outsiders.

For Japanese companies that are about to be taken over by a foreign firm, the imposition of a shareholder-oriented management philosophy by outsiders who have no sense of the *shigarami* to bind them to the status quo has serious implications for the future of organisational practices that are based on the communitarian precepts. Again, the experience of the case companies and the institutional framework will provide valuable pointers to the likely direction of organisational change.

This framework clearly can be applied to studies involving other geographic areas. It is evident, for example, that, as institutionally distant nations such as China continue their rapid integration into the global economy, those nations' companies will increasingly become acquisition or alliance targets for western firms. Institutional forces will be at work in the organisational architecture of those countries just as much as in the case of Japan, and the framework developed in this book will be of interest to academics and practitioners alike in trying to assess the impact of those forces on the outcomes of cross-border alliances and mergers involving those countries. However, it may have an application beyond geography. For example, in a rapidly consolidating industry such as automobile manufacturing, there may be deeply institutionalised organisational forms or work practices that have developed that are peculiar to that industry and that are quite separate from the national contexts in which they apparently operate. An institutional analysis would shed some light on the trajectory of the consolidation process.

As for Japan, since the bubble burst in the early 1990s one has been tempted on frequent occasions to declare that Japan is an important turning point. After fifteen years of stagnation, the economic environment over the last two to three years has been characterised by, if not outright optimism, then at least a lack of the bleak pessimism that has dogged business confidence for such a long period. During the fifteen years of economic weakness, questions were asked about the legitimacy of the Japanese employment system and the Japanese way of organising.

In the late 1990s, as I observed the increasing number of Japanese firms falling into foreign hands, I myself felt there was a turning point ahead. Extrapolating forward, there seemed to be a distinct possibility that the opening up of the market for corporate control, for foreign as well as domestic buyers, would be an important element in the development of a new, more market-driven form of capitalism. That might lead to significant changes in societal perceptions about the purpose of the firm and the relationship between the firm and its employees: in short the end of the community-based firm. As we approach the end of the first decade of the twenty-first century, it is clear that Japan has chosen not to follow this trajectory. While there has been a steady increase in "out-in" transactions, and even a few large-scale acquisitions by foreign firms, such as Wal-Mart/Seiyu and Citibank/Nikko, the level of these transactions is still extremely low compared to other industrialised nations. Rather, in the last few years, the debate that has gripped the media and has preoccupied the management of Japanese firms has been focused on how Japan can defend itself against foreign predators. However, little attempt has been made to distinguish between types of foreign acquirer, with the boundaries of discussion being framed by the activities of a small number of activist funds that in other major economies would receive only minor coverage. The implicit premise in these discussions is that foreign control of any kind represents a threat to a corporate way of life exemplified by the welfare corporatist organisation and that this necessarily harms Japanese interests in a number of ways.

The development of the global capital market and rapid industrial consolidation have come hand-in-hand with a willingness on the part of multinational firms to make important strategic acquisitions in increasingly institutionally distant markets. While my hunch that Japan, at the end of the twentieth century, was about to enter a new age of a more open form of capitalism has so far proved incorrect, it is only a matter of time. Just as Japanese firms must be willing to cross institutional barriers to establish a more meaningful global presence through acquisition, so the stakeholders of Japanese companies must eventually be persuaded that foreign ownership and control is not necessarily the unpalatable outcome it still seems to represent.

What I hope I have demonstrated in this book is that there are no pre-determined organisational outcomes where foreign firms acquire Japanese ones. Institutional factors played a role in shaping the trajectory of change, but a key role also seemed to be played by individual decision makers who were responsible for making the change vs continuity judgements and who exercised a profound influence on how employees responded to foreign control.

I hope I have demonstrated that foreign firms can have a constructive role to play in helping to create real improvements in Japanese competitiveness in a rapidly globalising economy where institutional distances appear to be rapidly shrinking.

References

Abegglen, J.C. (1958) *The Japanese Factory: Aspects of Its Social Organisation.* Boston, MA: Massachusetts Institute of Technology Press

Benedict, R. (1967) *The Chrysanthemum and the Sword.* Cleveland, OH: Meridian Books

Biggart, N. and Guillen, M.F. (1999) "Developing Difference: Social Organization and the Rise of the Auto Industries of South Korea, Taiwan, Spain, and Argentina", *American Sociological Review*, 64: 722–747

Child, J., Faulkner, D. and Pitkethly, R. (2001) *The Management of International Acquisitions.* New York, NY: Oxford University Press

Dore, R. (1973) *British Factory – Japanese Factory: The Origins of National Diversity in Industrial Relations.* Berkeley, CA: University of California Press

    (2006) *Dare No Tame No Kaisha Ni Suru Ka* (*For Whose Benefit the Corporation?*). Tokyo: Iwanami Shoten

Financial Times (2005) "Japan Sees Record Year for M&A". 6 January

Fligstein, N. (2001) *The Architecture of Markets: An Economic Sociology of Twenty-First Century Capitalist Societies.* Princeton, NJ: Princeton University Press

Giddens, A. (1984) *The Constitution of Society.* Cambridge: Polity Press

Greenwood, R. and Hinings, C.R. (1996) "Understanding Radical Organizational Change: Bringing Together the Old and the New Institutionalism", *Academy of Management Review*, 21: 1022–1054

Hanami, T. (2004) "The Changing Labour Market, Industrial Relations and Labour Policy", *Japan Labour Review*, 1: 4–16

Hirsch, P.M. (1986) "From Ambush to Golden Parachute: Corporate Takeovers as an Instance of Cultural Framing and Institutional Integration", *American Journal of Sociology*, 91: 800–837

Iwaisako, T. (2004). "Corporate Investment and Restructuring", Institute of Economic Research, Hitotsubashi University Discussion Paper Series A. Tokyo: 45

JIL (2003) "Unionization Rate Drops to Record Low 20.2 Percent", *Japan Labor Bulletin*, 42: 4–5

Kang, T.W. (1991) *Gaishi: The Foreign Company in Japan.* Tokyo: Tuttle

Kato, T. (2001) "The End of "Lifetime Employment" in Japan? Evidence from National Surveys and Field Research", *Journal of the Japanese and International Economies*, 15: 489–514

Kerr, C., Dunlop, J.T., Harbison, F. and Myers, C.A. (1964) *Industrialism and Industrial Man.* New York, NY: Oxford University Press

Marks, M. and Mirvis, P.H. (1985) "Merger Syndrome: Stress and Uncertainty", *Mergers and Acquisitions*, Summer: 50–55

    (2001) "Making Acquisitions Work: Strategic and Psychological Preparation", *Academy of Management Executive*, 15: 80–84

Nitta, M. (1997) "Business Diversification Strategy and Employment Relations". In M. Sako and H. Sato (eds.) *Japanese Labour and Management in Transition.* London: Routledge

Oliver, C. (1992) "The Antecedents of Deinstitutionalization", *Organization Studies*, 13: 563–588

Rebick, M. (2001) "Japanese Labor Markets: Can We Expect Significant Change?" In M. Blomstrom, B. Gangnes and S. La Croix (eds.) *Japan's New Economy: Continuity and Change in the Twenty-First Century* Oxford: Oxford University Press

    (2005) *The Japanese Employment System.* Oxford: Oxford University Press

Rohlen, T.P. (1974) *For Harmony and Strength: Japanese White-Collar Organization in Anthropological Perspective.* Berkeley: University of California Press

Shibata, H. (2002) "Wage and Performance Appraisal Systems in Flux: A Japan–United States Comparison", *Industrial Relations*, 41: 629–652

Tett, G. (2004) *Saving the Sun: Shinsei and the Battle for Japan's Future.* London: Random House

Walter, G.A. (1985) "Culture Collisions in Mergers and Acquisitions". In P.J. Frost (ed.) *Organizational Culture.* Beverly Hills: Sage

Weinstein, D. (2001) "Historical, Structural, and Macroeconomic Perspectives on the Japanese Economic Crisis". In M. Blomstrom, B. Gangnes and S. La Croix (eds.) *Japan's New Economy: Continuity and Change in the Twenty-First Century.* Oxford: Oxford University Press

Westphal, J.D. and Zajak, E.J. (1998) "The Symbolic Management of Stockholders: Corporate Governance Reforms and Shareholder Reactions", *Administrative Science Quarterly*, 43: 127–153

Yoshimori, M. (1995) "Whose Company Is It? The Concept of the Corporation in Japan and the West", *Long Range Planning*, 28: 33–45

Index